INTERSUBJECTIVITY

PHILOSOPHY & SOCIAL CRITICISM

Series Editor: David M. Rasmussen, Boston College

This series presents an interdisciplinary range of theory and critique emphasizing the interrelation of continental and Anglo-American scholarship as it affects contemporary discourses. Books in the series are aimed at an international audience, focusing on contemporary debates in philosophy and ethics, politics and social theory, feminism, law, critical theory, postmodernism and hermeneutics.

Other books in this series

INTERSUBJECTIVITY

The Fabric of Social Becoming

Nick Crossley

SAGE Publications
London · Thousand Oaks · New Delhi

SAGE Publications Ltd
6 Bonhill Street
London EC2A 4PU

SAGE Publications Inc
2455 Teller Road
Thousand Oaks, California 91320

SAGE Publications India Pvt Ltd
32, M-Block Market
Greater Kailash - I
New Delhi 110 048

British Library Cataloguing in Publication data

A catalogue record for this book is
available from the British Library.

ISBN 0 8039 7903 7
ISBN 0 8039 7904 5 (pbk)

Library of Congress catalog record available

Typeset by Type Study, Scarborough, North Yorkshire
Printed in Great Britain by The Cromwell Press Ltd,
Broughton Gifford, Melksham, Wiltshire

For Michele

Contents

Preface
A Book About Intersubjectivity

'Intersubjectivity' is a complex and multilayered concept. There are many quite different understandings and theories of it. It is also a popular concept which, for many writers, forms a central linchpin in the work in which they, as philosophers or social scientists, are engaged (Giddens 1993; Honneth 1995; Joas 1985). Furthermore, it is an interdisciplinary concept. It appeals to philosophers, sociologists, psychologists and political thinkers alike, seemingly offering them insights into both their specific discipline and the connections between that discipline and others.

For these reasons alone a book on intersubjectivity is both justified and warranted. Its different versions need to be explored and perhaps combined. Certainly they need to be introduced in a comprehensible form to students. Moreover, the interdisciplinary potential of the concept needs to be tested out in some way. We need to consider or to demonstrate how and in what ways different disciplines can engage with the idea, what they may contribute to our understanding of it and what they may wish to take from it. This book will, I hope, do all of these things to the reader's satisfaction. It aims to provide a comprehensive map of intersubjectivity, outlining the key theories in the intersubjectivist tradition and, importantly, putting forward the many arguments in favour of intersubjectivism in philosophy and social science.

In addition to these introductory functions the book offers a systematic attempt to join the various theories of intersubjectivity that it considers into a common perspective, or, rather, a system of interlocking perspectives. Specifically it traces a common path through the work of Merleau-Ponty, Wittgenstein, Mead, Schutz and Habermas and it considers their work against a background formed by the work of Husserl, Buber and Hegel. This is not an arbitary eclecticism or a postmodern shopping spree in the supermarket of ideas. Despite their often very different contexts and methods, all of the theorists whom I discuss are united in their intersubjectivism and in their rejection of the subjectivist and objectivist alternatives to it. Even if their versions of intersubjectivity are different, even if they don't use the word, the writers whom I discuss are all groping towards a common ground, as is evidenced in the many studies which have compared them separately (Coulter 1979; Habermas 1987a, 1991a; Heinzig 1987; Roche 1973; Rosenthal and Bourgeois 1991; Spurling 1977). What I am doing in constructing a theory of intersubjectivity is explicating this common ground, showing where paths or at least interests and concerns overlap, where one theory takes over from another.

My final purpose in writing the book has been to introduce an element of critique and coherence where I feel it is needed and to develop some of the points raised by the various theorists. I have entered into dialogue with the theorists whom I have discussed, replying to the questions which their theories raise and responding to those points which have provoked me. This dialogicality constitutes the book's own intersubjective situation and I can only hope it will be continued by you. Books are acts of communication. They are designed to convey, convince and provoke. And they call for a response.

The Plan

It is usual at the beginning of a study, to provide some definition of the central concepts to be used and to map out the structure which it will adopt. In the present case this is not possible. Defining 'intersubjectivity' is partly what the main body of the book as a whole is about. I do offer three definitions of 'intersubjectivity' in my first chapter, however, each of which represents an important statement in the history of the concept. These should suffice to give the reader a preliminary sense of 'intersubjectivity'. I have also deferred my exposition of the plan of the book to the first chapter. The plan is easier to follow when the various definitions of the concept have been discussed because the book itself is based around these definitions, or at least around my engagement with them.

Acknowledgements

Thanks to staff and students at the Centre for Psychotherapeutic Studies for listening to and commenting upon some of the ideas discussed in this book. Thanks to Bob Stern for reading and commenting upon an early chapter. Thanks to my mum and dad for being interested and encouraging me. Finally, very special thanks to my wife and colleague Michele Davies. Her advice, criticism, encouragement and the time she has taken to read over drafts have been invaluable. The book is dedicated to her.

1

Dimensions of Intersubjectivity

The concept of intersubjectivity is multilayered. In this chapter I unpack some of these layers through a discussion of three important philosophical analyses of intersubjectivity: Husserl's (1991) *Cartesian Meditations*, Buber's (1958) *I and Thou* and the analysis of the 'struggle for recognition' in Kojève's (1969) *Introduction to the Reading of Hegel*. None of these analyses provide an adequate account of intersubjectivity and their respective limitations are not overcome by a synthesis of the three. It is important to discuss them as a preliminary step in our investigation for three reasons, however. Firstly, they each argue persuasively for the importance of the concept of intersubjectivity. Secondly, they each provide a (different) map of the conceptual terrain of intersubjectivity, which together provide us with a comprehensive account of both the issues which we must address in our study and the relationships between them. Thirdly, each has been of considerable significance in the recent history of academic debate on 'intersubjectivity'. They have raised the questions and posed the problems which have provided the point of departure for later writers in the intersubjectivist tradition, including many of those discussed in subsequent chapters of this book.

Through the course of the chapter I will be identifying issues which are taken up and discussed at later points in the book. In addition, I use the chapter to outline a conceptual distinction (between radical and egological modes of intersubjectivity) which I take to be central and which I use to structure the earlier part of the book. The general structure of the book is outlined in the concluding section of the chapter.

Husserl's Other: Against Transcendental Solipsism

Husserl (1859–1938) begins *Cartesian Meditations* (1991) by retracing the *Meditations* of the seventeenth-century French philosopher René Descartes (1969). Like Descartes, he elects to doubt, for methodological purposes, everything of which he cannot be absolutely certain. And as with Descartes, he is thereby led to doubt the existence of a 'real' world beyond and external to his thoughts and perceptions. He even doubts all empirical facts about himself, such as the existence of his own body and the contents of his memories and biography. Such phenomena could, he argues, be halluci-nations or dreams. How would he know the difference? All that he can be certain of is that he thinks and that he must therefore exist qua thinking being. This truth is still affirmed if everything that he believes and thinks is incorrect because incorrect thoughts are no less thoughts than correct thoughts and as thoughts they presuppose the existence of a thinker.

Descartes's strategy from this position was to prove the existence of God, to reason that God is good and that a good God would not completely deceive him, at least with respect to his fundamental ways of thinking, and thus to gradually reinstate the beliefs that he had previously doubted. He thus advocates a realist epistemology. Husserl takes a different path. He does not reason his way back to 'the real world'. What we learn from Descartes's method of doubt, he argues, is that nothing is changed in the world of our conscious experience by suspending the belief that this world of experience refers to a world external to it. We still continue to experience a meaningful world of objects, even if their claim to external reality is suspended. This fact has two implications for Husserl. Firstly, it suggests that, for us, the world can never be anything other than the world of our conscious experience. We can never know if there is a world beyond our conscious experience. And if there is, we can never know what it is like. Secondly, it suggests that consciousness is necessarily 'intentional'; that is, it is the very nature of consciousness to be consciousness of something or other. One cannot be conscious without being conscious of something.

From this position, Husserl outlines a philosophical project, phenomenology, which is concerned to investigate the various ways in which different objects are 'intended' in consciousness; that is, the ways in which different objects are presented to consciousness. In order that this project be carried out rigorously, moreover, he advocates that phenomenologists swap the Cartesian method of doubt for a process of 'phenomenological reduction'. This entails a similar bracketing out of the external world to that achieved by Cartesian doubt, but rather than doubting the existence of the world beyond their experience, which would always involve the possibility of reaffirming the existence of that world, as Descartes did, phenomenologists merely suspend their belief in it, so that they can examine how it or parts of it are intended in consciousness. The existence of the world is neither doubted, rejected nor affirmed in this process of reduction. All such possibilities are bracketed out of consideration so that its manner of being-for-consciousness can be examined.

This position involves a direct criticism of Descartes. His attempt to affirm the existence of a world beyond consciousness is taken to be an impossible project because it entails that we must know that which is, by definition, beyond our knowledge and experience. This is rejoined by a further criticism regarding his failure to examine the 'transcendental ego' that was left over after he had doubted all empirical facts about himself; that is, the disembodied thinker that knows that it exists because it thinks. In Husserl's view, the existence and character of such an ego was the key discovery of Descartes's *Meditations*, but it was a discovery which Descartes himself remained largely ignorant of.

Following this criticism, Husserl advocates a thesis of 'transcendental idealism'; that is, he argues that the contents of consciousness are necessarily meaningful to it and that these meanings are dependent upon its own constitutive actions qua transcendental ego. The transcendental ego is said to bestow meaning upon the objects intended in consciousness. Furthermore, he argues that the phenomenological analysis of modes of intentionality should therefore necessarily entail an analysis of modes of constitution. Phenomenology thus becomes an analysis of the active constitution of the objects of experience. This thesis begs an important question for Husserl, however, which he spends a large part of *Cartesian Meditations* attempting to answer; namely, the question of the existence of other consciousnesses and his relationship to them. This is the Husserlian version of the question of intersubjectivity.

The question is posed in relation to the problem of solipsism or, more particularly, in relation to Husserl's anticipation of the objection that his thesis leads to and is inevitably solipsistic. Critics, he speculates, might object that transcendental idealism necessarily reduces the other (i.e. other conscious subjects) to the consciousness that one has of them:

> But what about other egos, who surely are not intending and intended *in me*, merely synthetic unities of possible verification *in me*, but, according to their own sense, precisely *others*? (Husserl 1991: 89, original emphasis)

The importance of this question and of avoiding solipsism is argued for, by Husserl, on ethical, epistemological and, later in *Cartesian Meditations*, social-ontological grounds.

At the ethical level, the problem of solipsism and the corresponding necessity for an intersubjectivist position is quite clear. Recognition of other (autonomous) subjectivities or consciousnesses is fundamental to any ethical relationship. We enter into ethical relations with others precisely to the extent that we recognise that they exist in their own right and have projects of their own, that they are not reducible to our thought about them but are precisely 'other'. If the other is nothing more than the idea which I have of them, as the solipsist claims, then I can have no obligation towards them because there is nobody, in a strict sense, to be obliged to.

At the epistemological level, Husserl expresses concern regarding solipsism because, he claims, other perspectives on the world than my own are necessary if the objectivity of the world is to be established. Objectivity, in this sense, is intersubjective. It is a view of the world arrived at through mutual confirmation and negotiation between different and independent perspectives. Rationality is also at stake here. Rationality, for Husserl and other phenomenologists, is not an individual but an intersubjective attribute. It manifests in a form of interpersonal persuasion and decision-making which relies neither upon force nor upon deception but upon an appeal to common evidence and argument, and thus to a reciprocity of individual perspectives and an interchangeability of individual standpoints. Such interchangeability is, of course, impossible in the solitary world of the solipsist because there are no others with whom one's perspective can reciprocate or interchange.

Finally, Husserl is concerned about the problem of solipsism and intersubjectivity because he aims to provide a philosophical elaboration of collective human phenomena, such as culture and community, and such phenomena are strictly inaccessible to the solipsist. They rely upon the possibility of a human 'interworld', a world of shared meaning which transcends individual consciousness. This is antithetic to the solitariness of solipsism.

Having established the importance of intersubjectivity, Husserl states that his method of establishing it philosophically will be phenomenological. Given the importance of transcending solipsism, he notes, the temptation is to opt for a Cartesian realism which rushes to establish the concrete existence of the other. But this road is not open to us because we cannot transcend the world of our own consciousness. And it is not necessary, in any case, because (in phenomenology) we do not doubt that existence. We have only suspended our belief in the independent existence of the other, and we have done so only to know better how they are intended and constituted in our consciousness of them.

The first stage of Husserl's analysis of this mode of intentionality addresses the manner in which other consciousnesses are routinely present to our consicousness in mundane situations. He suggests three ways. Firstly, others are presented to us as wordly, psycho-physical objects which are governed psychologically by motives, reasons, cognitions, etc. We experience them as intelligent but nevertheless as objects. Secondly, we experience others as subjects who experience and know the world and who experience and know us as a part of that world. In this way we can experience ourselves as experienced by the other (e.g. when we feel that we are being watched). Finally, Husserl maintains that we experience the world as an intersubjective world; that is, as a world experienced by others. This is exemplified when we point things out to others, or when we argue with them about things. Such argument presupposes that they can see the world as we do. Together, Husserl notes, these three elements comprise an 'empathic intentionality'.

What particularly impresses Husserl in this analysis is the genuine sense of otherness that is embodied in our perceptions and experiences. We seem able to transcend the particularity of our own perspective and to actually experience the experience of others. Or again, to experience our world as experienced by others. This observation raises the next and most important question for Husserl: how is this possible? How can one, as a particular consciousness, experience the consciousness of another? The question is perplexing because the consciousnesses of others are not tangible and visible percepts, as are our usual objects of experience. They are not objects and do not assume the form of objects. They are intentional experiences in their own right and seem only to be accessible, therefore, from within.

As a first step to solving this problem, Husserl performs a further methodological reduction. Having bracketed out of consideration the question of the external reality of that which he consciously perceives, he now reduces this phenomenological level to his 'sphere of ownness'. This involves a (methodological) bracketing of all traces of otherness which were revealed in his brief description of mundane consciousness. Others are no longer perceived as subjects. They are perceived as objects of his perception. And his experience of the world is deprived of its objective feel. It is reduced to his singular sense perception of it. This considerably affects his experience of his world, he claims, but it does not affect his sense of his psyche.

There are two purposes behind this second reduction. Firstly, given that his experience of his psyche remains intact at this level, it reveals a level of experience more primordial than that in which otherness is experienced and it thus reveals that the psyche is monadic at its most fundamental level. Secondly, it reveals the nature and forms of his psyche to him. He is able to identify himself both as a transcendental ego and as an empirical, psycho-physical ego which is composed of perceptions, memories, imaginings and is irreducibly embodied. This self-knowledge and the fact that it is still available in the reduced sphere of ownness is important to Husserl's case because it indicates a knowledge base (of consciousness and subjectivity) from which knowledge and experience of others might be constructed.

Having explicated his sphere of ownness, Husserl is finally ready to explain the empathic intentionality that constitutes otherness within consciousness. This explanation involves the interrelated processes of 'analogical apperception' and 'pairing'.

'Apperception', in this context, is a process which phenomenologists commonly identify in relation to perception. It refers to the manner in which our perceptions are informed by prior expectations and understanding, such that we perceive more than we actually see. A common example of this involves the perception of a house. When we look at a house we inevitably see it from a particular perspective and, as such, we do not see a whole house. We see a house front or a house back etc. We do not say that we see a house front, however, and neither do we experience our perception in this way. At our most pedantic we experience and say that we experience a house from the front, which entails that the whole house is there but that we are seeing it from an angle. The significance of the difference between perceiving a house front and perceiving a house from the front is revealed in the shock that we experience when the expectations that inform our apperception are revealed to be incorrect; when, for example, we discover that we are on a film set and that the houses don't actually have backs and sides. This shock reveals that there was an assumption, embodied in our perception, that we were seeing a house from the front and not merely a house front. It indicates that we perceived more than we actually saw. A similar process to this happens between the senses. Visual materials, for example, provide us with an expectation about and a sense of taste, smell or weight, as is revealed when that expectation is found to be incorrect; for example, when something which we perceived to be heavy is found to be quite light and we tumble backwards as a consequence of the excess of force that we applied to lifting it.

This process of apperception is relevant to the question of our perception and experience of others because it addresses the manner in which our perceptions go beyond what we see, to incorporate invisible dimensions. Just as we apperceive the back of a house when we see it from the front, so too we can apperceive consciousness in the movement of a body or face. There is a problem here, however, concerning the source of our apperceptions. I apperceive the back of a house from the front view, and I am able to do so because I have seen numerous house backs which are connected to fronts and sides. I have a wealth of direct experiences of houses to draw from in my apperception. But this is not true of others, because I have never seen another consciousness directly. If I had, then 'intersubjectivity' would not be a philosophical problem, or at least it would not be the problem that Husserl takes it to be. Thus, in itself, 'apperception' is not a solution to the problem of intersubjectivity. This is where the 'analogical' aspect of 'analogical apperception' comes in.

We do not have direct experience of other consciousnesses, Husserl notes, but the earlier stages of his meditations have already shown that we do have direct experience of our own conscious, subjective life. Thus our experience and perception of others qua conscious subjects, which is an undeniable aspect of our conscious life, must be based upon an imaginative analogical transfer of our own experiences onto others. Empathy is an imaginative process, or at least a conjunction of perception and imagination (Ricoeur 1967a). This analogical transfer is not a process of conscious reasoning, according to Husserl, but it is nevertheless a reasonable process which might be reconstructed (consciously) as follows: the other has a body which is identical to mine and they move as I do, my body and movements embody conscious life and experience, therefore the other's probably does too. Furthermore, there is always room for verification or refutation of this imaginative hypothesis. One will continue to believe that the other is a conscious subject and to imaginatively transfer experiences onto them for as long as they continue to behave in a way which is understandable from the point of view of a conscious subject. Hammond et al. (1991: 217) liken this situation to a sci-fi thriller scenario, where an android replica is distinguished from the red-blooded conscious hero on the basis of its lack of all-too-human traits; for example, it doesn't appear anxious when it should from a human point of view.

Integral to this process is what Husserl refers to as pairing. Whenever we perceive things (any things) that are alike we transfer attributions and treat them alike, he argues. We treat them as a pair. There is nothing peculiar about the perception of the other in this respect, except that it is ourself qua embodied ego which we pair with the object of our perception.

From this point in the argument, Husserl moves on to consider how the different position of our body, relative to the other, further facilitates a sense of otherness. We perceive the other as 'there' in relation to our 'here', he observes, and thus we recognise both that they have a distinct point of view on the world and that the world can be seen from different points of view and under different perspectives. This (again tacit rather than reflective) imaginative process is the origin of objectivity, rationality and community in the senses already discussed for Husserl and he spends the final pages of *Cartesian Meditations* adding the finishing touches to his discussion of them. The main work is already achieved, however, in the form of 'analogical apperception' and 'pairing'.

Husserl Assessed

Husserl's account of intersubjectivity is of considerable value. His concern with the problem of solipsism emphasises the importance of establishing 'intersubjectivity' as a grounding concept and thus of intersubjectivism more generally. Moreover, his account of the manner in which otherness is given to us in ordinary experience provides a useful account of the types of phenomena which must be considered in our discussion of intersubjectivity. He is at least correct in this respect, or partly so. There are major problems with the Husserlian account of intersubjectivity, however. These problems, which I outline below, do not completely undermine it. There is a place for the Husserlian version of intersubjectivity, as I show in Chapter 3. Nevertheless it cannot serve the fundamental role which Husserl would seem to believe that it can.

The first and most general objection which one can make to Husserl is that his methodological position of phenomenology, particularly in its transcendental and idealist form, seems condemned to a form of solipsism. Transcendental phenomenology will always have a solipsistic element because it begins and ends with an analysis of the constitutive operations of a solitary consciousness. It focuses exclusively upon an individual flow of experience and, as such, otherness will always be reduced in it to the experience of otherness which is constituted in that flow. In this respect, I suggest, Husserl does not completely set the criticisms which he anticipates to rest, and he cannot do so. His 'other' is always necessarily created by him, through an imaginative, analogical process. It can only ever be what he makes it. Thus a full transcendence of solipsism requires a break with transcendental and idealist phenomenology and with the focus on consciousness which this entails. We do not necessarily want to revert back to Cartesian realism, but Husserl fails to offer us an adequate alternative.

It is not just methodological bracketing that is the problem here. A large part of the difficulty with Husserl's approach lies in the manner in which he conceives of human consciousness and subjectivity. Three aspects of this conception are particularly problematic. Firstly, his 'subject' is constituted exclusively through 'observation'. It observes and experiences others but never interacts with them or becomes engaged with them in any way. Taking this stance ensures that others can never be anything other than that which is observed and thus further ensures that they are always reduced to the consciousness which self has of them. Following on from this, secondly,

Husserl's 'subject' or 'consciousness' (at least in *Cartesian Meditations*) is constituted exclusively by way of perceptions and imaginings (where the images are perceptual in form) to the exclusion of a consideration of the role of speech and language. This is a significant omission because much of our conscious life is precisely constituted through what we say either to ourselves or to others. What we think takes a linguistic form and it is only by way of language that we become aware of what we think. Moreover, speech and language, as phenomena in the life of consciousness, are more obviously related to intersubjectivity than perception and imagination. It is by way of speech, for example, that we participate with others in mutually meaningful situations. Speech is a form of interaction. Furthermore, as I discuss in the next chapter, the dialogical structure of conversation is strictly irreducible. By entering into dialogue, subjects transcend their individuation and become components in a larger whole.

The third problem with Husserl's characterisation of the subject also concerns language and speech but this time in relation to 'meaning'. For Husserl, meaning is reducible to a constituting act of consciousness. Consciousness bestows meaning upon the world. There are many problems with such a view, some of which are discussed in the next chapter. Most problematic from an intersubjectivist point of view, however, is that this conception precludes the possibility that meanings might be shared or communicated by subjects in an interworld or community. All meanings must necessarily be reduced to the particular consciousness which constitutes them and, as such, each consciousness will have its own meanings to which it alone has access. Meaning is thus a private affair and communication is only apparent; nothing is passed between subjects but meaningless sounds or inscriptions whose sense is constituted individually and separately by speakers and listeners. The implication of this, at the very least, is that Husserl's theory cannot account for 'rationality' and 'community' as he understands them. The world of experience, as he theorises it, is necessarily monadic and incommunicable.

Again a focus upon language and speech could circumvent this problem. As I show in the next chapter, recent philosophies of language and speech argue persuasively that linguistic meanings are strictly irreducible to individual consciousnesses. They are, it is argued, dependent upon social and intersubjective relationships and conventions and they are therefore necessarily shared. Speech is necessarily meaningful, irrespective of the operations of consciousness, according to this view, and this meaningfulness is intersubjectively constituted. It derives from language, which, in turn, derives from social life.

For critics of phenomenology such as Habermas (1987a, 1991a), the importance of language and speech in relation to intersubjectivity leads them to focus exclusively upon them. Habermas explicitly rejects the idea that perception has any role in our discussion of intersubjectivity and dismisses the perceptual focus altogether. Indeed he rejects any reference to 'consciousness' in the philosophy of intersubjectivity. I would not go as far as this, however, for a number of reasons. Firstly, we cannot dispense entirely with a consideration of perception, since language is always necessarily either read (and thus seen) or listened to. It must be received and thus an account of language must involve a proper account of perception. This is not to say that linguistic consciousness is reducible to perceptual consciousness. It is not (as will be become apparent later in the book), not least because of its necessarily participatory character. It is an extremely important and irreducible component of subjectivity which any account of intersubjectivity must necessarily account for. Nevertheless, some account of perception is involved in any account of language and this too must be accounted for. Secondly, as my discussion of Merleau-Ponty in Chapter 2 will show, there are better accounts of perception than the idealist version outlined in *Cartesian Meditations*, ones which are more appropriate to a discussion of intersubjectivity. Combined with a discussion of speech and language, these accounts allow us a more comprehensive understanding of intersubjectivity than an exclusively linguistic version. Thirdly, it is obvious that much of our conscious life is composed of perceptions and imaginings. Thus an account which functions through their exclusion is very fragile and is limited in what it can say about human life. Linguistic, perceptual and imaginary aspects of subjectivity must all be considered with a full weighting in our analysis of intersubjectivity. It should be added here, finally, that subjective life has an affective component which is crucial to our relations with others. Both Husserl and Habermas miss this point.

Three further lines of critique of the Husserlian position are suggested in Alfred Schutz's (1970) discussion of *Cartesian Meditations*. Schutz's first criticism concerns the reduction to the sphere of ownness. To reduce to the sphere of ownness, he argues, necessarily presupposes a definition of ownness, which in turn presupposes some sense of what does not belong to self and is therefore other. A consciousness of self, in other words, always already entails a sense of the other. They are relational terms, each meaningless without the other. This is quite a devastating criticism of the Husserlian position, which makes consciousness of the other dependent upon a prior consciousness of self, and it is sustained even if disconnected from the reduction to the sphere of ownness. To attribute consciousness to another being one must be aware of one's own consciousness as a particular consciousness, and this seems necessarily to entail a consciousness of alterity from which self can be comparatively demarcated.

It follows from this, importantly, that there can be no self-consciousness and no self-knowledge without awareness of the other. Therefore the thesis of the monadic psyche, at one level at least, collapses. Insofar as consciousness is monadic, it cannot be self-consciousness. We will see how this view of self-consciousness can be developed in an intersubjective theory when we discuss Kojève and Hegel.

Schutz's second criticism concerns the asymmetry between the perception of one's own conscious life and the perception of that of the other (by way of their behaviour). Husserl's conception of pairing assumes that the life of consciousness looks the same from the outside-in as from the inside-out, Schutz argues. This is how we (as constituting egos) know to pair the two and it is the only way in which we could know this in the terms of Husserl's account. But the inside-out and outside-in views are not the same. The experience of pain, for example, feels quite different to the sight of a display of pain behaviour. Likewise, the experience of perception is quite different from the sight of another person's eyes or ears, or indeed of the bodily movements involved in perception. Indeed, with respect to much of our perceptual life, we might say that we do not experience it (and thus do not experience ourselves in it) at all. Perception is a vehicle by which we experience but which we do not experience in itself. Furthermore, we seldom see that part of our own body which is most expressive of our intelligence and consciousness; that is, our face. It is very unlikely, therefore, that our experience of otherness is based on analogy with ourself. Or at least, insofar as we do understand others by way of analogy, this process must be mediated by a prior process or factor in which the inside-out and outside-in views are already paired. The obvious contender for this job is again language or other significant symbols. In language our experiences are coded with those of others under common labels. I will discuss this in more detail in Chapter 2.

It might be objected here that social technologies such as mirrors, cameras and videos give us a fair idea of our own externality, which could then be used in analogical apperception. This does not suffice to rescue Husserl, however. There are many reasons for this. Most important amongst these is that the ability to recognise an image of self, and thus to identify self, already presupposes consciousness of not self or of the other (in the sense discussed above) and thus it could not be invoked in an attempt to understand our conception of the other. One already needs to distinguish me/not me in order to recognise oneself in a mirror, as I will show in my discussion of the 'mirror stage' in Chapter 3.

Schutz's third criticism of Husserl is that we cannot develop a phenomenology of community around the model of face-to-face interaction. Communities involve wider and more divergent forms of relationship than this, he maintains. And these need to be explicated in their own terms. I will discuss how Schutz does this in Chapter 4. For the moment, however, I will turn to examine the work of Martin Buber.

Martin Buber and the Between

My exposition of Buber (1878–1965) must begin with a major qualification. *I and Thou* (1958) is as much a theological work about our relations with God as a philosophical work about intersubjectivity. It is based in the author's faith. I do not share the author's faith, however, and whilst I find the book fascinating with respect to the question of (wordly, material) intersubjectivity, I achieve this only by ignoring its theological component. Therefore my (atheistic) reading of Buber necessarily ignores much of what he argues. Indeed it completely misses the point as he presumably intended it. The reader must decide if such exegetic butchery has been worth the effort.

Buber's central contention, with which he opens *I and Thou*, is that the world is 'twofold' for human subjects, in accordance with their 'twofold attitude'. What this means is that human subjectivity is necessarily directed towards alterity (Husserl would say that it is necessarily intentional) and that it can take up this directedness and live it out in one of two ways: I–It or I–Thou. These alternatives, as their names suggest, are ways of addressing alterity. In the first case, the address is objectifying. It constitutes the other as an object (an 'It') to be *experienced* and *used*. In the second instance, by contrast, a *mutual relationship* is initiated. Following from this, moreover, the first case entails that the other is experienced as consisting in parts and being located in space, and that it is mediated by a knowing consciousness, whilst in the second case the relationship is immediate and space is shared with the other, who is present as a whole. The other is not experienced in this case. We may not even be aware of them, as such, because we are too closely involved and harmonised with them. This can be summarised by saying that in the first case the other is an *object of our experience*, whilst in the second they are a *subject who is in communication with us*. The I is privileged in the first case, reducing otherness to itself and to its ideas. The 'It' is an object to be controlled and manipulated. In the second case, by contrast, both partners are equal and ideas move between them in a communicative exchange.

It is integral to this distinction that the I is not constant across both attitudes. The I is not a fixed substance for Buber. It is a relation and is constituted in the attitude assumed towards the other. In the first case, this relation is constituted through objectification; the I is a subject of knowledge and experience. It is reflective and is reflectively/reflexively aware of itself. In the I–Thou case, by contrast, it is an interlocutor, irreducibly bound to the other with whom it is engaged. There is no sharp sense of distinction in this case, no reflective awareness of either self or other. Self is too engaged and involved with other to be reflectively aware of either its own existence or theirs.

Buber's intent, in identifying I–It and I–Thou relations, is chiefly ethical and critical. Whilst he argues that both I–Thou and I–It relations are necessary to human subjectivity and to practical social life, he is nevertheless concerned that I–It relations are begining to predominate in modern rationalised, industrialised societies and he sees this as a deterioration in the quality of human relations. For him this valuation is based on the view that I-Thou relations are an extension of our relations to God, but we need not accept this religious baggage in order to accept the point. Although there is room for equivocation (see Chapter 7), we would not ordinarily view objectification as the proper basis for an ethical and qualitiative relationship. Objectification, as Buber notes, is related to the need to control our environments, which is sometimes necessary but is potentially dangerous when applied to other persons. This is much the same view as I noted with respect to Husserl. However, having said this, what Husserl describes as intersubjectivity seems to conform more to what Buber describes as an I–It relation and could not therefore be described as an ethical relationship in Buberian terms (Levinas 1989).

It is not just on the ethical front that Buber provides a critical alternative to Husserl. He does so on the ontological front also. Buber's I–Thou can be regarded as a completely different manner of being to that accounted for by Husserl. This point has been argued by both Levinas (1989) and Theunissen (1984), who both maintain that Buber takes us beyond the subject-centred ontology of Husserl, towards an ontology of the 'interval' or the 'between'. That is to say, Buber does not reduce the meeting and relationship of persons to the consciousness which either of them have of it (neither, by the same token, does he take the objectivistic line of viewing it in terms of a coincidence of coordinates in space); rather, he takes the meeting of participants and the space which links them as an irreducible and primordial structure. Such a situation is meaningful and thoughtful but the meanings and thoughts that it entails are strictly irreducible to either participant. They are formed in and belong to the interworld which forms between them. Moreover, each participant is decentred in relation to the joint situation. Their thoughts and experiences are dialogically interwoven with those of their other.

This common linkage is possible by virtue of language and speech. In speaking we assume a common basis for our thought, and our thoughts are made available to others (potentially at least) in the very same way, at the very same time, as they are made available to us. Furthermore, in conversation ideas literally pass between us:

> Ideas are no more enthroned above our heads than resident in them; they wander amongst us and accost us. (Buber 1958: 27)

The situation of the other in I–Thou relations is also quite different to that described in *Cartesian Meditations* (and to I–It relations). They are, to paraphrase Levinas (1989), radically other. There are two basic differences involved here. First, the other is not reduced to the ego's conscious comprehension and constitution of them. They remain irreducible to the thought process of the ego. Secondly, they are not apprehended by way of their similarity to the ego (as in analogical apperception) and need not be similar. Indeed, Buber is quite clear that the other involved in I–Thou relations need not be another human being. It might equally be an animal, a plant or a landscape. Having said this, however, he does privilege human-to-human relations because they involve language and dialogue. This makes possible a special form of shared understanding, mutuality and reciprocity. Linguistic beings can confer and ask and answer questions. The fabric of language holds them closely together.

Human subjectivity ordinarily swings between I–Thou and I–It relations for Buber. Or, rather, it consists in this swinging. We continually move between the two. Having said this, however, Buber argues for the primacy of I–Thou relations at both an existential and an ontogenetic–psychological level. At the existential level he maintains that I–Thou relations are primary since they must be presupposed in I–It relations. I–It relations involve objectification, he notes, but objectification is always objectification of something that already exists for us and thus it presupposes a prior, non-objectifying mode of being-with otherness.

This primacy is replicated at the ontogenetic–psychological level in the respect that the child is born with an innate Thou, according to Buber, without it yet being capable of I–It relations. The innate Thou is exemplified, he maintains, in the fascination and enjoyment which the infant appears to derive from 'conversing' with its environment and with its apparent lack of any reflective awareness of itself in this process. The infant, like the interlocutor in the I–Thou relation, has no sense of its own distinctness from the other. This is not identical to the mature I–Thou relation, in Buber's view, because the infant cannot yet speak and lacks even the sense of self necessary for ordered, reciprocal dialogue. These are features which will only be acquired by way of interaction, he argues, and by way of the acquisition of language. These same processes also give rise to the possibility of reflective objectification, however, and thus to the I–It relation. The child becomes capable of genuine meaningful exchange with others, but it equally becomes capable of the sharp sense of distance and distinction.

The implication of much of Buber's work is that there is a symmetry in relationships. Partners stand either in I–It relations or in I–Thou relations. He does refer to the possibility of asymmetry, however, and particularly to the possibility of a 'demonaic thou' who is universally recognised as thou but does not recognise others in this way. Napoleon is the example which Buber uses of such a figure, which suggests that such figures are public and political. There is no necessity for this, however. It seems evident that such asymmetry can manifest in a range of different types of relationship, both personal and public. Intersubjectivity, in this sense, is always a potential site of power. It is always political.

The Importance of Language

Language plays a central role in Buber's philosophy of intersubjectivity and he advocates a very specific conception of it. He is concerned with the role of speech as a constitutive action. This is particularly important in relation to the word couples I–It and I–Thou. These couples aren't so much descriptions, he argues, as ways of opening and initiating relationships. It is by utterance of the word 'Thou' that an I–Thou relation is begun. This is not to say that those particular words need be spoken, nor that the meaning and effect of such words is not affected by context. Furthermore, modes of address can be spoken insincerely. Buber's point, however, is that it is in taking up a particular form of address that our relations to others are constituted. And these modes of address will ordinarily be linguistic.

This point is illustrated in Buber's historical critique of the increasing preponderance of I–It relations. This historical shift is indicated, he argues, by the difference between modern European languages and more traditional or 'primitive' languages. The latter, which are rooted in more communal ways of living and experiencing, embody a much more concrete and relational form. They both indicate and constitute a greater preponderance of I–Thou relations.

This example also illustrates the extent to which language is, for Buber, an intersubjective and social structure. Language is not transcendental in this view. It belongs to the life of a community, as an institution, and it is activated in praxis as the structuring principle of that praxis. In this respect Buber believes that subjectivity, in his sense of the word, is subtended by a belongingness to a linguistic community and to the common fabric of language. In contrast to Husserl and his notion of a sphere of ownness, Buber emphasises the extent to which subjectivity (even I–It subjectivity) depends upon participation in a common intersubjective space, a between:

> . . . in actuality speech does not abide in man, but man takes his stand in speech and talks from there. (Buber 1958: 57)

The subject is not an isolated monad, in the Husserlian sense. It is always already situated in a social-linguistic between world or interworld. And its capacity for making sense and meaning is dependent upon this. This point is recognised to some extent in Husserl's later work. In *The Crisis of the European Sciences and Transcendental Phenomenology* (1970), he posits the concept 'lifeworld', a concept which identifies shared and acquired cultural 'maps' and assumptions in the substructure of our thought and action. For the later Husserl, as for Buber, conscious subjectivities belong irreducibly to shared interworlds of meaning. I will return to this concept of the lifeworld, as developed in the work of Schutz and Habermas, later in the book. For the moment, suffice it to say that, for Buber, the basic structure of the interworld is formed through the conventions and forms of a shared language.

Buber Assessed

The concept of I–Thou relations captures an element of intersubjectivity which is completely absent in Husserl and it serves to highlight the egological bias in his conception of intersubjectivity. Furthermore, Buber's recognition that self and other are always relational terms is a considerable advance on the Husserlian perspective. Self and other, as I argued in my critique of Husserl, must always be accounted for, as Buber accounts for them, as elements of a common structure. Buber's twofold typology is limited, however, because it is unable to account for the type of relationship with otherness that Husserl describes, a relationship which is, I suggest, confirmed by our experiences and which is equally as common as either of the two experiences described by Buber. The other is clearly 'experienced' by self in Husserl's account. His *Cartesian Meditations* precisely concern the possibility of such an 'experience'. Thus, Husserlian intersubjectivity must be interpreted as a variation upon I–It relations. The other qua object of experience which is constituted by self is clearly not addressed as 'thou'. They are reduced to self, neither speaking for themselves nor relating with self. Moreover, the I of the Husserlian account is a subject of experience and contemplation who observes rather than engaging with the other. Nevertheless, the other is not constituted as an 'it' in *Cartesian Meditations*. They are precisely constitued as another consciousness or ego. They are experienced as experiencing. They are a subject–object or an It-Thou. And as such they form a third possibility between Buber's two alternatives.

There is, moreover, a moral element to the Husserlian position which is missed in Buber's account of ethics. Although the other is reduced to an experience of self, in Husserl's account, this process is nevertheless empathic. Self puts itself in the place of the other, acknowledging the other as a subject and thus recognising a moral status for that other. A strict Buberian might reply to this that putting onself in the place of the other is tantamount to displacing them and is not therefore ethical. The only truly ethical relationship, they would argue, is one in which partners are each able to represent themselves in an open dialogue. There is perhaps some truth to this but we must concede that empathy has some place in our ethical life. At the very least it seems preferable to the instrumental relationship to otherness adopted in true I–It relations.

The distinction between the Husserlian other and the radical other of Buber's I–Thou relation is a more important distinction than that between I-Thou and I–It relations, in my view, since we tend to fluctuate more along that axis, in human relations, than between I–Thou and I–It relations. That is to say, we fluctuate between genuine, open dialogue with others and imaginary (perhaps paranoid) constructions of them which we (re-)create for ourselves. Sometimes we genuinely engage with others in communicative relations, other times we anticipate, imagine, empathise. I will thus drop the Buberian distinction between I–Thou and I–It relations, replacing it with a distinction between radical (I-Thou) and egological (Husserlian) intersubjectivity. Or rather, given the stated problems with Husserl's position, I will do so when I have reconstructed a position from which we might refer meaningfully to analogical apperception.

This reconstruction, which is outlined in Chapter 3, will involve the further incorporation of many Buberian elements into the Husserlian view. In particular I will be arguing that self and other are necessarily relational terms and that neither can be conceived as pre-existing the other. Moreover, following Buber and using contemporary psychological analysis, I will be suggesting both that there is an innate thou and that radical intersubjectivity is prior to egological intersubjectivity. The egological sense of self and other,

I will argue, is the result of a specifiable social-developmental process. Finally, I take from Buber the idea that subjectivity consists in a swinging between attitudes. Our lives are inextricably bound up with those of others, I contend, but our ways of being with others are continually shifting between the radical and egological modes. And they may, on occasion, involve both. Importantly however, it will be a fluctuation between radical (I-Thou) and egological (Husserlian) modes of intersubjectivity that I will be addressing, not between I–Thou and I–It relations.

My prioritisation of the radical–egological duality does not preclude the possibility of I–It relations in the Buberian sense. We clearly do objectify each other, on occasion, and I–It relations are most common in our relations with non-human things (notwithstanding occasional animism). I will be clear to consider this throughout the book. In particular I will discuss it in relation to Habermas's understanding of labour in Chapter 5, and to certain forms of prejudice and conflict. I have not dropped the 'It' from consideration. I have simply moved it to a less central position in our understanding of intersubjective relations.

Buber introduces many other useful innovations in his discussion of intersubjectivity, some of which I will be returning to later in the book. In particular his introduction of the concept of power and asymmetry is important, as is his discussion of the historical transition towards objectifying forms of social relationship. Notwithstanding this, however, his discussion of each of these issues is too brief and sketchy to be of much use to us. We will need to look beyond Buber if we are to discuss these issues substantively.

The Struggle for Recognition

The final theory that I will consider in this chapter concerns the human desire and struggle for recognition. This notion has a long lineage in Western philosophy (Fukuyama 1992). Our concern, however, is with the Hegelian (Hegel 1770–1831) version of the thesis, specifically the version posited in Alexander Kojève's (1969) influential *Introduction to the Reading of Hegel*. This text, which has been the subject of some controversy amongst Hegelians (Kelly 1965), focuses upon Hegel's (1979) *The Phenomenology of Spirit*. The idea of a struggle for recognition is also discussed in Hegel's (1971) *Philosophy of Mind*, however, and as both Axel Honneth (1995) and Jürgen Habermas (1974) emphasise in their reading of Hegel, it was first introduced in his 1805–6 Jena lectures.

The struggle for recognition is posited in Hegel's work during a discussion of the origins of self-consciousness. Hegel is concerned to identify the conditions which give rise to this state, and he duly traces through various levels of consciousness (each dialectically contained within whilst superseded by the next) to identify these conditions. The first three levels that he considers, which are given with the organism in isolation, are 'sense certainty', 'perception' and 'understanding'. At each of these stages, though they are different, he argues, consciousness loses itself in that which it is consciousness of. It is absorbed in and by the objects of its experience and fails to distinguish itself from them. This is slightly altered at the next level of consciousness, 'desire'. In desire, Hegel argues, consciousness becomes partly aware of itself through the experience of lack (e.g. in the desire for food it experiences itself through hunger, the lack of food). However, ordinary desires are not sufficient to explain full self-consciousness according to Hegel. All animals have these desires, he notes, but not all animals are self-conscious.

Only the human species is capable of full self-consciousness in Hegel's schema and this is explained by a desire that is peculiar to human beings alone: the desire for desire or rather the desire to be desired, the desire for recognition. Human consciousness desires to be recognised as consciousness, for Hegel. Moreover, such recognition is required if consciousness is to achieve full self-consciousness. Only through the mediation of the consciousness of the other can consciousness turn back upon itself and identify itself:

> Self-consciousness exists in and for itself when, and only by the fact that, it so exists for another; that is, it exists only in being acknowledged. (Hegel 1979: 11)

Desire, recognition and self-consciousness are intimately and inseparably bound in this schema. Consciousness only becomes aware of itself when and to the extent that it identifies the existence of other consciousnesses. It must decentre itself, identifying and acknowledging its own particularity as a perspective upon the world amongst other perspectives. Prior to this it makes and can make no distinction between the world and its particular view of the world or between itself and the world. This decentring leaves a tension or a gap, however. Consciousness is pulled out of itself when it identifies the consciousness of the other. It is alienated from itself, experiencing itself only as an object in the experience of the other. And only the recognition of the other will return it to itself. Only when the other acknowledges that it recognises consciousness as consciousness will consciousness be able to experience itself as such. Self-consciousness is an intersubjective phenomenon in this sense, achievable only through mutual recognition between consciousnesses. Furthermore, our sense of self-esteem, pride and dignity is integral to this. These are feelings that we can only have relative to the other and they are thus bound to our relations and interactions with others.

However, recognition is not automatically granted, according to Hegel. The desire for recognition is expressed in the first instance in a 'fight to the death'. Hegel's explanation of this fight is obscure. It involves three central claims. Firstly, in order to be human and to be recognised as such, one must place and be seen to place one's human desire above all animal desires, particularly the animal desire for self-preservation. Secondly, this implies that one must risk one's life for one's humanity. Thirdly, this is expressed in a contest in which each risks his or her life and this is a fight to the death. One proves oneself in the fight to the death.

One possible ending to this fight, in Hegel's view, involves one contestant killing the other. This is not satisfactory for either party. The loser dies whilst the winner loses his or her only possible source of recognition. Another possible ending involves one party surrendering to and fully recognising the other, without enjoying such recognition for him- or herself. They succumb to their animal desire for self-preservation and become a slave to the other, thereby giving rise to a relationship of master and slave. Historically, both of these outcomes may have been realised. But the former can only give rise to human extinction, whilst the latter can and does give rise to a historical dynamic. History, in this view, is a sucession of sets of social relations which are animated by way of a struggle for recognition.

At this point, Hegel's level of analysis shifts. Self-consciousness is identified as being dependent upon the historical dynamic of social relationships. An analysis of consciousnesses is thus displaced by an analysis of concrete historical beings in concrete historical circumstances and intersubjective relations of recognition are conceived as social and political structures. Moreover, Hegel shifts his focus from individual actors to collectivẹ actors. He now considers the slave and master classes, rather than individual masters and slaves.

The historical form of the master/slave relationship involves the slave working for the master, producing the goods that will satisfy the master's biological needs. This further liberates the master from the base realm of animal desires, whilst simultaneously tying the slave more closely to it. The slave's life is devoted to the satisfaction of animal needs, whilst the master is liberated from such concerns almost completely (they must of course still eat). In this situation, Hegel argues, the slave lacks *citizenship* (Kojève 1969: 47). To be a citizen, in this conception, is to be part of a community in which one is recognised as such; that is, recognised officially and institutionally, at the level of law and the state, as an autonomous consciousness. Citizenship is the concretisation of full recognition and self-consciousness.

It is not only the slave who suffers in the master/slave relation, on Hegel's account. The master suffers because they are only recognised by a slave, who is unworthy of bestowing recognition since they are not recognised themselves. To be recognised by a slave is to achieve slavish consciousness, not full self-consciousness. Recognition is only satisfactory if one is recognised by those whom one recognises as worthy of recognising one. Thus the master/slave relation is unsatisfactory for both parties. For the master, this results in an impasse. The master has risked life itself for recognition, but failed. There is nothing more that they can do. They have nothing left to fight against and nothing else to risk. There is hope for the slave, however. The slave, because not recognised, appreciates the value of recognition and they still have it to fight for. Moreover, the slave's work, their transformation of the material environment, provides the basis for recognition.

Work provides a basis for the recognition not achieved in the fight to the death in three respects. Firstly, because work, as Hegel defines it, necessarily involves a transformation of and mastery over nature (e.g. through tools, farming techniques, etc.), it liberates the slave from nature. Workers are not slaves to nature, even if they are slaves to a human master. Secondly, because the slave qua slave is working to satisfy the needs of another person as well as their own, they are transcending and subordinating their own immediate animal desires (as they would have done by risking their life) and freeing themselves from nature. Finally, because they transform nature and fashion it according to human need (making it into things that belong to the human, social world), they have an external object through which they can recognise their own humanity. Work is an externalisation of human consciousness or spirit, for Hegel, and as such it provides the mirror through which self-recognition can occur. However, of course, the slave will still want this humanity to be politically recognised in the form of rights and civil status, and they will have to overthrow the system of slavery if this is to be achieved. Work provides a glimmer of self-consciousness but not its full realisation.

From this point, Hegel describes the various ideological stages which the consciousness of the slave has passed through in the course of history, before achieving full recognition and ending history – a point which Hegel identified with the French revolution. These ideologies are stoicism, scepticism and Christianity, respectively. Each of these ideologies prevents the slave from fully recognising their position and its injustice, he argues, and they have therefore acted as countervailing forces working against the development of slave consciousness into revolutionary consciousness and thus to liberation. In Christianity, for example, the slave alienates their own powers by projecting them into an imaginary God figure, and they imagine that their slavery on earth is cancelled out by an equality before this imaginary figure.

One final point which should be made regarding the Hegelian account of intersubjectivity concerns its understanding of the mediations of desire through objects. Hegel's account of intersubjectivity qua mutual recognition and the struggle for recognition is intimately bound with an understanding of human beings' relationships to their immediate environment and to the objects in that environment. Relations with 'things' are said to be mediated, in many instances, by relations with others (they are intersubjectively mediated), whilst relations with others are said, in some instances, to be mediated by relations with things. We have seen how this works in the case of master/slave relations, but there are other variations. Our desire for objects and artefacts, for example, may often be a sublimated desire for the desire of others. Kojève emphasises this when he discusses the human desire (during battles or competitions) for the capture of flags and other symbols. These symbolic goods serve no basic animal desire, he argues, but they bestow status, which, in turn, bestows desire and recognition. Likewise, Fukuyama (1992) argues that much of our desire for modern consumer goods is, in fact, a sublimated desire for recognition. Our basic animal desires for food and shelter could be satisfied many times over in the modern world, he argues, and yet our desire for goods seems insatiable. This is because these goods symbolise the desire of others and because owning them is therefore the key to self-respect and self-worth. That is, until the wheel of fashion turns again.

Hegel Assessed

There are some interesting similarities and contrasts between the Hegelian and Husserlian positions. Although Hegel makes recognition by the other a precondition of self-consciousness, and thus almost reverses the Husserlian view (whilst injecting a necessary relational element into it), his concern to account for self-consciousness is very similar to Husserl's concern to explain how consciousness manages to transcend itself and recognise others. In both cases there is a common concern for the manner in which consciousness transcends its own particularity, by recognising that particularity, and then moves forward towards the possibility of a universality constituted through collective, rational agreement. Recognition involves consciousness cooperating with others and decentring itself. Furthermore, much of what Hegel says regarding the desire and struggle for recognition conforms to what I have termed the egological form of intersubjectivity. Subjects experience each other as experiencing beings and experience themselves as experienced. Indeed this is the basis for the desire for recognition. Where Husserl has the advantage over Hegel, I contend, is that he attempts to account for this consciousness of consciousness (Hegel does not). Where Hegel has the advantage, however, is that he identifies both the relationalism of self and other, and the desire and tension which manifests between them. Desire and tension are important, I would suggest, because they go some way to explaining the motivation that animates human interaction. Some of this motivation is, of course, accounted for by our need for food and our sexual drive. But not all of it is, and the desire for recognition would seem able to account for much that is not. In particular it explains the apparent human motivation for status and distinction (Bourdieu 1984), or again the moral sentiments of dignity, pride, guilt, shame, love and justice (Honneth 1995; Sartre 1969).

Interestingly, the version of Hegel that we have been discussing, that is, Kojève's version, also reproduces the Husserlian prioritisation of observation, with all of the problems that this entails – this is not true of the early Hegel (Honneth 1995). Subjects are aware of each other and fight with each other but seemingly fail to communicate. This point is drawn out sharply in the contrast between Sartre's (1969) appropriation of the struggle for recognition in *Being and Nothingness* and Merleau-Ponty's (1962, 1964b) discussions of it in *The Phenomenology of Perception* and *Signs*. Sartre focuses much of his discussion of the struggle around 'the look'; that is, he examines the anxiety and alienation that we experience when we realise or feel that we are being looked at. The look of the other captures us, he maintains. We are made acutely self-conscious, but at the same time we feel as if we are an object in the experience of the other. This indicates, for Sartre, an irresolvable conflict at the heart of intersubjective relations. We have a basic choice in relationships, he argues: we can either experience ourselves as alienated and objectified in the gaze of the other or we can objectify them. We either dominate or are dominated. For Merleau-Ponty, by contrast, the possibility of speech provides a third alternative. The anxiety and conflict of 'the look' emerge only out of a (communicated) refusal to communicate in his view. Subjects must draw back from each other and objectify each other. This tension and conflict is broken for Merleau-Ponty, however, when good communicative relations are restored (Crossley 1993, 1994).

It doesn't follow from this that speech puts an end to the struggle for recognition. Speech might fail to truly communicate for many reasons and the struggle for recognition can be as much conducted through speech as circumvented by it. Nevertheless, Merleau-Ponty's position advances two interesting points. Firstly, it introduces language and speech squarely into the discussion of recognition. Secondly, it suggests that the desire and struggle for recognition might be a function of a particular type of intersubjective relation. They occur when we take refuge in reflective self-hood, standing back from open communication and experiencing ourself through the other. This feeds in to the schema of radical and egological intersubjectivity that I have introduced in this chapter. The desire and struggle for recognition are a function of egological intersubjective relations but not of radical intersubjectivity. The communication involved in radically intersubjective relations overcomes or resolves the struggle for recognition – though, given that we swing between the radical and egological forms, such resolution will never be permanent.

Hegel's relational conception of self and other compares, at one level, to that of Buber. Like Buber he recognises the interdependency of individual consciousnesses and identities. The advantage of Buber over Hegel in this respect is that Buber recognises two possible types of social relation (which are historically coexistent) to Hegel's one. The advantage of Hegel, however, is that he explores interdependency in more detail and depth. His conception of self is, at one level, more dialogical, for example. He considers how self is formed in relations of recognition and how our sense of pride and dignity are related to the esteem in which others hold us. Furthermore, he introduces a sense of material dependency into the picture. His subjects aren't bare consciousnesses. They are constituted through concrete social relations which, in turn, form part of a wider historical context. This is not to say that Hegel's conception (as read by Kojève) of these concrete social relations and of society are faultless. They are not. There are problems, particularly in the grand leap which Hegel makes from face-to-face relations to historical totalities and in his substitution of individual agents by collective agents. It is not at all clear that individuals and classes can be treated analogously (Hindess 1988) and there is certainly a conceptual gap to be filled between the movement of the individual dyad and that of history. Nevertheless, it is important that Hegel makes the transition from individual interactions to the social structure and to collectivities. This is one of his key contributions to the intersubjectivity debate. Moreover, it is important that he firmly establishes the concept of citizenship at this level. This takes us beyond the political hints of Buber, towards a firm understanding of the political enshrinement of intersubjectivity. This is a notion that I will deal with in Chapter 7.

Axel Honneth (1995) makes an interesting contribution to this debate on 'levels' in his recent study *The Struggle for Recognition*. Honneth argues that recognition is essential to proper social agency and thus that it might serve as the moral linchpin of a critical social theory. Moreover, he posits three distinct levels (or rather three levels which have become distinct in the course of the history of our societies) at which different forms of recognition should take place: the family, civil society and the state. At the level of the family, he argues, there is a struggle between infants and carers, in which infants must achieve recognition in the form of love. This will allow them to achieve basic self-consciousness, trust and self-confidence. This is an interesting point which rejoins a number of Hegel-inspired studies of child development, all of which tend to illustrate that the achievement of a sense of self is, in fact, a product of social interactions in childhood (e.g. Benjamin 1991; Merleau-Ponty 1968b). There is a cross-over with Buber here, moreover. These studies tend to suggest (as Buber does) that self-consciousness, such as Buber identifes with I–It relations, is not inborn but is acquired. I will discuss this in more detail in Chapter 3.

At the level of civil society, Honneth argues, we are concerned with rights and the self-respect which these afford us. There are no end of struggles which exemplify this level. Struggles over gender and race are two good examples, however, and Honneth is particularly concerned to focus upon these. The Hegelian understanding of a struggle for recognition allows us to see these as moral struggles, he argues, rather than examples of a (Hobbesian) war of all against all. We can recognise that they are premised upon serious moral claims. That they are struggles and that Hegel allows us to conceive of them as such is also important, however, since it allows us to identify our moral sensibilities with concrete historical processes and practices. Honneth's concerns at this level are rejoined by a great many political writers who have used the struggle for recognition to make sense of the position and identity of subordinated groups or their psychology and lack of agency (Easton 1987; Fanon 1986; Habermas 1974; Lloyd 1985; Merleau-Ponty 1969; Sartre 1948).

Honneth's final level is that of the state. The concern at this level, for him, is that individuals have the possibility to (competetively) develop their own potential to its full. It concerns their need to be an individual and to have a sense of individual self-worth. The 'prize' at this level is self-esteem.

This schema is certainly useful. Like all other schemas, there will always be ambiguous cases which do not fit perfectly within it. Nevertheless, it allows us to see that recognition must be achieved at different levels and in relation to different issues. I would suggest, with respect to the middle level of civil society, that Honneth would have done better to differentiate between formal rights and the substantive treatment that different groups receive in different interaction contexts. Much contemporary debate is as concerned with the substantive realisation of rights as with their legal enshrinement. But this is only a further development of Honneth's model. It is not a rejection of it.

The final point to discuss in relation to Hegel is the notion of the fight to the death. This strikes me as a particularly obscure notion, which cannot be understood other than as a fable. Notwithstanding this, however, like all myths it points to something real. In this case, that reality is not only bloody wars and revolutions but also the human desire to prove oneself, to compete and test onself and to win. The intersubjective fabric is at once a site of sharing and agreement, and of competition and contestation.

Dimensions of Intersubjectivity

In this chapter I have discussed and critically assessed the different versions of 'intersubjectivity' posited in the work of Husserl, Buber and in Kojève's reading of Hegel. This discussion has effectively mapped out the terrain that I will be examining in more detail in the rest of the book. It has identified the concepts, the levels of analysis and the deficits that we must consider. Moreover, as such, it provides a rationale for what follows in subsequent chapters.

A fundamental distinction which has been established in the chapter is that between radical and egological phases of intersubjectivity. The radical phase, according to this typology, is equivalent to Buber's I–Thou relations. It involves a lack of self-awareness and a communicative openness towards the other, which is unconditional. Self engages with other in this modality but has no experience of them as such. Egological intersubjectivity, in contrast to this, derives from Husserl. It involves an empathic intentionality which experiences otherness by way of an imaginative transposition of self into the position of the other. These two phases of intersubjectivity and the issues which they entail (e.g. self-hood) will form the subject matter of the next two chapters. The remaining four chapters will then address the other central concerns that have emerged out of the chapter: Chapter 4 deals with the question of the lifeworld; Chapter 5 deals with the question of social structure and its relations to the lifeworld; Chapter 6 deals with the issue of power; and Chapter 7 deals with the question of citizenship.

2

Subjectivity, Alterity and Between:
On Radical Intersubjectivity

In this chapter I develop and further consider 'radical intersubjectivity' as defined and discussed in Chapter 1. This discussion will be based around four central claims. Firstly, that human subjectivity is not, in essence, a private 'inner world' which is divorced from the outer (material) world; that it consists in the worldy praxes of sensuous, embodied beings and that it is therefore public and intersubjective. Secondly, that subjectivity consists, in the first instance, in a pre-reflective opening out onto and engagement with alterity, rather than in an experience or objectification of it. Thirdly, that human action, particularly speech, necessarily assumes a socially instituted form and that this form is essential to its meaningfulness. Fourthly, that much human action and experience arises out of dialogical situations or systems which are irreducible to individual human subjects. Taken together, these four points enable us to conceptualise intersubjectivity as an irreducible interworld of shared meanings and to understand human subjectivity as necessarily intersubjective.

I will be developing these claims, mainly, through a critical discussion of the work of Maurice Merleau-Ponty. There are problems with Merleau-Ponty's work, some of which I will be discussing (see also Crossley 1994). Notwithstanding this, however, it is my contention that his work provides a strong philosophical basis for the concept of radical intersubjectivity. It is the purpose of this chapter to support that contention.

In arguing this position I will be standing in opposition to Emmanuel Levinas (1985, 1987a, 1987b), who has argued that Merleau-Ponty's philosophy fails to break sufficiently with Husserl's idealist and egological reduction of 'the other' (see Chapter 1). For Levinas, Merleau-Ponty reduces otherness to the perception of otherness by a subject. I object to this on three grounds. Firstly, it fails to consider the radical nature of Merleau-Ponty's understanding of perception, which precisely posits it as a pre-reflective engagement with alterity rather than an objectifying reduction of it. Secondly, if perception is not accounted for in theories of intersubjectivity, then those theories will stumble whenever they are forced to consider it. Thirdly, perception is only one part of Merleau-Ponty's account of intersubjectivity. He also examines the role of speech, gesture and emotion, and he integrates these elements with his perceptual account.

Although Merleau-Ponty's work is the main focus of the chapter, it is not the exclusive one. Throughout I supplement Merleau-Ponty's position with the views of Mead, Schutz and Wittgenstein. These writers, I argue, allow us to overcome some of the weaknesses in Merleau-Ponty's thinking and to develop and extend his ideas further than he takes them himself. They have a similar view of human subjectivity to him but each differs in emphasis and in the insights which they provide.

The chapter begins with an analysis of perception. This is followed by a discussion of interaction and dialogue. Finally, I consider emotion. In the conclusion to the chapter I identify the limits of a radical conception of intersubjectivity, suggesting that radical intersubjectivity is only one phase in the complex process of intersubjectivity.

Perception and Alterity

Perception enjoys a privileged position in Merleau-Ponty's philosophy. He maintains that all consciousness is based in perceptual consciousness and that '[we] never cease living in the world of perception' (1968b: 3). Perception, in this sense, includes all perceptual modalities: visual, tactile, auditory, saporous and olfactory. And Merleau-Ponty was keen to stress the interrelation of these modalities. Nevertheless, most of his examples and arguments focus upon visual perception and most of his conceptual innovations are explicitly oriented to this modality. This is a problem but I do not have the space to correct it here. I must reproduce Merleau-Ponty's bias.

Merleau-Ponty's discussion of perception begins with a critique of two opposed strands of thought: empiricism and intellectualism. The former of these, empiricism, posits that perception is physical sensation and is the caused effect of a determinate object or 'stimulus' upon the visual system (understood itself as a physical object or mechanism). Merleau-Ponty's first objection to this view is that its concept of physical sensation precludes consideration of perceptual meaning; that is, it fails to consider that perception entails something being seen by somebody and that the something seen is significant for the one who sees it. Even where empiricists do recognise perceptual meaning, however, he continues, empiricism is atomistic and objectivist. It assumes a pre-given, isolated object which is able to impose itself upon the visual system, failing to recognise that perceptual objects always emerge in the context of a structured visual field, which provides the necessary relief for their outline and the contextual condition of their meaning. A pencilled dot can only be seen as a dot, for example, against a background which is different to it. If the pencilled area filled the whole of our visual field – e.g. if we moved in so closely as to not allow anything else into our field – then we would not see a dot. Moreover, its meaning, the way in which we see it, will be quite different depending upon the background against which we see it. If it is situated on a drawing of a face, just under an eyebrow, then we will see it as an eye; if it is placed over the top of a vertical line in the context of a page of written text, we will see it as part of the letter 'i'; if it is placed at the end of a string of words, we will see it as a full stop, and we will see the string of words as a sentence, etc. The meaning of the object and thus its very existence for us as an object is determined by its structural relation to a background.

In addition to challenging the atomism of empiricism, the notion of a structured visual field challenges empiricism in two further respects. Firstly, by pointing to a background structure in the visual field, it identifies aspects of that field which are taken into account in what is seen but are not actually seen in themselves. This is problematic for the empiricist because empiricism maintains that things are either seen or they are not. It cannot account for such ambiguous presences. Secondly, the notion of the field suggests that the object is structurally dependent upon the organisation of the visual field for its existence as an object and that it cannot, therefore, be the determinate factor in perception. It cannot 'cause' perception.

Ambiguous images such as Wittgenstein's (1953) duck/rabbit illustrate some of these criticisms. The visual meaning or object of such images changes without a change in what empiricists would identify as the stimulus. Furthermore, one or another of the objects in the picture can often prove difficult to find. Such phenomena strongly challenge the idea that the object is determinate. They suggest that the object is dependent upon the organisation of the visual field and that the organisation of the field is not fixed. Indeed they suggest that what we see (the object of perception) is at least in part determined by the way in which we look.

Many of these criticisms of empiricism have been posited by what Merleau-Ponty refers to as the intellectualist tradition. Intellectualists, such as Descartes (1969), share the empiricist conception of the body (and visual system) as an object, but they posit a distinct substance, an immaterial mind, to account for meaningful perception and other 'mental' phenomena. Perception is a judgement or constituting act of consciousness, according to these writers. We see with our minds, they maintain, not our eyes.

The example which Descartes gives in support of this intellectualist view involves the view of men passing on the street below his window. In this case, he argues, he does not really see men. He sees 'hats or cloaks, which cover ghosts or dummies' (1969: 110). But he judges them to be men and, in this sense, constitutes the meaningful sense of his perception: 'I understand, by the sole power of judgement which resides in my mind, what I believed I saw with my eyes' (ibid.).

This intellectualist view has the advantage of taking the meaningful nature of perception seriously but it still has many flaws in Merleau-Ponty's view. In the first instance, its account of perception-as-judgement presupposes a (meaningful) percept which is judged, and thus it begs rather than resolves the question of meaningful perception. Descartes's account, for example, presupposes the meaningful perception of hats and coats (which are judged to be men) and thus it cannot account for meaningful perception. Another way of putting this would be to say that intellectualism presupposes the subject of perception, as empiricism presupposes the object of perception, in its very account of perception.

Secondly, in locating the meaningful aspect of perception in a separate realm to the body, intellectualism raises the manifold problems of mind/body dualism. Not least of these problems is the inability of dualists to explain how these two distinct 'substances' can interact – a problem which comes into sharp relief in relation to perception because perception precisely entails an interface of consciousness and the world.

The third problem of intellectualism, for Merleau-Ponty, concerns its inability to account for perceptual errors. If meaningful perception is constituted by means of an act of consciousness, he argues, then it is not clear how our (initial) perceptions could ever be deemed incorrect on the basis of closer inspection. A mind that is responsible for bestowing meaning on the world could not do so incorrectly unless it were playing tricks upon itself – which one assumes that it would not do – because there could be no standard of correctness by which to judge its judgements other than those which it sets for itself. But we clearly do make perceptual errors.

Merleau-Ponty therefore rejects the intellectualist view and, in effect, any view which would reduce the visible world to an act of judgement or constituting consciousness. In perception, he argues, perceivers must go beyond themselves. They must open out onto what is other than them. Perception, he argues, must be a dialectical process which is effected between the organism and its environment. It involves a 'gaze' which 'questions', 'ranges over or dwells on' a world which is 'pregnant with form' and which resists it, allowing and also disallowing certain views of itself (1962: 53). Perception is an opening out onto and engagement with otherness, which neither reduces it nor is reduced to it. It is an active interrogation in search of form.

The mistake of both the intellectualists and the empiricists, for Merleau-Ponty, is that they effectively presuppose what they seek to explain. Empiricists presuppose the object of perception, whilst intellectualists presuppose the subject of perception. Both fail to see that these elements are relationally constituted, that neither therefore can explain the other and that both are in fact the outcome of perception rather than its cause. Perception, according to this account, is an originary process, rooted in the dialectical relationship of the organism and its environment, which gives birth to both the subject and the object of perception.

The (perceptual) 'subject' and 'object' which emerge out of this process are not the fully formed reflective types assumed by traditional philosophy, however. Perceptual consciousness is, in the first instance, practical consciousness and as such it is pre-reflective, pre-objective and pre-egological. The seer remains largely self-unaware, at a reflective level. Furthermore, they are even unaware (at a reflective level) of what they see. What they see calls forth a responding action from them and they often respond without the mediations or awareness of reflective thought. Furthermore, what is seen is framed by the activity in which the seer is engaged, such that there is a dialectical movement between perception and action; action frames perception whilst perception calls forth action. Perception, in this sense, enjoins the seer to a field of action. The seer's world is neither contemplated nor observed, as such. It is participated in.

Merleau-Ponty's main example of this centres upon football, a case which also serves to highlight the role of acquired cultural rules and habits (a 'habitus') in perceptual activity (1965: 168). Footballers don't ordinarily contemplate the pitch and the game at the time of playing, he notes. They are absorbed in it and it moves too quickly for reflective thought. The pitch is a background against which they act and their perceptions are a means of involving them in it. They read the game and no more notice the figures or 'objects' on the pitch than readers notice the shapes of the letters in the words and sentences which they read. They see openings, passes, off-sides, goals; that is, specific meaningful events which are appropriate to the game of football. Furthermore, the significance of these sights is not reflective but practical. They call forth responses from players which must be immediate and 'without thinking'. Strikers see an opening and immediately move into it. They do not have the time to reflectively realise that what they see is an opening, nor do they have the time to reflect upon whether to move into it.

This view of perception has a clear parallel with Buber's understanding of I–Thou relations, as discussed in Chapter 1. Perception is not, in the first instance, an 'experience of' objects, for Merleau-Ponty. It is an enjoinment and an involvement with them. It is a 'communion' with otherness.

Embodiment and Perception

A further central component of Merleau-Ponty's analysis of perception is his concept of the 'body-subject', a concept which is intended to replace both the problematic mind/body dualism of the intellectualists and the mechanistic view of the body as a physical object which these philosophers share with the empiricists. Against the dualistic view, Merleau-Ponty posits that we are our bodies and that all of our experiences and the meanings which animate our lives are based in our active corporeal (and intercorporeal) involvement in the world. I will be fleshing out this idea throughout this study (see also Crossley 1994, 1995a, 1995b). For the moment it will suffice to briefly consider Merleau-Ponty's view of the corporeal basis of perception.

At one level, the role of the body in perception is to provide perspective. Phenomenological analysis reveals that perception is always a view from somewhere (e.g. above, to the side, near, etc.) and that the idea of a view from nowhere is incoherent. A perceived 'thing' always presupposes the point from which it is seen, and the body, given that it extends in and occupies space, is this somewhere. We can see because, as bodies, we have the power of taking up a position in our world and standing in relation to it. Embodiment provides more than a standpoint from which to see, however, according to Merleau-Ponty. His view of perception as an 'interrogation' which meets 'resistance' necessarily entails that seer and seen are made of the same 'stuff' and thus that it is only as (physical) body-subjects that we can be seers. A genuinely different substance to the body, such as Descartes's 'mind', could not see the world, according to this argument, because there could be no point of contact between it and the world. The two could not engage.

The implication of this is that, having criticised the empiricist identification of perception with sensation, Merleau-Ponty posits his own version of this idea. He modifies the idea in two crucial respects, however, so as to overcome its aforementioned problems. In the first instance, he maintains that sensation cannot be separated from meaning in the context of perception. The field of perceptual sensations forms a gestalt structure which is meaningful for the body-subject, he argues. This point relates to a more general point that all meanings and ideas must be embodied (e.g. in words, gestures, artefacts, rituals, etc.). Secondly, he expresses reservation about the connotation of privateness that accompanies the notion of sensation. He refuses to locate perceptions 'in' the perceiver. We don't see things in our head, he argues. We see them in the world, where we can touch them, manipulate them and point them out to other people. Perception is not an inner representation of an outer world. It is an opening onto and into that world, as is clearly revealed in the aforementioned notion of the perceptual dialectic. Whilst individuated sensations form one pole in the perceptual relation then, they cannot pre-empt the notion of perceptual consciousness or the perceptual field. The latter must be understood to form in *the space between* the perceiver and the perceived, by means of *the active engagement of the two*. The perceptual field is a 'between' or 'interval' in Buber's sense.

Interspecular Relations: The Between

The implication of Merleau-Ponty's view of perception, as it has been developed so far, is clearly positive in terms of the notion of radical intersubjectivity. By defining perception as an opening onto otherness which functions at a pre-reflective, pre-objective and pre-egological level, it challenges the solipsistic idea of private perceptual worlds, positing instead that our looks open out into a common space where they overlap and intertwine:

> There is here no problem of the *alter ego* because it is not *I* who sees, not *he* who sees, because an anonymous visibility inhabits both of us, a vision in general. (Merleau-Ponty 1968a: 142, original emphasis)

Our perceptual openness enjoins us to an interworld. We open out into a shared visual world or 'intermundane space' (1968a: 269). Moreover, given that perceptual consciousness is the basis of all consciousness for Merleau-Ponty, human consciousness itself is therefore defined as an opening onto alterity.

This is not to say that the perceptions of those involved in an intermundane space will be identical. All perceptions are, as I have said, necessarily perspectival for Merleau-Ponty. Moreover, as no two people can occupy the same place at the same time, they will not necessarily see the same things. Indeed there are many factors which might account for discrepancies in visual experiences, ranging from social position and 'cultural capital' (Bourdieu 1984) through to purpose, mood and momentary inclination. All of these factors may lead us to interrogate our environment differently. Nevertheless, even in cases of disagreement and difference, the intersubjective fabric is not broken. Perceivers can argue and debate about what they see and can show and teach each other how to see the same things in the same ways. They can enter into each other's perceptual fields.

Having said this, it is important to add two caveats. First, as Lefort (1990) notes, our perceptual explorations and negotiations are not as free as Merleau-Ponty's work would sometimes seem to suggest. Our earliest (learning) perceptual experiences, as infants, he argues, are mediated by adults who, to some extent, reserve the right to define perceptual reality for us and to insist that we see it as they do (the mediation of language is central here). We are, in other words, initiated into a specific version of the visible world at an early age. We acquire culturally specific perceptual schemas. Secondly, as empirical work by both Pollner (1975) and Coulter (1975) suggests, disagreements over 'perceptual asymmetries' tend to be based upon the realist assumption that there is a single perceptible reality to be seen, with the consequence that irresolvable disagreements tend to result in one person being deemed right and the other being defined wrong; that is, being defined as biased, shortsighted or perhaps mad. As Pollner argues, there is a 'politics' to perceptual experience, in which the perceptions of some are validated at the expense and to the disadvantage of others (see Chapter 4).

A further important factor in the constitution of intermundane spaces, for Merleau-Ponty (1968a), is the 'reversibility' of the perceiving subject. Body-subjects are visible-seers, tangible-touchers, audible-listeners, etc., he argues. They form a part of the perceptible world that they open onto. This means, importantly, that they open onto each other. Each body-subject is visible to the others. This is fundamental to Merleau-Ponty's theory of intersubjectivity. It explains how subjects are enjoined to each other. He is clear that it is not the sheer visibility of the body-subject which effectively institutes intersubjectivity, however. It is the meaningful behaviour of the other which counts. To perceive another person, for Merleau-Ponty, is like reading a written text or hearing a spoken word (and clearly it may involve either or both of these). One doesn't see a physical object (e.g. a body or a string of letters), rather one is affected by a meaning. The other body-subject is animated and its animation communicates. Furthermore, as a communication this behaviour calls for a response. We don't contemplate the communications of the other, we are affected by them and we reply to them. The behaviour of the other asks questions of us and our first inclination is towards an answer rather than towards the question or the questioner.

There is an implication of mutuality in this account which political observers of human behaviour will doubtless object to. Gazes are identified by many feminist or black critics, for example, as sources of objectification, power and conflict (Beauvoir 1988; Fanon 1986; Young 1980). Such an objection must be modified if it is to be sustained against our position. Firstly, it must be noted that our view does not imply harmony in interspecular relations. To say that I am affected by the meaning of the other may well mean that I am angered. Secondly, reciprocity is only one possibility in interspecular relations from a Merleau-Pontyian position. He equally acknowledges, as I noted in Chapter 1, that objectification of the other or feelings of being objectified by the other, such as are described by feminist and black critics, are possible (though only in the egological mode). Where the Merleau-Pontyian position may be criticised, however, is that it fails to fully recognise the extent to which the visible is a site of political differentiation, wherein groups engender a sense of their own distinct visual identity (cf. Hebdidge 1988; Wilson 1985) and where ideological influences increase the likelihood of members of certain groups being objectified by members of other groups; for example, it would be difficult to deny that our society constitutes women, for men, as objects of visual contemplation and consumption and that this considerably decreases the likelihood of their being seen and responded to as interlocutors. We must incorporate this political dimension into our view. We must recognise that our visibility is invested with a symbolism and a political value, and that, as such, it serves as a locus for relations of conflict and control.

Intermundane Space and Conversation

The grasp on alterity afforded by perception and the mutuality and sharedness of this grasp is ordinarily complemented through action and speech, according to Merleau-Ponty. Perception, action and speech combine in a mutually informing way to provide a cohesive grip on the world. In some cases (of speech) this can involve a fundamental transformation of the subject's manner of being. By speaking, the body-subject can transform itself into a reflective and reflexive subject (see Chapter 3). In many instances, however, this is not so. The body-subject acts in a meaningful way, which we would describe as involving both knowledge and understanding, but neither the knowledge, understanding nor meaning assumes a reflective or reflexive form. They are not present to consciousness. A clear example of this is driving a car. This act involves purpose, knowledge and understanding. Drivers must know where they are going, they must be responsive to changing events and conditions on the road, they must know where the controls are on the car and how and when to use them, and they must know where their limbs are relative to the controls such that they can operate the controls at appropriate moments. All of this is usually performed in a pre-reflective fashion, however. Drivers understand how to drive but this is not something which comes before their mind when they actually do drive. They brake, steer, swerve, pull out and change gear 'without thinking'. These actions are not planned but are called forth by the environment as it is given in perception. Only an unusual event, such as an instrument failure, will provoke reflective thought.

This view leads Merleau-Ponty to posit the idea that the body-subject forms a 'system' with its environment. The body-subject is constituted through action, he maintains. If it is not active, then it is no more than the material object of the empiricist. If it is active, however, then this is necessarily relational to the circumstances of its action, as given in the perception–action dialectic. The body-subject responds to an environment. It is in dialogue with its environment and this dialogue is irreducible. Its actions can no more be understood without reference to 'its environment' than 'its environment' can be understood independently of the perception–action which gives that environment its nature.

When applied to interactions with other human beings, this notion adds considerably to our understanding of radical intersubjectivity. Merleau-Ponty is now able to talk of an intersubjective 'system' forming between body-subjects, which is unbroken by reflective objectification, a system which is irreducible to either party but which calls forth the action of each. Subjects stand together in an I–Thou relation. Their actions interlock and engage, each motivated and coordinated by and through an orientation to the other, but without conscious positing and reflective awareness of either self or other. They do not think about their other. They respond to them and are absorbed in a common action. Each action by the one calls forth an action in the other, which calls forth an action from the first, and so on.

Such pre-reflective interactions are also theorised by Mead (1967), who refers to them as a 'conversation of gestures'. These conversations, in their most basic form, are not only found in the human world, according to Mead. They exist in other species too. Indeed his most famous example of such a conversation is of a dog fight, in which each animal 'squares up' to the other, changing position in accordance with that assumed by the other, who must change again, and so on. Like Merleau-Ponty, Mead views this 'conversation' as a primary unit of analysis, a system which is more basic than the parts (individuals) of which it is composed and which functions below the level of conscious reflection. To understand human behaviour, in this view, it is necessary to understand the intersubjective systems in which human beings are involved. The system is more fundamental that the individual.

For Mead, the form of such intersubjective systems changes slightly when conversations are linguistic. Though responses are still immediate, he maintains, speakers hear themselves speaking and therefore anticipate the likely response of their interlocutor. They effectively answer their own questions. There is thus a certain element of reflexivity involved in linguistic communications that is not involved in other forms. Notwithstanding this, however, Mead, Merleau-Ponty and the hermeneutic philosopher Hans-Georg Gadamer (1989) all identify a similar intersubjective system in linguistic communication. They identify dialogue as a communicative system which is immediate and which both subsumes and is greater than the sum of the two speakers involved.

In dialogue, Merleau-Ponty notes, a 'common ground' is constituted between self and other; they are 'woven into a single fabric':

> . . . my words and those of my interlocutor are called forth by the state of the discussion, and they are inserted into a shared operation of which neither of us is the creator. (Merleau-Ponty 1962: 354)

In this process, he continues, 'perspectives blend' into a shared 'common world'. We grasp the other's thoughts 'the moment they come into being':

> . . . indeed, the objection which my interlocutor raises to what I say draws from me thoughts which I had no idea I possessed, so that at the same time that I lend him thoughts, he reciprocates by making me think too. (ibid.)

Or, as Gadamer puts it,

> The way one word follows another, with the conversation taking its own twists and reaching its own conclusion, may well be conducted in some way, but the partners conversing are far less the leaders of it than the led. No one knows in advance what will 'come out' of a conversation. (1989: 383)

It is only after such conversation, Merleau-Ponty concludes, when one is recalling the event, that one reintegrates it into one's own personal life and personal history; that is, that one attributes certain ideas to oneself and some to the other. At the moment of the discourse all thoughts belonged only to the system of interactions which forms between the interlocutors. This system is irreducible to the actions which compose it; they derive their sense and raison d'être from it. It is in this sense, for Mead, Merleau-Ponty and Gadamer, that our decisions, choices and ideas can be regarded as genuinely shared. Ideas are not a property of the individual in such cases but a property of the pair. They form in an interval or between.

Privileged Access?

A number of objections might be levelled against this view. It might be argued that it ignores the social structure of speech, or the power relations that are often involved in speech and other symbolic exchanges. Or again, it might be argued that our actions are seldom so immediate and absorbing as the above quotes suggest. It is more usual, it might be argued, for us to be guarded in our interactions with others, to plan and rehearse how we will act and to stage-manage our encounters so as to ensure that we achieve the results that we desire. Moreover, it might be argued that the intersubjectivist position only considers 'external' behaviours, that it ignores our 'inner world', a world to which we alone have access. The existence of this world and of our privileged access to it, it could be argued, ensures that our relationship to our self comes before any relations which we may have with others, and thus negates the supposed primacy of intersubjective relations identified by Mead, Merleau-Ponty and Gadamer. Our relationship to the subjectivity of the other cannot be immediate, according to this view. Their subjectivity is an inside which can only be inferred from external expression, and intersubjectivity is therefore a secondary structure.

I will be discussing the social structure of interaction in Chapter 4 and I will discuss power in Chapter 6. I do not intend to address those objections here, except to say that power and social structure need in no way obfuscate the immediacy described by Mead, Gadamer and Merleau-Ponty. In reply to the objection concerning 'stage-management', I concede that this does of course occur, and is well documented. People do have public selves and private selves. This has been studied ethnographically by Goffman (1959, 1968) and Hochschild (1979, 1983) and historically by Elias (1978a). It is by no means obvious that conscious stage-management occurs all of the time, however, or that it precludes us from being 'carried away' in a conversation. Even a stage-managed action must be open and adaptive to the responses of the other. We must improvise and we must do so in concert with the improvisations of the other. Furthermore, the evidence of all studies on such phenomena suggests that private spaces are not inner spaces but are carved out of intersubjective space, by way of intersubjective agreement; that is, we tend to keep private those matters that it is generally (intersubjectively) agreed that we ought.

But what about privileged access? Are our mental states essentially private? And can our relationships to the subjectivity of others only ever be inferred and secondary? Following Merleau-Ponty (1962, 1965), I would suggest not. If we wish to transcend mind/body dualism, Merleau-Ponty argues, then we must concede that what we ordinarily take to be 'mental events' are inseparable from embodied performances or behaviours which are equally visible from the outside as from within. Moreover, it follows from this that we become aware of our own mental states in the same way that we become aware of the mental states of others. Thus our mental states are, in principle, always intersubjectively available by way of our performances. I will give a number of examples of this in the course of this chapter. For present purposes, however, we can consider the example of 'understanding' – an example also discussed in a similar vein by Wittgenstein (1953).

To say that a person understands, Merleau-Ponty argues, is not to refer to anything extraneous to their verbal and motor behaviours; that is, to anything 'internal'. It is to note their ability to perform a given task competently, according to certain public criteria; for example, we say that a person understands long division when they are able to *do* long division, irrespective of any internal sensations. Moreover, this applies equally with respect to ourselves. If I want to know whether or not I understand long division, for example, I have no way to judge other than to consider my past and present performances. I would not trust to vague sensations such as a 'click of comprehension'. Or at least I would be prepared to say that such a click is no guarantee of understanding and that one can understand without it. A further argument for this, from Wittgenstein, is that words such as 'understanding' must refer to publicly available performances since they belong to a public language. Words in a public language can't apply to a private state, according to this argument, because we could never have common rules of application for them. I will return to this line of argument later.

These arguments apply to all mental predicates (believing, intending, meaning, etc.), as is shown clearly in the work of Merleau-Ponty, Mead, Wittgenstein and Gilbert Ryle (1949). In all of these cases we ascribe to ourselves or to others on the basis of what we do or the way and style in which we do it, not on the basis of 'inner' events.

Sensation and the Other

A possible test case in relation to this issue of privileged access is sensations. Are sensations, such as pain, not private states? Merleau-Ponty never explores this question in any depth. He seems to assume that sensations, insofar as they are bodily feelings, are private, but he equally seems to think that they are not of any great significance. This is probably true with respect to most cases, but there are some sensations, such as pain, which are of significance (e.g. in relation to ethics) and cannot be ignored. To account for such sensations and their place in intersubjective life, we will turn to Wittgenstein's (1953) famous analysis of 'pain'.

Wittgenstein's analysis and his method of analysis, both of which will be discussed in more detail later in this chapter, are based, in part, in an analysis of language and the 'grammar' of words (the other part is broadly phenomenological); 'grammar', in this sense, refers to the logic of the use of words. Many deep philosophical issues are, for Wittgenstein, the result of the philosopher's misuse of language and the confusion which this creates. One particular illustration of this argument is his analysis of 'pain' and of knowing whether oneself and others are in pain. He opposes the notion that only an individual can know whether or not they are in pain.

The first step of this opposition is an analysis of the grammar of 'know'. To apply this word in a situation, Wittgenstein maintains, one must equally be able to apply the concepts 'doubt' and 'learn' to it. 'Doubt' and 'know' are interdependent terms, each being the negation of the other, from which it follows that we must be capable of doubting that which we claim to know. Moreover, 'know' is grammatically tied to 'learn' insofar as we must 'learn' what we 'know'. The second step of the argument is to note that it makes no sense to say that one doubts that one is in pain or that one learns that one is in pain. Consequently, the conclusion is drawn that it is strictly inappropriate to maintain that one 'knows' that one is in pain or to interpret such phrases as 'I am in pain' as knowledge claims or descriptions. For Wittgenstein, the

phrase, 'I am in pain' is an exclamation rather than a description or knowledge claim. It is similar to 'ouch!' or 'agh!' and is an acquired cultural
replacement for natural pain behaviours such as a baby's cry.

What Wittgenstein is driving at here, at a more phenomenological level,
is the notion that pain is not an object which can be known: 'It is not a
something but not a *nothing* either!' (1953: 102, original emphasis). This
point has baffled many Wittgensteinians. From a Merleau-Pontyian point
of view, however, it makes perfect sense. We are our bodies and can
therefore never completely stand in the distantiated relationship to them
which is demanded in regarding them as an object or a 'something'. Parts
of our body, as Merleau-Ponty notes, can't be said to hurt us in the way
that external objects (such as a large stick) might be said to do. At most
they can constitute a 'pain-infested space'. Wittgenstein agrees with this
analysis, I contend, when he claims that he cannot learn of his own pains
because 'I have them' (1953: 89). To know of one's pain would presuppose
that it existed as an independent phenomenon to one's own being, but it
doesn't. Therefore one cannot know of one's own pain.

The other side of this point is the question of whether we can ever know
the pain of others. At the grammatical level, this is a perfectly meaningful
possibility. It is reasonable to say that one can doubt that others are in pain
and that one can learn that they are in pain, so there is no immediate
grammatical objection to the idea that one can know that they are in pain.
The non-Wittgensteinian objection to this, however, is that because we can
only see the exterior of another's pain (their pain behaviour), we can never
actually know whether they are in pain. Pain behaviour, whether in the
form of a linguistic avowal or a gesture and pain itself are, as Wittgenstein
himself admits, two quite distinct things in principle and it is therefore
possible for a person to pretend that they are in pain when they are not and
to hide their pain when they are. Their pain can be a strictly private matter,
which does not open out into intermundane space.

In responding to this objection, Wittgenstein again combines a grammatical and a phenomenological analysis. Those who say that we can never
know whether another is in pain, he maintains, are applying the wrong
criteria for the word 'know'. What they are effectively denying is not that
we can never *know* another's pain but that we can never *have* another's
pain (which we obviously can't). In the ordinary sense of 'know', 'doubt'
and 'learn', it is perfectly possible both to doubt another's pain and to
know it.

This is not the end of the issue, however. Interestingly, Wittgenstein
seems to hint at a possible relationship to the pain of others which is
beyond or beneath the grammar of 'knowledge' and 'doubt'. This notion
emerges, on the one hand, in the form of an experiential challenge which
seemingly places the pain of others beyond doubt and, consequently,
beyond knowledge: 'Just try – in a real case – to doubt someone else's fear
or pain' (1953: 102). The point here, assumedly, is that we do not and
cannot doubt genuine fear and pain in others – which implies that our

primary relation to the pain of others is not one of knowledge either. Furthermore, Wittgenstein questions whether our own conviction regarding the pain of another does not take the form of our reaction to it: 'Pity, one may say, is a form of conviction that someone else is in pain' (1953: 98). In this sense, Wittgenstein seems to suggest that our relation to the pain of others, like our relation to our own pain, is more immediate than that of reflective knowledge. We don't think about the pain of others, in the first instance, we respond to it. On this point, I contend, Wittgenstein returns us to our notion of the conversation of gestures, where the other is not an object of reflection or knowledge but rather an interlocutor. We don't know the pain of others, rather it communicates to us and we are affected by it.

The outcome of this brief discussion is that sensations, at least as long as they can be compared to the sensation of pain, do not challenge our understanding of radical intersubjectivity. We can never *have* the pain of others but we can *know* that they are in pain. Moreover, at a pre-reflective and radically intersubjective level, we can respond to the pain of others prior to any reflective knowledge of it. Their pain can communicate to us and call us into action.

The possibility of this conversation of gestures is, of course, dependent upon the 'attitude' of the other. We can only respond pre-reflectively and pre-reflexively towards their pain if they do. If they elect to hide their pain and to contain it within a private space, then there is nothing we can do.

Temporality and Mutual Tuning In

The stress upon perception and behaviour, hitherto, paints a particularly spatial picture of intersubjective interworlds. We occupy interworlds, I have argued, because we open onto common spaces, because the intentions and understandings of others unfold before our eyes and because our own understandings and intentions occupy a visible, tangible space by means of our behaviour. Even the terms 'interworld', 'interval' and 'between' are suggestive of space and its (mutual) occupation.

Temporality is equally important in the constitution of an interworld, however, as is shown by Alfred Schutz's (1964) notion of 'mutual tuning in'. The meanings of our actions and utterances are not given at once, Schutz argues. They unfold through time, with a rhythmic and melodic structure. Furthermore, if subjects are to join in an action or a meaning, then the temporal horizons of their respective actions and words must fuse to form a shared horizon. They must share the same lived time horizon. Schutz illustrates this by reference to music. Two pieces of music can last for the same period of time, objectively, he notes, whilst their 'lived' temporal structure is quite different; one might be quick and racing, whilst the other drifts along slowly. Correspondingly, when we listen to the music, if we are to appreciate it, we must either race or drift with it. We must, as it were, listen to it as quickly or as slowly as it is played.

Most of Schutz's discussion of this issue is taken up with the music example but he is clear that the fusion of lived temporal horizons is necessary to all communicative and interactive situations, including the conversation of gestures mentioned above. In linguistic communication, for example, the meaning of words and utterances is only discernible when they are correctly sequenced and when the temporal continuities between them are correctly identified. We must, for example, identify answers with what has gone before them (i.e. questions), if we are to make correct sense of them. Or alternatively, we must correctly identify the punctuation pauses in an utterance if we are to understand it. A pause can change the whole meaning of a phrase. This applies equally to conversations of gesture. Gestures make very little sense independently of their situation in an ongoing sequence. None of this is possible at all, however, without a fusion of lived time horizons. Interaction requires a common rhythm and a basis for the organisation and coordination of turn-taking.

As I will discuss in the next chapter, this point is borne out in one of the most fundamental of our conversations of gesture: that between a parent and a baby. Some research would seem to suggest that rhythm and turn-taking exchanges are the key constituents of the relations between parents and babies when the latter have not yet fully acquired a linguistic, perceptual and behavioural repertoire (Coyle 1987; Stern 1977).

Speech and Language

The key medium of most social inter-actions, for Merleau-Ponty, Wittgenstein, Schutz and Mead, is language. Furthermore, all agree that language is central to the constitution of intersubjectivity. The role of language in this process is manifold and I will return to it at several points in this study. My consideration begins here, however, with a discussion of Merleau-Ponty's understanding of the relationship of thought to language.

Merleau-Ponty identifies an intimate relationship between thought and language. He believes that language is, for the most part, a tool with which we think. This position is argued for on two fronts. In the first instance he considers the language disorder aphasia. Two aspects of this disorder particularly interest him. Firstly, aphasics tend to experience 'thought disorders' along with their linguistic problems, thus suggesting that thought and language are intertwined. Many aphasics experience problems in categorising activities, for example. Secondly, aphasics tend to be able to use some words in some contexts and for some purposes but not others, which suggests that speech is not simply a third person, mechanical process but is intimately bound to the meaning of what is said; that is, to its thoughtfulness. In addition to this, Merleau-Ponty points to more general levels of experience which suggest thought/language intimacy. He notes that we must speak (albeit perhaps 'internally') to find out what it is that we think and that objects remain, to an extent, indeterminate for us until we can name them or articulate them; that we can only think around an issue once we have named it. This is not to say that thought determines language or that language determines thought. On the contrary. Merleau-Ponty identifies a much closer relationship than this. Thought and language are two sides of the same coin, he argues. Each needs its 'other half' for its own existence. We think in and through language.

It might be objected here, from a Wittgensteinian position, that Merleau-Ponty's argument essentialises 'thought' and 'thinking'. These terms, it might be argued, are used in a plurality of ways in ordinary speech, not all of which are directly referential and, of those which are, not all of which refer to 'verbal thought'. Indeed, it could be argued, we sometimes use 'thinking' in a way which pre-empts any close identification of thought and language; for example, 'I said it without thinking!' Furthermore, Merleau-Ponty's claim might be challenged from a more psychological position, by reference to the apparent independence of 'thought' and 'language' in both phylo-genetic and ontogenetic stages of human development. Vygotsky (1986), for example, whilst he maintains that thought and language are two sides of the same coin in most adult human cases, nevertheless maintains that it is possible to discern pre-linguistic thought (i.e. problem-solving) and pre-intellectual speech in both infants and some primates.

These criticisms are far from devastating and can be absorbed into Merleau-Ponty's position quite easily. His own analysis of the body-subject, for example, clearly posits that (non-verbal) human behaviour is intelligent, and thus he only disagrees with Vygotsky on the issue of whether such activity should be termed 'thought'. And in relation to Wittgenstein, it can be conceded that we use 'thought' in a multitude of ways, without significantly detracting from what Merleau-Ponty argues; namely, that a great many of the reflective and cognitive processes that human beings effect are conducted by and are dependent upon the use of symbolic forms, and, moreover, that these symbolic forms are the means by which human beings themselves become aware of these processes. Merleau-Ponty simply wanted to draw attention to the dependency of many of our conscious ideas and reflective experiences upon symbolic forms, and in this sense both Vygotsky and Wittgenstein are in agreement with him.

The identity of thought and language is important for Merleau-Ponty because it establishes that thinking is an activity which takes place only by way of shared (intersubjective) social resources and that it is therefore always potentially intersubjective in character. It shows that thought is an intersubjective action and that there is no private mental world of thoughts behind the world of social coexistence. Moreover, it means that we can genuinely make our thoughts public and can communicate. If thought and language were separated, he argues, we would never know whether we meant the same things by what we said. Words would be empty carriers which everyone would interpret in their own way. Furthermore such processes as learning would be impossible since each person would have to know how to interpret what they are taught before they are taught it; that is, they would have to understand what they are to be taught before they have been taught it.

In order to fully elaborate this position, Merleau-Ponty needs an account of the social nature of language and linguistic meaning. There are several attempts to provide such an account in his work (Edie 1987), but he is not successful in providing an adequate and full account (Crossley 1994; Ricoeur 1967b). For this reason I propose that we take a brief detour into the philosophy of Wittgenstein. This will provide us with a philosophical view of language which is appropriate to Merleau-Ponty's general approach (Heinzig 1987) and it will further reinforce the intersubjectivist model that we are outlining.

Wittgenstein and Language Games

The aspect of Wittgenstein's philosophy that I am concerned with is drawn from his later writing and was written (at least in part) in opposition to a theory of meaning and truth that he had outlined in his first published work, *Tractatus Logico-Philosophicus* (1961). In this early work, Wittgenstein had argued that words refer to and thus correspond to objects, and he had maintained that this relationship of correspondence effectively constitutes their meaning. Furthermore, he had argued that meaningful sentences effectively purport to describe states of affairs in the object world and that they can be defined as true or false according to whether the state of affairs that they describe corresponds to a state of affairs in the object domain. According to this theory, whilst the meaning of a word may be given in the form of another word or words (i.e. dictionary definition), the process of definition must ultimately lead to simple words which are defined ostensively; that is, by direct reference to the object which they represent. The typical form of an ostensive definition consists in repeating a name and pointing to that which it names.

This theory implies that much of what we say in ordinary, everyday speech is literally non-sense – because it doesn't refer to any object. Wittgenstein (1953) recognised this in his later work, *Philosophical Investigations*. In this study he argued against the representational theory of meaning and posited an alternative approach. To determine the meaning of a word, according to this later approach, we must examine its use:

> For a large class of cases – though not for all – in which we employ the word 'meaning' it can be defined thus: the meaning of a word is its use in the language. (Wittgenstein 1953: 20)

Wittgenstein expresses hesitation in his definition of the word 'meaning' here because he is clear that a single word can be used in a number of different ways and a number of different situations, thereby having a number of different possible meanings. Indeed context is central to his later approach to meaning. Nevertheless, to inquire into the meaning of a word in the context of Wittgenstein's later philosophy is to inquire into the work it does when uttered in a specific context. Wittgenstein uses the phrase 'language game' to denote this combination of context and use and he lists a number of such games; for example, joking, commanding, asking, questioning, explaining. These are the sorts of things that we do with language, the games that we play.

In order to play a language game and thus to use a word meaningfully, Wittgenstein observes, one must understand and follow its rules. Rules are central to meaning, in his later philosophy, replacing the earlier notion of ostensive definition. Indeed the notion of ostensive definition is subjected to considerable criticism in *Philosophical Investigations*. Ostensive definition works, Wittgenstein maintains, if and only if the person for whom a word is being defined already understands some language or, at least, shares a form of pre-understanding with the person defining. For example: it is relatively easy to define 'blue' to another person if one is able to point to an object, a cup for example, and to explain that 'blue' is the colour of the cup; but if they don't understand the words 'colour' and 'cup', how are they to know that it is the colour that I am pointing to and not the cup qua artefact or its texture or shape or location? Moreover, if they are pre-linguistic, how do they know that pointing and uttering, in this particular situation, is defining and not, for example, claiming ownership rights ('that's mine') or passing judgement ('tasteless')? How do they know what language game I am playing? And even if they do realise that I am defining, how are they to know that they are supposed to allow their eyes to follow the direction of my finger from my hand to my finger nail and then forwards until they reach something? Why not follow the finger 'backwards' along my arm and over my shoulder, or why not simply look at the hand as dogs tend to do?

What Wittgenstein is effectively challenging here is the idea that language can be justified or grounded in terms which do not already presuppose shared linguistic conventions and presuppositions; that is, that do not presuppose language itself. And this is, in effect, a critique of any attempt to ground language in anything outside of itself. There is no foundation beyond convention for Wittgenstein. This negative conclusion has a positive flip side, however, in the sense that it suggests that effective language rests in human agreement and shared understanding. Language, for Wittgenstein, is based in an irreducible agreement between language users about the rules of language, the ways in which it used. It is a necessarily intersubjective institution.

It is important to add here that this agreement does not imply reflective or conscious agreement. It is more fundamental than this: 'they agree in the *language* they use. This is not an agreement in opinions but in forms of life' (1953: 88, original emphasis). The definition of the concept 'forms of life' has been a subject of great controversy amongst Wittgensteinians (Hunter 1971). It will suffice for our purposes, however, to suggest that what Wittgenstein means is that, prior to any conscious reflection, there is a concordance or consensus between the linguistic practices of human beings.

There is agreement between the actions of language users. This might be
based in a common biological constitution (Hunter 1971). It might be based
in a common cultural heritage (Winch 1958). But it is probably based in a
mixture of the two.

The Possibility of a Private Language

Wittgenstein further explores this perspective on the shared basis of
language by considering the possibility of a private language; that is, a
language which only one individual could understand or follow. This
'private language argument' has been the subject of many controversies and
it has been interpreted in many different ways (e.g. Ayer 1981; Hanfling
1989; Kripke 1982; Malcom 1981; Perkins 1981). It is of importance for this
study because the idea of a private language, in the strictest sense, is
antithetic to the idea of radical intersubjectivity. It suggests that the meaning
of what we say is determined by individuals alone, in isolation, and thus that
meanings are never genuinely shared or exchanged. A rejection of the
notion of a private language, conversely, would be a great step forward for
intersubjectivism. It would suggest that (linguistic) meaning is necessarily a
radically intersubjective phenomenon. This debate is a continuation, in
different form, of our earlier discussion of privileged access. We are now
asking whether the meaning of what we say is determined by a private act of
consciousness.

The first stage of Wittgenstein's analysis of the possibility of a private
language consists in considering whether any aspects of our ordinary public
language could be said to have private meanings. His consideration of this
issue falls into two parts. In the first instance he asks whether the meaning of
words could be said to be conferred by any private mental process,
independent of the uttering of words and the language game. He approaches
this in a broadly experiential fashion, by asking his reader, firstly, to say
something and mean it, then to say it without meaning it, to mean it without
saying it and to say it whilst meaning something else. Readers are expected
to fail. There is, of course, a sense in which it is possible to say something and
not to mean it or else to say something and to mean something else: the
language games of irony, parody and such like make this possible. In all such
cases, however, the complex structuration of the meaning belongs to the
relationship between utterance, context and performance and does not
belong to any mental process which accompanies the act. Thus, for
Wittgenstein, the meaning of a word does not depend upon a private mental
process.

He follows this up by asking whether our words for sensations, such as
pain, presuppose a private definition and thus private meaning. If the
meaning of the word 'pain' is dependent upon a reference to a feeling within
one's body, he observes, then that meaning must be private because only the

individual can refer to feelings within his or her body – nobody else has access to them.

The resolution of this problem has already, in part, been given (above): 'I am in pain!', as I noted, is an exclamation, for Wittgenstein, and not a description or report. Moreover, it is an exclamation which we learn (from others) to substitute for our more natural pain exclamations and behaviours; for example, a baby learns to replace crying with 'It hurts!' (Coulter 1989). It is of course essential to this that pain sometimes coincides with pain behaviour. Wittgenstein accepts this presupposition. In particular he believes that the coincidence of the two is closest in babies because babies do not yet know how to pretend or lie: 'Lying is a language-game that needs to be learned like any other one' (1953: 90). Thus, the use of the word is a common usage which is learned without reference to any private experience, less still any private object.

In conjunction with the points made earlier on sensation, pain and pain behaviour, this is the basis of Wittgenstein's rejection of the notion that words in our common language might refer to private objects. In addition to considering what is the case, however, he wants to consider what could be the case. *Could* sensation words be given a private meaning? He considers this by imagining a person who writes a sign 'S' in their diary every time they experience a particular sensation – which already assumes that they know how to play the language game of definition. For the sake of argument, as Hanfling (1989) notes, Wittgenstein assumes that the association between the sensation and the sign is made. But he questions whether it has a purpose: 'But what is this ceremony for? For that is all it seems to be!' (1953: 92). The diary writer has formed an association but that is not language or meaning and it is not clear how it could be because there is no purpose for it to serve. Moreover, it has no function because it cannot serve as a proper definition. A definition would presuppose independent criteria by which the use of the word could be checked, but this does not apply in the present case: 'whatever is going to seem right to me is right. And that only means that here we can't talk about "right"' (ibid.). What Wittgenstein is doing here is taking us back to the idea that linguistic meaning has no absolute foundation, which was raised in the critique of ostensive definition (above), and which was resolved with recourse to the question of agreement, and he is arguing that without such agreement the definition could not be either justified or made effective. Thus there can be no private language.

Many commentators leave their reflection on the private language argument at this point. Hanfling (1989) takes it further, however. He notes that there is far more to language than sensation names and he maintains that the meaning of words and their function is dependent upon their relation to other words – which is why the single sensation name is useless and meaningless. 'S', for example, is the name of a sensation and it has its meaning in relation to the word 'sensation'. How, Hanfling asks, would 'sensation' be defined privately, particularly if it is to be distinguished from the names of particular sensations, such as 'S'? The definer would need to make a distinction between the particular ('S') and the generic ('sensation'), but how, we might add, are they to define 'particular' and 'generic' privately? Wittgenstein's reflections upon the possibility of this are even more pessimistic than in the former case:

> . . . in the end when one is doing philosophy one gets to the point where one would just like to emit an inarticulate sound. (Wittgenstein 1953: 93)

This argument leads us back to where we came from; that is, to the argument that language and thus linguistic meaning are based, in the final instance, in shared agreement and understanding concerning the use of utterances. They necessarily depend upon an irreducible agreement 'between' people and are always, therefore, radically intersubjective.

Speech Acts and the Social World

A further development of Wittgenstein's view is provided in the work of Austin (1971). Austin's contribution, from our point of view, is twofold. Firstly, he argues that speech is action and that many of our common social actions are, in essence, speech acts. We perform many tasks by speaking; for example, we declare, prohibit, invoice, command, request. Secondly, he argues that the effectiveness of our speech acts, in performing their tasks, is dependent upon certain 'felicity conditions', some of which depend upon prior agreement in forms of life. Asking questions, for example, is only effective to the extent that those asked recognise the speaker's actions as questions and deem them appropriate to the situation. Or again, whilst calling an election is a speech act, not everybody's speech is socially sufficient. Only a prime minister can call a general election because only their speech acts are invested with the commonly (intersubjectively) recognised authority to do so. In this sense, then, we can say that much of our social world is the achievement of speech acts, whose effectiveness rests in intersubjective agreement in forms of life and in the types of legitimacy afforded different speakers within those forms of life. This is our first key to understanding the intersubjectivity of the social world and social action.

Austin's work has provoked much response amongst social theorists. One important response, for our purposes, is that of Pierre Bourdieu (1992). Bourdieu argues that the rights of speech that Austin discerns constitute the basis of one of the most significant forms of power in the social world: symbolic power, the power to define and determine what we take to be true. Linguistic models of the social order ordinarily portray that order to be the achievement of free negotiation, Bourdieu argues, but Austin's arguments challenge that. They show that speech situations are embedded in institutional conditions which, in turn, determine who is able to speak and what they are able to say. We are never simply speakers, for Bourdieu. We are always bearers of institutional roles with rights and privileges of speech attached to them. In this sense, following Bourdieu, we might say that symbolic power is woven into the very fabric of intersubjectivity.

Affect and Emotion

Having described how we are enjoined to others and to a common world by means of our perceptions, actions and spoken thoughts, one crucial issue remains: affect or emotion. We must account for the fact that the encounters between body-subjects are often infused with love, hate, jealousy, pride, shame and other affective dynamics. Our relations with others (and with objects) are always 'mooded', for Merleau-Ponty. Moreover, there is no escape from such moodedness. Even an apparently emotionally neutral attitude is an emotional attitude. Moreover, insofar as intersubjective relations are understood as concrete interpersonal relations (Barrel 1985), their affective constitution is one of their key features.

Much (empiricist) work on emotion has tended to conceive of it as a configuration of physical sensations. Merleau-Ponty is critical of this, however. The same sensation, such as a racing heart, might constitute a qualitatively different emotion (e.g. fear or love) depending upon its context, he argues, which suggests at least that 'emotion' refers to the contextual significance of a sensation. This significance is further and more determinately fixed, however, by the ways in which we act, what we do in situations and the style or way that we do it. Indeed, these ways of acting may continue long after the subsidence of any particular sensation and may even be present without such sensations. These actions are the key to emotion for Merleau-Ponty. Emotion is a situated corporeal attitude, a way of being in relation to the world. Moreover, he maintains that it is inseparable from the other aspects of subjectivity hitherto mentioned in this chapter. It manifests in our perceptions, our speech/thought, our motor actions, gestures, and in our ways of understanding and interpreting. Thus our anger and love might consist in our gestures, in the way in which we speak or respond to events, and, in the longer term, in the patterns which unite our actions across different situations: my love, for example, might consist in my patience towards my loved one, my impatience towards all those who stand between us, my detailed care and attention in all matters concerning her and my inattention to other matters, etc.

As with the other aspects of subjectivity mentioned in this chapter, Merleau-Ponty maintains that our emotions function, primordially, at a pre-reflective level, and thus that we may not necessarily be reflectively aware of them. Indeed, the more we are absorbed in an emotional attitude, the less likely we are to realise the fact. We might be angry or jealous, for example, without realising it.

Three important points regarding intersubjectivity and emotion can be gleaned from this brief account. Firstly, emotions are not inner states. They manifest in the way in which we act and they are, potentially at least, publicly and intersubjectively definable states. Secondly, emotion is defined as a way of relating. It forms part of the 'system' that we form with others. We are joined to others by emotion. Thirdly, following on from this, emotion must therefore be dialogically constituted; that is, it shapes and is shaped by our interactions with others. We might be angry, for example, creating fear in the other, which then makes us feel guilty because we didn't want to hurt them. And we will carry this guilt into our next situation, which might make our other suspicious, making us angry with them, etc.

A further intersubjective aspect of emotion, noted by Jeff Coulter (1979), is its accountability. That emotion is rooted in conduct (rather than sensation) and that it is intersubjective, for Coulter, is exemplified by the fact that we expect people to be able to account rationally for their emotions and that we reserve the right both to criticise them for their emotions and to talk them out of their emotions. We tell a friend that they are wrong to feel jealous, for example, and we might present a case to them for not feeling this way. Clearly this is not the way that we would behave with a private sensation such as headache. Coulter's argument further reinforces Merleau-Ponty's position, then, and it adds to it by showing the way in which emotions are woven into the intersubjective fabric.

This doesn't mean that people cannot or do not hide their emotions, keeping them to themselves. Nor does it deny the often very private sense which we attach to emotion. It does suggest, however, that emotion does not take this private form in the first instance, a fact reinforced historically by Elias's (1978a) work. Elias shows how the privacy which we afford our emotions is a product of a slow historical process and that once it was common for many currently privatised emotions to be openly manifest. This privatisation is an intersubjective process for Elias, however; that is, he argues that it has become intersubjectively unacceptable for much emotion to be shown publicly. Social members 'agree', if only in their forms of life, to hide certain emotions or to reserve their expression for particular social situations.

From Radical to Egological Intersubjectivity

This chapter has sought to develop the notion of 'radical intersubjectivity' introduced in Chapter 1. I have argued for a non-reductive understanding of the irreducible 'systems' of interaction, coordinated through both time and space, which bind individuals. Furthermore, I have posited an understanding of language as an irreducibly intersubjective phenomenon which, at the same time, is central to the constitution of human subjectivity. The implication of this is that human subjects are necessarily intersubjective beings.

Integral to this argument has been a description of the pre-reflective being of the human subject qua body-subject. Radical intersubjectivity has been shown to be possible because human beings are able to adopt pre-objective and pre-reflective attitudes in which they open out onto and commune with alterity.

A critic might object that this argument has only been possible by ignoring the more private dimension of our subjective life. Clearly, they might suggest, we have a private world of feeling and thought which we do not make accessible to others. Furthermore, whilst we may be capable of adopting a pre-reflective way of being, we do reflect also, and we reflect about others. My response to this is twofold.

Firstly, returning to several points raised in the chapter, I would suggest that many of our 'private spaces' are in fact intersubjectively constituted, both in the sense that they rely upon intersubjective resources (such as language) for their construction, in the sense that they are demarcated for privacy by the intersubjective order, and in the sense that they occur in depopulated 'outer' spaces rather than in literally 'inner' spaces. A number of sociological studies can be used to support this point. Firstly, there are the historical studies which show that and how an emphasis upon privatisation of the self has emerged within the intersubjective fabric of contemporary societies, such that certain thoughts, actions and feelings are now expected (intersubjectively) to be kept to the self (Abercrombie et al. 1986; Elias 1978a; Foucault 1979). Of these, Elias's study is particularly interesting as it suggests that this historical process is miniatured in the psychological development of infants. Infants, he notes, are taught to keep certain feelings, thoughts and actions for themselves or for particular contexts. In addition to these historical studies, moreover, are ethnographic studies such as Goffman's (1959) *The Presentation of Self in Everyday Life*. This study illustrates clearly how subjects learn intersubjective scripts concerning the appropriateness of certain types of action to certain types of situation, and how they develop 'back regions' in which to let the mask slip. There is no ultimate back region in this account, no ultimately private space of the self. Different places serve as fronts and backs to each other. We can be certain things in certain situations, according to intersubjectively prescribed rules.

The case for this will be considerably sharpened in the next chapter where I argue that our sense of self and the possibility of our adopting a reflective attitude both derive from our relationships with others. Reflection and self-hood, I will argue (following Mead), are internalisations of the dialogical process.

Having said this, my second point is that the account of radical intersubjectivity hitherto outlined offers no account of human imagination and of the forms of privacy which this makes possible. Through imagination we are able to detach ourselves, in part, from the world of shared perceptions and thus to (partially) escape the intersubjective world as described in this chapter. We can, through imagination, carve out a world where private fantasies rule supreme. Moreover, this world of imagination also allows for different forms of relationship with other people. We can put ourselves in their place, imagine their response to things, rehearse what we intend to say to them, etc., without them actually being there to speak for themselves; that is, without being joined with them in a dialogical system. This possibility tends away from the type of intersubjective relations that I have been discussing in this chapter, suggesting a rather more egological mode of intersubjectivity. This egological mode and the relations between it and the radical mode form the focus of the next chapter.

3

Imagination, Self and Other: On Egological Intersubjectivity

The concept of radical intersubjectivity which was discussed in the previous chapter relies strongly upon an account of the social structuration of experience and action. I referred, for example, to acquired perceptual schemas, to the cultural shaping of 'natural' expressions and behaviours and to the grounding of thought and reflection in the (shared) institution of language. This raises an important question concerning the intersubjective orientation of the under-socialised being, the infant. Are infants always already other-oriented or is that orientation itself a result of socialisation? If the latter, what characterises pre-intersubjective subjectivity and how can it be made intersubjective? This is the first key cluster of questions for the current chapter. Reviewing theories and studies of child development, I will be considering whether radical intersubjectivity is primordially rooted in the human organism or whether it is a secondary construct on top of something more primordial.

Following this and considering Mead and Merleau-Ponty's theories of child development in particular, I will be discussing the development of 'self' and of the human sense of separateness that I began to consider at the end of the last chapter. This will allow us to consider both the character of the egological moment in our intersubjective experience, in which both self and other are objects of our experience, and the more reflective and reflexive aspects of our being more generally.

Discussion of these issues inevitably raises the question, also introduced in the last chapter, of imagination and of the imaginary worlds which provide us with escape routes from the mundane intersubjective world. These worlds, as I argued in the last chapter, pose a prima facie challenge to many of the ideas outlined in that chapter because they seem to indicate the existence of a private (rather than intersubjective) world of consciousness. This is the final issue addressed in the chapter.

The Child and the Other

In *I and Thou*, as I noted in Chapter 1, Buber (1958) suggests that infants, whilst they remain outside of the conventionalised or instituted practices of communication and sociality, are nevertheless communicative beings. They 'converse' gesturally with their parents in accordance with an innate predisposition. Moreover, self-hood and the world of private experience is, for Buber, a secondary structure which is constructed through and on the basis of such interactions. This view is shared by Merleau-Ponty and Mead, but it is by no means the only view or even the most popular. There is a long tradition in theories of child development, which includes the work of such central figures as Piaget (1961) and Freud (1984), of viewing the mental state of children as 'autistic'; that is, as closed in upon itself in an 'imaginary' reality and thereby insulated from the world around it. The socialisation of the child, in this (latter) view, is not only a matter of teaching and intitiating the child into the rituals, rules and conventions of its social world and of its particular place in that world (which is what it involves for Mead and Merleau-Ponty); it is equally a matter of 'opening out' the mind of the child to others and to a world shared in common. The child literally has to be *made* social and made to share in intersubjective reality.

Castoriadis's (1987) thesis of the 'monadic core of the psyche' is a recent and extreme version of this view. Castoriadis understands the psyche to be, in its essence, monadic and closed in upon itself. Socialisation, in his view, is a 'violent' process which pulls the child out of its 'monadic core', in order to introduce it to the instituted world of its parents and community. This violent wrenching of the subject out of itself is never complete, for Castoriadis. There is always a residue of private imagination which remains. It is the necessary basis of the social and intersubjective world, however. The social–intersubjective world, in this case, is a secondary structure, imposed upon an otherwise monadic psychological life.

Castoriadis's position has a certain appeal, not least because it accounts for both the role of imagination in human life and the sense of privacy which we enjoy in relation to that world. It is flawed, however, at both a theoretical and an empirical level. Theoretically it is flawed because it is not clear how an imaginative monadic core, turned in upon itself, could ever be wrenched away from itself by something outside of it and made to identify with an intersubjective world. If the outside has an influence upon the psyche, then the psyche is open to or oriented to the outside and not, in any strong sense, monadic. We can add to this point by drawing from one of Castoriadis's (1990, 1991) own qualifying statements, namely, that the 'violence' which is alleged to pull the subject out of itself and into the intersubjective world is not violence in our common understanding of the word. It is not physical violence. It is violence only in the sense that it negates the imaginative world of the child. This adds to my criticism because it suggests that parents do not need to go to any (physical) extremes in order to orient their children towards them or their shared world, again suggesting, contrary to the monad thesis, that babies are always already oriented (in one way or another) to the world (and thus to others).

In addition to this, there is a problem in suggesting that newly born infants are locked in an imaginative monadic core because it is not clear what their 'images' could consist in, if they have no prior ('real world') experiential materials with which to work. Imaginings, however creative and unusual in form, are constructed out of visual and linguistic images which are derived from the intersubjective world (Cohen and Mackeith 1991; Ricoeur 1991). Thus the idea of an imaginative realm which predates our relation to reality is inconsistent and begs more questions than it answers. What could the images and hallucinations of the child with no experience of reality consist in? Castoriadis (1987) anticipates this criticism and argues for a distinction between a secondary imagination (which is derivative) and a radical imaginary which is psychically primordial and generative of all other cognitive functioning (particularly perception). This doesn't solve the problem, however, because it still fails to account for the contents of infantile, monadic psychological life.

This line of criticism is supported at the empirical level. Daniel Stern (1977), for example, echoing a considerable consensus amongst developmental psychologists, has argued that infants, from the moment of birth, are active stimulus seekers. Indeed, rather than identifying the necessity for a violent imposition of 'reality' upon the infant, Stern argues that infants appear to exhibit a drive towards both perceptual and cognitive stimulation. This drive allows them to form sensori-motor schemas by which they can accommodate to and assimilate 'reality', including the reality of their carers, in their earliest weeks and months. Moreover, Stern adds, the infant seemingly has an inborn capacity to habituate to 'normal' experiences. It disattends to the familiar and concentrates upon new and different stimuli, which afford a greater opportunity for learning. It is true, of course, that the child can be overstimulated, particularly in very early infancy. It is also true that the infant will take steps to avoid such overstimulation. The schematic appropriation of the shared sensori-motor world takes time and the infant cannot face the complexity of that world all at once. Nevertheless, it does appear that the infant 'opens onto' that world from the moment of birth and that it is, in part, the agent of its own assimilation into it.

Recent research into infant's imitation, by Meltzoff and Moore (1977, 1983, 1991), takes this view further in the innate-intersubjectivity direction. They found that children, whilst characterised by considerable sensori-motor immaturity, are nevertheless motivated and able to imitate certain adult facial gestures (such as sticking out one's tongue) from as early as *forty-two minutes old*. This strongly suggests that the propensity and capability to imitate is innate, and it is significant in two respects. Firstly, it suggests that children are equipped to play a very active role in their own socialisation. They are not passive recipients of external 'violence'. Secondly, it effectively shows that the infant's (lived) body is pre-reflectively 'paired' and thus intersubjectively bonded with that of its other. It sticks out its tongue, in reply to the same action by the other, before it has even realised that it has a tongue, thereby demonstrating a lived sense of corporeal equivalences (your tongue/my tongue) at the very earliest stages of development.

This point can be developed through a consideration of Merleau-Ponty's (1968b, 1979) discussion of the infantile body-subject. Referring to slightly older infants, Merleau-Ponty makes a number of observations regarding the imitation which is central to learning. First, he observes that infants often imitate the results of action rather than the specific movements that they entail (e.g. if an adult turns his or her eyes to look at something then the infant may turn its whole head to look at it). This is significant, for Merleau-Ponty, because it suggests that the child is oriented to and responds to the meaning (qua purpose) of the gesture as a whole, rather than to the empirical extension of the adult's body through space. It is, in other words, always already oriented to the meaningful actions of the other. Secondly, he observes that infants often imitate what they cannot see on either themselves or the other (e.g. when learning to speak they imitate the correct modulation of the larynx without being able to see either their own larynx or anybody else's) or what they see the wrong way round (because the parent is facing them). This reinforces the first point and, additionally, makes a strong case for the notion of a lived sense of corporeal equivalence between body-subjects. It suggests an innate intercorporeality.

This is not to suggest that the child is born with a complete orientation to intersubjective reality. Neither does it deny either the agency and mediations of the caregiver in the process of orienting the child towards an intersubjective reality or the cultural specificity of the 'reality' towards which the child is oriented. Both the psyche of the child and the orientation of that psyche towards a symbolically and politically ordered world will require enormous work before the infant is ready to take its place as an agent of a specific social formation. The point is, however, that this is only possible because the child is always already 'open' to its environment and thus to the formative influences of that environment. The child is an active participant in its own formation. Moreover, and this brings us to our next point, it is able to enter the intersubjective order through the influence of the practices of that order because it is always already involved in intersubjective relations. This point requires elaboration.

I have argued eleswhere (Crossley 1994) that the social practices which shape and control our subjectivities (which we may resist) are intersubjective practices. They depend upon shared meanings and the dynamics (in the broadest sense) of relationships. This is equally true of socialisation and, as such, is borne out in many recent studies of child development. The work of Stern (1977; Stern et al. 1977), Newson (1977, 1979) and more particularly Trevarthen (1977, 1979; Trevarthen and Hubley 1978), for example, clearly reveals that entrance into the intersubjective world of adult society is achieved by way of stages of 'primary' and 'secondary' intersubjectivity, the former of which is made possible by the apparently innate communicative and intersubjective propensities of the child. Infants are born with a propensity for intentional or purposive action, Trevarthen argues, and in particular they are motivated by a desire (as well as some rudimentary ability) to communicate. In the early intersubjective stage ('primary intersubjectivity') this desire to communicate is seemingly divorced from an interest in the objects of their world. Infants either want to play with their caretaker or (at a slightly later age) they want to manipulate other aspects of their world, but not both at the same time. At the secondary stage, however, there is a gradual bringing together of the two, such that the environment and its objects mediate relations between infant and caregiver. They play with an object and share in an object world together. Through the course of the secondary stage, moreover, the child begins to show an interest in the interest of the carer. The interest of the carer in an object will interest the child in it and the child will realise that the carer has an interest to be stimulated. This intertwining of interests can be a major controlling influence upon the child. It will look for the approval of the carer before acting and will trust in that approval when trying out new or risky experiences.

Primary and secondary intersubjectivity are, without doubt, very different to the intersubjectivity described in Chapter 2. The infant does not speak a word of language and most of the common rules of adult interaction must be broken if the child is to respond; temporal and spatial exaggeration of gesture, extended eye-to-eye gazing and 'baby talk' are all examples of this (Stern 1977). Nevertheless, many of the features of intersubjectivity, as I have described it in Chapter 2, are present in a rudimentary form. Particularly evident amongst these features is 'mutual tuning in'. The sharing of a temporal frame, of rhythm and tempo, it would seem, is a crucial constituent of infant-caregiver relations (Coyle 1987; Fogel 1977; Stern 1977). Most important, however, Trevarthen maintains that a 'correct description' of infant–carer interactions,

> . . . to capture its full complexity, must be in terms of a mutual intentionality and sharing of mental state. Either partner may intitiate a 'display' or 'act of expression' and both act to sustain a sharing and exchanging of intitiatives. Both partners express complex purposive impulses in a form that is infectious for the other. (1977: 241)

In order for this to be possible, according to our account in Chapter 2, infant and carer must share in (in addition to a perceptual world) both a language game and a significant symbol; that is, a gesture must have the same significance for both partners. This, it would seem, is the case. Gestures, according to both Trevarthen and Newson, appear to have the same meaning for both parties and that is a meaning tied to certain types of 'doing' or social activity. Of course these meanings are 'infantile' and the process of their exchange must be sharply transformed before the infant will be a competent member of the adult social order. Moreover, it would appear that many language games (e.g. naming) are precisely learned during this period and are not therefore innate. Nevertheless, the rudiments of communication appear to be innate.

The evidence of child development research supports the general thesis of Buber, Mead and Merleau-Ponty, then, and it allows us to criticise the monadic view of Castoriadis. Infants are always already oriented to their environment and to others, in a number of sophisticated ways, and it is this primordial intersubjectivity which provides the basis for their passage into the adult intersubjective order. Socialisation is communication not violence. This is not to suggest that socialisation is conflict free, however.

Motherhood, Recognition and Struggle

During the period of primordial intersubjectivity, particularly in the context of the socialisation process, the child is very dependent upon the carer. The carer provides the child with food and warmth and protects it from potential dangers. Moreover, as Kaye's (1991) research reveals, the child's socialisation and education is dependent upon the carer framing his or her interaction with the child. Framing involves controlling the time and space of interactions to afford infants the situations and aids that they need to develop. Furthermore, it involves the carer interpreting the actions of the child as meaningful social actions or communications, sometimes complementing them so that the child learns to develop them into proper social actions, at other times just teaching the child to translate its natural gestures into a conventional cultural form (Clarke 1978; Schaffer 1991).

This notion of translation between natural and cultural gestures vindicates Wittgenstein's analysis of pain behaviour and thus lends further support to the intersubjectivist case. It is important to note, however, that not all learning is translating. Newly acquired schemas can actually change the world of the child. They create new experiences and possibilities for experience and they pose new problems for the developing infant to resolve. When a child imitates an adult way of acting, it actually achieves, as an unintended consequence, greater access to the adult world of meaning and experience.

Integral to framing and to development more generally is the child's aforementioned interest in the interest of the carer and its desire for approval by that carer. This is a third dimension of dependency between infant and carer. Importantly, however, as Benjamin (1991) observes, this dependency is two-way. The primary carer, whom Benjamin identifies as usually the mother, needs recognition from the child, both for herself and in order to maintain her interest and recognition of the child. The child, by contrast, needs recognition both in order to motivate its interest correctly through the socialisation process and to establish its sense of self. What this amounts to, Benjamin notes, is a need for mutual recognition in the Hegelian/Kojèvian sense (see Chapter 1). As in the Hegelian account, however, this desired state is struggled over. Both parties want to be recognised by the other but both equally experience the other as a threat and seek their independence.

Benjamin's point is suggestive and interesting. It allows us to identify the relation of carer and infant as an irreducible system, based in recognition, and it therefore adds considerably to our understanding of the situation of primordial intersubjectivity which precedes adult intersubjective relations. The mother is able to fulfil the infant's need for recognition to the extent that the infant is able to fulfil the mother's. Moreover, Benjamin raises the important point that the infant, in the context of these primordial relations, begins to develop a sense of self. Unfortunately, however, like Hegel and Kojève before her, Benjamin is not very specific in her account of what 'self' consists in or of the manner in which it develops, and she does not support her account with much empirical evidence, at least not of the direct observational kind. To fill in this gap in her account we can return to the work of Merleau-Ponty and Mead, and to some recent studies of child development.

The Process of Self

For both Merleau-Ponty and Mead, self is a socially instituted and temporally mediated reflexive process. It involves the subject 'turning back' upon themself (through time), to view themself from 'outside' or, rather, as another would view them. In this sense it is very similar to the notion of self-consciousness which was discussed in connection with Kojève in Chapter 1. Furthermore, like Kojève, both Merleau-Ponty and Mead maintain that this reflexive process is made possible through the interaction of the subject with others. Indeed, like Kojève, they maintain that, without such interaction, consciousness remains largely unaware of itself. Mead is the most useful of the two for allowing us to conceptualise this process and I will therefore use his schema as a means of giving form to the ideas of both writers.

Mead posits two concepts which allow us to separate the aspects of the self process: the 'I' and the 'me'. The precise definition of the 'I' has been a cause of controversy amongst Mead scholars. He is notoriously ambiguous on this point. For our purposes, however, it will suffice to identify it with the active agency of the (Merleau-Pontyian) body-subject, as described in Chapter 2. The I is the perceiving, acting, speaking, feeling body-subject, which is not (yet) reflectively aware of either itself or its world:

> It is because of the I that we say that we are never fully aware of what we are, that we surprise ourselves by our own action. It is as we act that we are aware of ourselves. (Mead 1967: 174)

The I, Mead continues, only knows itself in the past tense; that is, as 'me':

> As given, it is a 'me', but it is a me which was the 'I' at an earlier time. If you ask, then, where directly in your own experience the 'I' comes in, the answer is that it comes in as a historical figure [i.e. as 'me']. (ibid.)

The me is the I's objectification, recollection or image of itself. It is the conception which the 'I' forms of itself. This conception involves the I taking an outside view upon itself; that is, conceiving of itself as another would conceive it ('taking the attitude of the other', as Mead calls it). Furthermore, as such, it necessarily entails a sense of the perspective of the other.

It is important to note here that one's relationship to one's self qua me compares directly with one's relationship to others in the Husserlian schema (Chapter 1). The self 'experiences' itself. It constitutes itself as an object of experience. This is central to the egological mode of intersubjectivity and it contrasts sharply to the radical mode, where the subject is largely self-unaware.

Much of the emphasis in Mead's discussion is on the historical nature of the me. The I is portrayed as an active and reactive force which plunges forward into situations, the me as a passive construction in the retrospective accounting of that process. This is not the whole story, however. One of Mead's central reasons for introducing the I and the me into his discussion is to account for the possibility of reflection, planning and anticipation, and it is clear that the me has a central role in these processes. On the one hand, the me is the image through which the I can imaginatively project itself into future events and into which it can invest its hopes, fears, dreams and ambitions. On the other, it is the reflexive looping of I and me which effectively allows the subject to engage in dialogue with itself and thus to decide, with a fair degree of conscious awareness, what it wishes to do. It puts forward a view which, assuming the attitude of the other, it then turns back on and responds to, and it then responds to this response, and so on, until a decision is made and action ensues (or until action disrupts the process of debate). In this sense the me is constituted not through the actual past responses of others towards the subject, but through anticipated responses to action which the I constructs and runs through in an imaginary modality. Moreover, these responses may tend to be based less in the assumption of the (imagined) attitude of specific others and more in the assumption of the attitude of what Mead refers to as 'the generalised other'; that is, the view of nobody in particular but rather the community as a whole. The me is instituted from the point of view of the community as a whole.

The implication of this point, for Mead, is that the me is effectively an internalised locus of social control. Insofar as the self process is a dialogue between I and me it entails individuals policing their own intentions in terms derived from the wider community ('the generalised other'). As a dialogue this can involve no guarantee that the individual will capitulate to the communal view, nevertheless it is sufficient in Mead's view to ensure the effective basis of liberal democracies. We are able to enjoy the benefits of liberal democracy and to live without the threat of excessive punishment regimes, Mead maintains, only because we have this internalised control function; that is, because we take the attitudes and views of others and of the community as a whole into account before we act. In addition to controlling action, moreover, this process equally coordinates it. Individuals anticipate each other's responses to events and actions and are able to accommodate to them on this basis. This, for Mead, is quite fundamental to the possibility of social life in itself.

It is important to add here that Mead's notions of 'community' and 'the generalised other' can be pluralised to account for the plurality of social groups and identities in contemporary societies. This pluralisation does possibly pose political problems for Mead, as I discuss in Chapter 7, but at the analytic and psychological level there is no reason why his theory cannot incorporate the idea of multiple overlapping communities and identities.

The Emergence of the Self Process

For Merleau-Ponty, a prototype of the reflexivity which is constitutive of the self process is built into the very 'flesh' of the body-subject. There is, he argues, a reflexivity (1968b: 168), even a narcissism (1968a: 139) in all perception because we are visible-seers, tangible-touchers, audible-listeners; that is, because we are part of the (perceptible) world that we perceive. This extends, he continues, to our relation to ourselves. We can see ourselves and touch ourselves. We perceive our own perceptible being, at least to some extent. In *The Visible and the Invisible* (1968a), he contemplates the possibility that this extends to a complete reflexivity and reversibility, such that we might touch ourselves touching or see ourselves seeing. Experience falls short of this, however. Complete reversibility is always imminent but it is never realised in fact. We reach the 'verge' of coincidence but then it slips away, never to be realised:

> . . . the coincidence eclipses at the moment of realisation, and one of two things always occurs: either my right hand really passes over to the rank of the touched, but then its hold on the world is interrupted; or it retains its hold on the world, but then I do not really touch *it* – my right hand touching, I palpate with my left hand only its outer covering. (Merleau-Ponty 1968a: 147–8, original emphasis)

This, to use Mead's terms, is why the I can only ever experience itself as me and why the self is always necessarily a temporal process. The I can never completely coincide with itself. Moreover, given the difficulty of completely seeing oneself (in a metaphoric as well as a literal sense), this is why the view of others is necessary to complete the reflexive loop. Others see one in ways that will never be possible for oneself and it is only by recognising that they see one as such that one can actually achieve a recognition of one's perceptible being. My recognition of my visibility for the other, Merleau-Ponty maintains, makes it such that 'for the first time I appear to myself completely turned inside out under my own eyes' (1968a: 143). This is not achieved all at once for Merleau-Ponty or for Mead, however, and it is not achieved independently of social institutions. It is the result of a lengthy socialisation process. At birth and for some time after infants fail to identify or differentiate themselves in this way. They have no reflective consciousness of either self or other. At most they have a vague corporeal sense of themselves, manifest in their immature perceptions and sensations.

It is important to distinguish between this view and the view of innate intersubjectivity outlined earlier. The earlier view was that infants are born with an innate predisposition towards and ability for jointly meaningful interactions. What we are now suggesting is that they do this without any sharp reflective sense either of their self or of others. In other words, they are innately predisposed towards a form of radical intersubjectivity but not towards egological intersubjectivity. The latter is a secondary and derived possibility. This is a view which is supported by contemporary developmental psychology. Whilst there is evidence to suggest that newly born infants enjoy some sense of their self (Coyle 1987), most psychologists see this as a lived or tacit I which will only later be joined by the reflective self-consciousness of a me (Case 1991; Fein 1991). Moreover, they maintain that the early intersubjective engagements of the I are integral to the development of the me.

One particularly important process for the achievement of differentiation and the development of a reflective self-consciousness, for both Merleau-Ponty and Mead, is the entrance of the infant into the world of language and social symbols. The role of language in the production of self is multidimensional, but four aspects in particular are of importance.

In the first instance, language is, as I noted in Chapter 2, a means by which thought is achieved, according to both Merleau-Ponty and Mead, and it is equally a means by which thoughts are made apparent to the thinker. When we speak we quite literally hear ourselves thinking and this initiates for us a relationship (mediated through time) to ourselves. We can both speak and listen to ourselves. Mead's discussion of this issue is more detailed than that of Merleau-Ponty. He breaks it down into four points. Firstly, he maintains that speech, whilst it is clearly an action, can equally be regarded as a shortening of action, something which falls short of action whilst communicating the intent of an action. Secondly, following on from this, he maintains that verbal thought can therefore mediate our relationship to our environment, presenting our possibilities for action to us before we act upon them. In this sense, subjects are distanced from their environment and turned towards their own possibilities within it. They do not simply respond. They think. The third point is that this thought, because of its linguistic form, represents possibilities to subjects. Subjects speak (perhaps silently to themselves), hear themselves and respond. They can have an 'internal dialogue' with themselves. Finally, Mead maintains that the internal dialogue, because it relies upon significant symbols whose meaning is ubiquitous throughout the linguistic community, involves subjects taking the attitude of the other towards their thoughts; that is, in replying to their own suggestions, subjects play the role of the other in relation to themselves. They respond to themselves as they would to another speaker and thus become an-other to themselves. Speech, in this sense, effects the reflective and reflexive process that is constitutive of self.

A second role of language in the constitution of the self process, which is of more concern to Merleau-Ponty than to Mead, is the use of linguistic self-referents and particularly names and pronouns (see also Harré and Gillet 1994). Linguistic behaviour differs from other forms of behaviour in that, in some instances at least, it explicitly refers back to and demarcates both the speaker and their audience. Moreover, forms of address configure us in specific relations; for example, to refer to 'mum' is to imply a relation to 'child'. This may sound unremarkable but the cultural variability of different forms of address and different naming practices has raised important and interesting questions about the cultural variability of our identities and forms of self-hood (Hirst and Wooley 1982; Mauss 1979). Questions have been raised, for example, about the experiences of self of those who do not use individual names or who have no direct equivalent to the English personal pronoun 'I'. Could we experience ourselves in the way that we do without these modes of address? Moreover, the symbolic construction of particular ways of identifying and differentiating persons (e.g. gender) and their relationship to specific institutional arrangements and hierarchies can be of considerable consequence for those who come to occupy them. Our (linguistic) categories of human identity are integrally bound to specific forms of power and privileges (Butler 1990).

Following on from this, the me is often housed in an autobiographical narrative. Our sense of ourselves is based in stories which we tell about ourselves, which exemplify the sort of persons we feel that we are and which construct and sustain a sense of continuity over time. Autobiographies identify us both to ourselves and to others. Language is again central to this process. Indeed autobiography might be conceived as a special form of language game, which places certain demands upon the speaker and furnishes them with rhetorical devices for meeting those demands (Davies 1993, 1995).

At a slightly different level, for Merleau-Ponty (1979) the acquisition of language is important for the development of self because part and parcel of becoming an effective speaker is learning to recognise (albeit at the tacit level) the specificity of one's own perspective and to compensate for that when one communicates. To become a competent and effective speaker one must learn to account for the gaps between one's own experience and that of one's interlocutors. Without this 'filling in', one's speech will be heard as (egocentric) nonsense.

The entrance into language, narrowly conceived, is not the whole story of the construction of self for either Merleau-Ponty or Mead, however. Both identify processes over and above straightforward language acquisition and participation in autobiographical language games, and both maintain that the sense of me is something more than a linguistic objectification. I will discuss Merleau-Ponty's account of these processes first.

The Mirror Stage

For Merleau-Ponty (1968b), the key process for the development of self, over and above language acquisition, is the 'mirror stage'. As its name suggests, this involves a series of experiences prior to the acquisition of language, in which the child comes to recognise its self through the reflections of itself that it encounters in its environment. The child reflexively turns back upon itself, in other words, by means of a 'reflecting surface' and it identifies itself with what it sees. The me is thus a mirror image. For many of Merleau-Ponty's apologists, these reflections emanate principally from the infant's caregivers (Dillon 1978; Levin 1991; O'Neill 1986). The 'mirror' of their mirror stage is a metaphor. Much to their disappointment, however, Merleau-Ponty's own discussion tends to centre upon infants' relations to literal mirror images and it even seems to play down the parental (intersubjective) mediation of these relations. Merleau-Ponty fails to consider that infants are placed in front of mirrors, by carers, and that those carers actively encourage and help the child to recognise its image as its own. I will begin my discussion of the mirror stage by discussing this literal mirror imaging.

A child's ability to recognise itself in the mirror, as indicated by its ability to use a mirror to learn about or alter aspects of its appearance, is used by many child psychologists as an indicator of a child's objective sense of self (or me). Contemporary studies indicate that this recognition is achieved by about 65 per cent of children in their twentieth to twenty-fourth months (Amsterdam 1971). This achievement can be divided into three stages. At six to twelve months, according to Amsterdam, infants tend to treat their mirror images as a 'sociable playmate'. Then, between fourteen and twenty months, they begin to show self-conscious behaviour. Finally, starting at twenty months, they begin to achieve full recognition.

What this process involves, for Merleau-Ponty, is a gradual negation of the 'quasi-reality' of the mirror image. It is as much a process of learning not to treat the image as real as of learning that the figure in the mirror is itself. The 'quasi-reality' of the image is never completely diminished according to some Merleau-Pontyians, however. Romanyshyn (1982), for example, argues that the me in the mirror is never a simple reflection of the person standing before it. It is always an imaginary character, fitted into a plot of future plans and viewed from the point of view of the other. The mirror image is never I. It is always a me to be invested with fantasies and hopes.

Merleau-Ponty speculates that it is the child's experience of seeing others in the mirror which first enables it to see the mirror as a reflecting surface and thus to recognise that one of the figures in the mirror is itself. The discrepancy which the child experiences between seeing an image in front of it and hearing the voice that 'belongs' to that image behind it is, he argues, a considerable learning experience. He is less interested in the stages of experience and cognitive development that make such recognition possible, however, than in the consequences of it. Through the mirror, he maintains, the child learns that it is visible from the outside, that a view can be taken on it. Moreover, it identifies with this image, bringing about a narcissistic alienation that is definitive of the human self:

> I am no longer what I felt myself, immediately, to be; I am the image of myself that is offered by the mirror. To use Dr Lacan's terms, I am 'captured, caught up' by my spatial image. Thereupon I leave the reality of my lived *me* in order to refer myself constantly to the ideal, fictitious, or imaginary *me*, of which the specular image is the first outline. In this sense I am torn from myself, and the image in the mirror

prepares me for another still more serious alienation, which will be the alienation by others. (Merleau-Ponty 1968b: 136, original emphasis)

This specular/imaginary self-alienation is not experienced negatively, according to Merleau-Ponty. On the contrary, the child's experiences before the mirror, in many cases, are joyful. The child loves the image of itself and this is why and how it is able to identify with it, defining itself in terms of the image. This is alienation, however, since it pulls the subject out of itself, separating it from the immediacy of its experiencing being. To use Mead's terms, the I is confronted with the 'me' and, from that point on, will have reference to itself only as me.

It is important for Merleau-Ponty that this exteriorised, imaginary 'me' is a public me, a me who is experienced as capable of being experienced by others: 'others have only an exterior image of me, which is analogous to the one seen in the mirror' (1968b: 136). By seeing itself as visible, he maintains, the subject sees itself in a similar fashion to the way in which others see it and it takes the first step towards experiencing itself as existing for others. Moreover, it is only when the subject sees itself as others see it, when it assumes the 'attitude of the other', that the full self-consciousness of the me is achieved.

The experience of the me as existing for-others is again described by Merleau-Ponty as alienating, and again 'alienation' is not intended to connote a negative experience. Being experienced by the other can be pleasurable and self-confirming. This alienation can be threatening, however, in the sense that subjects experience themselves as captured in the experience of the other; that is, they experience a paranoid sense of being objectified from the outside and of losing the ability to determine the meaning of their own actions. In such situations, subjects become acutely self-conscious and consequently lose (temporarily) their capacity for pre-reflective spontaneity (Fanon 1986; Sartre 1969; Young 1980). Every movement is approached with anxiety and paranoic intensity. This is the phenomenon of 'the look' that I discussed in Chapter 1 (see also Crossley 1993, 1994) and it is particularly important, as I noted in my discussion of the politics of the visible in Chapter 2, in relation to those groups who are defined as 'other' within a particular culture. These groups, who include both women and some ethnic groups, are less likely to find themselves engaged in open communicative relations, more likely to find themselves objectified in the gaze of the other (Beauvoir 1988; Fanon 1986; Young 1980).

This account poses an important philosophical question; namely, how (after the mirror stage) does the infant pass from self to other? How does it have access to the experience of the other, such that it can experience itself as experienced? It is important to emphasise here that this access to otherness is quite different to that discussed in relation to radical intersubjectivity in Chapter 2. In the case of radical intersubjectivity the other is communicated with and responded to on the basis of their actions. In this (egological) case, by contrast, the other becomes an object of knowledge and thought and their actions are used as a basis from which to make certain explicit inferences about them. Moreover, in the egological mode the other no longer occupies their own place in the situation, rather self puts itself in their place and thinks for them.

There can be no doubt that this experience occurs in an imaginary modality. As Wittgenstein argued (see Chapter 2), we cannot *have* the experience of the other. But we can imagine it. With imagination we can feel the eyes of the other burning into us or, again, we can 'know', without talking to them, what they are thinking about us. In relation to this issue, with the philosophical modifications which are suggested by the first three chapters of this book, we can revive the Husserlian notion of analogical apperception (see Chapter 1). The other, we can argue, appears to us in the egological and alienating mode by means of our imaginative transposition of our own egological perspective onto them. One key difference between our version of this thesis and that of Husserl, however, would have to be that self does not attribute thoughts to the other on the basis of prior contact with itself. Following our critique of this idea in Chapter 1 and our critique of the notion of privileged access in Chapter 2, we would have to maintain that inferences about the other are made on the basis of shared symbols and shared understandings of the significance of particular types of conduct and gesture. We will get a clearer idea of how this might happen in the next section, where I consider Mead's views on our imaginative relations with the perspective of the other.

Play, Games and the Other

Merleau-Ponty's account and the implications that we have drawn from it are important for our discussion of intersubjectivity. There are, however, a number of problems with it. The most obvious of these, as Martin Dillon (1978) notes, is that self-consciousness would seem to be a relatively ubiquitous phenomenon amongst human beings, whilst mirrors and the availability of (literally) reflecting surfaces are not. Furthermore, to add to this point, infants who are blind from birth, despite the many problems which they face, nevertheless arrive at a coherent sense of self without the use of the mirror. This is not to say that mirrors have not had a tremendous impact upon those cultures which have variously invented them. It does suggest, however, that the self-consciousness of the me is not tied to a mirror in the strictest sense of the word.

For many of Merleau-Ponty's apologists (Dillon 1978; Levin 1991; O'Neill 1986) the role or function of the mirror can be assumed by a carer. Thus the need for a literal mirror is avoided and the problem (apparently) overcome. In Dillon's account, this is described in terms that are reminiscent of Castoriadis (above). The child's lack of a sense of differentiation, Dillon maintains, is broken down by a 'significant other' who 'forces the infant to recognise an alien perspective' (1978:91). The examples which Dillon provides of how this is done are punishment and withdrawal of approval. This notion is quite logical and it allows us to develop a further criticism of the mirror stage, by identifying a process which that stage would not seem to account for. For the infant to learn to recognise 'other conscious beings' or other perspectives and, thereby, recognise the particularity and peculiarity of its own (i.e. to recognise its self as self), Dillon is suggesting, it is necessary for those perspectives to impose themselves upon it. A consciousness which is unaware of other consciousnesses has no reason, even if it sees that it has or is a body similar to those with which it interacts, to infer that they are consciousnesses, unless they inform it of the fact. Why should it? They are facets of its world and function perfectly well for it without needing to seem conscious. The problem with this account, however, is that it still fails to explain how the child gains a sufficient degree of distance from itself to recognise the view of the other as another view. It doesn't explain why the child should understand the actions of the carer, however obtrusive and punitive, as indications of the perspective of another. Parental punishment, for example, whilst it must give a child a (tacit) sense of its own limits, might suffice only to produce physical aggression in that child. It need not lead the child to see that the parent has a point of view.

To overcome this problem and thus to achieve a better understanding of the development of self-hood and egological intersubjectivity we must turn again to Mead's work. Mead maintains that children develop distance from themselves, first, through play, particularly forms of play which involve role changing, and, second, through playing games.

In play, Mead argues, children pretend to be someone else. They take on social roles. This contributes to the development of a sense of self in a number of respects. Firstly, it particularises and relativises the child's own perspective qua infant. It learns to take a different relation to the world and thus to identify the particularity of its normal situation. Secondly, it enables it, at least in cases where it pretends to be one of its carers, to take an outside view on itself and to address itself from the outside. It can pretend to be its mother talking to it and can thereby assume the attitudes which its mother has towards it. Thirdly, at least in cases where the child takes two or more roles (e.g. it is nurse, doctor and patient in succession), it can assume, in loose form, the conversational relation to itself which is constitutive of the I/me relation. In other words, the play of the child involves an imaginative identification with others which allows the child to take an outside perspective on itself and thus allows it to develop the reflexive (processual) relation to itself that is constitutive of self.

It might be objected here that this process presupposes what it sets out to explain. In order to assume the role of the other, it could be argued, the child must always already have an understanding of the other and thus of self. This need not be so, however. As Merleau-Ponty (1979) notes, a child can imitate the action of the other without any conception of the attitude and perspective of that other, and only then discover within that action the attitude of the other. The perspective unfolds for the infant as it performs the routines that it involves. It acquires understanding by 'doing'. This point is particularly important in relation to the objections which I have raised against Husserl's account of analogical apperception (Chapter 1) because it allows us to see how an imaginative transfer of experiences might take place, how one might be able to assume the perspective of the other, without relying upon dubious notions of analogy and without presupposing a prior transparency of the subject to itself. For Mead, conceptions of self and of other are formed at the same time by the same process, and self has access to the perspective of the other by actually playing at the (public) role of the other and discovering through this exercise the 'inside' of the role. It is this role playing which allows for the pairing upon which apperception is based.

Mead's theory of play is supported empirically by the work of Fein (1991). However, Fein adds, in a manner which both confirms and refines Merleau-Ponty's note, that the play of children itself develops through stages which involve an increasing identification with the 'attitude of the other'. Simple forms of play afford and require less of an ability to take the attitude of the other, in other words, but they allow the child to develop the structures of behaviour, thought and experience that are necessary for it to engage in more complex forms and thus to progress to a more differentiated sense of self and other.

Play is only one stage in the development of the self process for Mead, however. It is limited in what it will enable. Through play we acquire the perspective of specific others but not the view of the community or 'the generalised other' that I mentioned earlier. For this attitude to develop the infant must be involved in games.

Mead is clear that games take many different shapes and forms and that they vary greatly in their degree of complexity and structure. What he is particularly concerned with, however, is team games. Such games require that each of the players view their own actions from the point of view of a number of their fellow players at once, and indeed from the point of view of the abstract and general purpose and rule structure of the game as a whole. This will require the reflexive capabilities that the child has acquired, through play, and it will, he believes, transform those capabilities to the point where the child can view itself from the view of the community as a whole and its institutional embodiment in the law and the constitutional structures of its society. This process involves a dialectic of particularism and universalism. The child learns to see itself as a particular member of a larger group and to judge itself, in its particularity, against the universal standards of this group. It at once learns to differentiate itself and to identify with its community and its traditions.

Two important implications should be drawn from this. In the first instance, it should be noted that, in contrast to Merleau-Ponty, Mead identifies the process of differentiation which forms a distinct sense of self (me) with a process of identification in which the child is introduced into the community as a member of it. The child distinguishes itself from the community but as a part of that community. It identifies the community as a distinct standpoint and assumes the values and standpoint of the community. The development of self-hood, in this sense, is equally an intitiation into citizenship (albeit local citizenship in the first instance). Indeed, Mead is quite clear that he believes that the rights and duties which (as an irreducible twin package) form the institutional structure of citizenship can and should only be made available to those who can and do 'take the attitude of the other'.

This identification of self and citizenship is, from our point of view, positive. It identifies a link between personal and political being which is vital to an intersubjective perspective. Moreover, it accounts for a sense of 'membership' and communal belonging in individual self or identity, which Merleau-Ponty's perspective is unable to account for – but which he clearly recognises. This is not to say, of course, that subjects always feel a part and always feel integrated. Neither does it deny that self is an alienation in Merleau-Ponty's strictly technical sense. But it is to stress that self is, in the first instance, the result of a social rather than a solitary (and narcissistic) identification.

The second point concerning Mead's understanding of the development of self is the role which it attributes to power:

> What goes on in the game goes on in the life of the child all the time. He is continually taking the attitudes of those around him, especially the roles of those whom in some sense control him and on whom he depends. (Mead 1967: 160)

This point allows us to see a conjunction between Mead's view and that of Dillon. The child effectively assumes the role and the attitude of those who impose themselves and their will (however benevolent) upon it. This suggests a modification to the citizenship view outlined above. It suggests a self process which is effected in and through relations of power; that is to say, it suggests that the child assumes the attitudes of those whose relations to it are relations of power. Furthermore, we can infer that the dialogue between the I and the me might take the form of an argument between the thoughts and intentions of the subject (I) and the view of the agents of power (me). The 'generalised other', in this sense, is less the voice of the community, more the voice of those who speak for it or are powerful within it.

It needs to be emphasised here that this political understanding of self remains dialogical and processual. Institutional authority qua the 'me' does not have the final word. There is a constant dialogue between the 'I' and the 'me' in which either can win out and, indeed, in which one may simply override the other. Warning by the 'generalised other' need not be heeded by the 'I'. It also should be emphasised, moreover, that 'me's' and sources of 'me' continue to develop throughout the course of an individual life. New power figures can constitute new 'me's' as and when they are encountered as power figures; for example, when individuals enter into new institutions and play the 'games' that constitute those institutions, with their rules, their roles and their goals.

Identity, Difference and Denigration

One's sense of self-consciousness as well as one's sense of self-worth is, for Mead, dependent upon recognition by those whom one deems worthy to recognise one (i.e. structures of mutual recognition), such that selves require and seek out this recognition. This bears close resemblance to the ideas of Kojève. Like Kojève's description of the master/slave relation, moreover, Mead's account falls short of identifying a liberal utopia. Much as selves strive for recognition, he maintains, and much as, as me's, they are instituted through the view of the community, they equally seek to differentiate themselves from the community and to individualise themselves. They tend, in many circumstances, to define and to seek to define themselves in relations of superiority to their others, both at an individual and at a more collective level. They struggle for distinction, to use the language of Pierre Bourdieu (1984).

This struggle for distinction, for Mead, is usually not harmful. It is this, he argues, which motivates fruitful competition, at least when properly channelled and regulated. The only danger which he identifies is at the level of collective identity and international society, where, he argues, some form of regulation is necessary to prevent nationalism, as an embodiment of the desire for distinction, from getting out of hand.

This is not intended to be a comprehensive view of nationalism. If Mead were discussing nationalism rather than self he would include a discussion of the economics and history of specific nationalist struggles etc. The limits of this view as a view of nationalism, then, are not particularly a problem for this book. What is problematic, however, is that Mead fails to follow through this notion of distinction to consider how certain distinctions have become institutionalised in modern Western societies and thus in modern structures of self. He fails to consider that we identify ourselves through social categories (e.g. man, young, middle-class, white), that these categories function through the differentiation of an other (man with woman, black with white), and that these differentiations often involve evaluations. Racism and gender relations are two very obvious examples of this. As a number of recent writers have begun to suggest, both women (Beauvoir 1988; Butler 1990; Young 1980) and black, Jewish and oriental subjects (Fanon 1986; Goldberg 1993; Said 1978; Sartre 1948), have all been positioned in the culture of the West as an inferior other to the ideal (white male) self; that is, they have been defined in accordance with characteristics that are defined as inferior or as lacking in relation to the ideal or normal. These differentiations are important because they affect both the way in which members of subordinated groups are treated and the way in which those groups themselves can construct an identity. This, in turn, has obvious effects upon both agency capacity and mental health (Fanon 1986).

The picture of the politics of self which this paints is rather more bleak than that of Mead. It suggests a me which is loaded with negative self-evaluation and a hostile 'generalised other'. Whilst the self is still communal, in this view, the community is not a welcoming place and intersubjectivity is experienced negatively. There are no end of autobiographies and studies which express such sentiments. The message from Mead's perspective, however, is that this negative me and the community from which it derives is only one pole in the dialectics of self and intersubjectivity. There is an I which engages in dialogue with this me and which can criticise it. Thus the denigrated self may be involved in struggle both with others and with itself, fighting the negative evaluations which others impose upon it and which it has internalised for itself. The dialogical conflict of these voices is only just beginning but it is already making its mark.

The Intersubjective Presentation of Self

What is suggested by this political reflection is that 'selves' belong to an intersubjective order which is equally a moral order. Selves can be deemed good or bad. They carry a moral value. This idea has been developed in depth, though in a less political vein, by Goffman (1959, 1968). For Goffman, the moral integrity of our 'self' is at stake in all of our interactions with others, and we must therefore work to preserve it. This is why, at one level, we go to great lengths to correct possible misunderstandings of our actions or to make sure that our actions appear rational even to those whom we do not know; for example, if we have to 'about turn' in the middle of a busy street because we have left something behind then we often visibly reprimand ourselves as a means of showing that there is purpose to our actions (that we are rational) and that we do not ordinarily walk in one direction only to turn back and walk in the other. A number of quite crucial points come out of Goffman's various discussions of this issue. Firstly, he stresses that our intersubjective situations are governed by rules of interaction and that a sustainable sense of 'self' is intimately bound to these rules. We must abide by or at least show that we are aware of such rules (e.g. by apologising for or qualifying our intransigences) if a 'respectable' sense of self is to be preserved. I will say more about such rules in my discussion of Schutz in the next chapter. The self connection is what is important for the present chapter. Secondly, in his discussion of *The Presentation of Self in Everyday Life* (1959) Goffman shows how we often stage-manage our interactions with others in order to sustain a particular sense and value of self and how we construct 'backstage areas' in which to drop the façade. This point suggests that we may often find private enclaves within the intersubjective fabric, where we can prepare ourselves for encounters with others. It suggests that we have private spaces of reflection and that there might be a discrepancy between our public and our private presentations of self. But it equally illustrates the extent to which such private reflections are oriented towards the public world and the extent to which our sense of our own self-hood is dependent upon the views of others or at least our view of their view. One is reminded here of the 'struggle for recognition': Goffman's subjects, as much as Hegel's, are driven to seek and maintain the respect of others. Why else would they be concerned with appearances? Finally, there is an emphasis in much of Goffman's work upon the ways in which self can be degraded and upon the struggles which certain groups can have to sustain their sense of self in an apparently hostile environment. The two strongest examples of this in Goffman's work concern the mortification processes of total institutions (Goffman 1961) and social stigma (Goffman 1968).

What these points illustrate is the extent to which the self process is routinely bound into our interactions with others. Through Mead we have learned that the self process is constituted through an internalisation of our relations with others, and now, through Goffman, we have learned the extent to which our external relations with others are still bound into this process. These points allow us a double-edged conclusion. Firstly, we can recognise that self-hood is inevitably intersubjective. Self is seen to be achieved only in relation to other. Secondly, we can identify a relationship to others which is less immediate than that discussed in Chapter 2, a relationship which is precisely mediated by way of our anticipations, our 'taking the attitude of the other' and staging. This double edge is the essence of the egological mode of intersubjectivity.

On Imagination

In discussing the egological mode of intersubjectivity and the notion of self and other which are constitutive of that mode, I have repeatedly relied upon a notion of human imagination. Relations to the other, in this mode, I have argued, are based upon an imaginary transposition of one's thoughts and feelings to the other. Furthermore, self, in this mode, whilst apprehended through a reflective turning back of the subject upon themselves, is equally invested by imagination and effected through imagination (e.g. putting oneself in the place of the other, assuming the attitude of the other). This raises an important question; namely, how does a notion of 'imagination' square with what we have said about intersubjective processes as we have described them hitherto? The force of this question comes from the fact that many characterisations of imagination contradict much of what we have said with regard to intersubjectivity hitherto. In Chapter 2, for example, we defined subjectivity (based in perception) as an opening out onto otherness, and we defined experiences and thoughts as shared or as emerging out of a shared context; but imagination, as commonly understood, seems to suggest private images and representations. We say, for example, that experiences or thoughts are 'just in his imagination' or that a person is 'in a world of their own', and this is more so in the case of dreams. Does this mean that imagination is the constituent of subjectivity which finally individualises us, breaking the intersubjectivity fabric? Does it mean that the difference between radical and egological intersubjective boils down to the reliance of the latter on imagination, and, by implication, that radical intersubjectivity is an unimaginative way of being?

The answer to these questions lies in the definition which we give to 'imagination' and the relations which we discern between it and perception/language. How could and should we characterise imagination?

Richard Kearney (1991) has detected a shift in the history of philosophical conceptions of imagination, away from vision and towards discourse, or, at least, to a greater concentration upon discourse. Contemporary theorists of imagination, such as Ricouer (1991), he argues, are more concerned with languaged narratives and stories, where their predecessors, such as Husserl (1991) and Sartre (1972), were concerned with visual images. From our perspective it is perhaps best to say that imagination might involve either or both together (which is closer to Kearney's own position). Imagination may involve visual images or discourse or both.

This doesn't get us much closer to a characterisation of imagination, however. What is it in visual or discursive images which constitutes them as imaginary phenomena? For a preliminary specification we can draw upon Sartre (1972), who defines imaginary experiences as those which involve that which we are conscious of as 'not being', in the sense: 'It was not real, I imagined it.' This does not imply that imaginings are explicitly recognised as imaginary at the time they are being experienced, but it suggests that they reveal themselves as such in the long run. One of the reasons for this, for Sartre, is that imaginary experiences do not have the depth of perceptual experiences: where the perceptual world can be infinitely explored, beyond one's current experience, imaginings end with one's current experiences. We might add to this, a point advocated by both Merleau-Ponty (1962) and Wittgenstein (Budd 1989), that imagination differs from perception in the sense that it encounters no resistance from the world and is entirely at the mercy of one's will (even if one is not always in control of one's will). This is intended to apply mainly to perception. Both writers want to suggest that perceptions encounter something which is beyond them (as corporeal beings) and which affects or resists them (see Chapter 2), whereas imaginings don't and can change form rapidly. The same might be said of discourse, however, if we consider it on the 'language game' model outlined in Chapter 2. In the sort of language game that we might call telling an imaginative story, for example, it is acceptable to say that pigs can fly (and those who object to this have missed the point), whereas in the type of language game which we call 'giving a factual account', the story given, whilst it might draw upon many of the same stylistic devices as the previous account, must necessarily be bound to that which could be verified.

It is this unresisted aspect of imagination and its tie to 'non-being' which seems to defy the notion of intersubjectivity, because it apparently takes away all common reference points which might serve as supports for intersubjectivity. Already, however, we have hinted that this is not so, at least in the case of (primarily) discursive imaginings. If imagination is constituted through stories and suchlike, and if stories are both constructed out of language and structured as specific language games (which they are), then there is no reason why imagination is not an intersubjective phenomenon because stories are usually shared. Indeed a good story-teller (with a good story) precisely grips an audience and weaves a common world with them.

Alfred Schutz's (1973) paper 'On Multiple Realities' gives us a clear idea of the manner in which such imaginative enclaves are firmly embedded within the social/intersubjective fabric. Imaginative activities are often collective activities, he argues, and they consequently rely upon a common recognition of imaginative content. We watch plays together, for example, sharing an involvement in their imaginary worlds as surely as we share in the 'real world'. Moreover, we share in the world of films or soap operas. And in all of these cases we share in rulings about what is appropriate to each 'province of meaning' and where each province itself may begin and end.

It could be objected here that I still have not dealt with the visual aspect of the imagination. I have and I haven't! I have, in the sense that I have pointed out that both films and soap operas can be part of our imaginary worlds and thus that visual images (qua aspects of the imaginary) need not be 'inside the head' or private in any way. Sartre (1972) bears this out with considerable argumentative force. Imagination is equivalent not to a particular visual material, he argues, but rather to the attitude we take towards such material (i.e. the way in which we use it and respond to it). It is not a separate world from our shared world but a way of acting in that world, and as such it can be either an individual or a joint and intersubjective venture. In this sense a painting or a sketch or a mime or any number of commonly available materials may function in our imagination. Children's games, where a finger may become a gun or a building brick a car, etc., all illustrate this in its intersubjective dimensions. They all depend upon an intersubjective, imaginative collusion, which takes place in shared spaces with shared materials.

This does not mean that imagination cannot be used as an escape from the intersubjective world. People can use imagination to transport them out of their intersubjective context, whether that be the immediate context (from the workplace to the home) or the wider context (to an imaginary world). Our analysis hitherto would suggest that such retreats need not be private, however. Certainly they are not private in principle. Are they not perhaps a privatised and internalised version of the shared fantasies that emerge more openly and outwardly in children's play?

A critic of this position may persist, however, by arguing that, whilst most imaginings do open into intersubjective spaces, they can nevertheless be attached to private ('internal') images; the dream would be the most obvious example of this. On this point I would concede that there is an apparently private mental domain. I do not think that this domain could truly be described as 'in the head', however, at least not phenomenologically, since we can experience our dreams kinaesthetically (e.g. the feeling that we are falling) and we sometimes respond to them as whole bodies (e.g. calling out, reaching out, sitting up). Rather than 'in our head', our private images seem to be projected around us, as they are in our shared imaginings. Indeed the only difference between them and our shared (waking) imaginings is an apparent absence of 'real' perceptual materials to work upon (cf. Sartre 1972 for an elaboration of this idea). Moreover, when we are in the world of dreams we are still not disconnected from the world of intersubjective, perceptual experience. This is attested to by the fact that we can be woken out of that state by events and persons in the 'waking world'. We are still enough in the intersubjective world to be affected by it, and, indeed, to affect it (if, for example, we shout in our sleep). The oneiric world is not so much a break or discontinuity with our waking, intersubjective world, then, as a space at its margins.

Radical and Egological Intersubjectivity

In this chapter I have considered the more egological aspect of intersubjectivity; that is, the aspect which entails our sense of self and our reflective and reflexive capacities. The key argument here has been that features of our experience are only made possible through our relations with others and that, at most, they are an individuated function of our relations with others. Furthermore, contrary to views which suggest that human beings are (primordially) imaginative monads who must be literally opened out to others, I have emphasised both that infants are innately attuned to others and that imagination, in large part, can be shared in.

It is my contention that human subjectivity and intersubjectivity, as Buber argues, swing between this egological mode of intersubjectivity and the more radical mode outlined in Chapter 2. Sometimes we are deeply engrossed with others, too engaged to be aware of either ourselves or of them. At other times, and rapidly, we can become sharply aware of both, constituing them as reflective and reflexive aspects of experience. All spontaneous interactions can be stultified by a reflective block, only to be undermined later by a genuine and spontaneous communication which collapses the reflective barriers of self and other. I's push their me's to the side and become joined.

It should be added here that the egological attitude always necessarily entails the radical attitude as an underlying foundation. Whenever we are reflectively aware of the other we are still, always, necessarily responsive to their moves at an unreflective level. We are always affected by what they do and say, by their movements and gestures. Egological intersubjectivity is only a relative reflective distancing. It is never absolute.

In my discussion of both of these aspects of intersubjectivity I have briefly mentioned the notion of the social structuring of intersubjective relations. In particular I argued that, for Mead, the ability of subjects to 'take the attitude of the other' is a necessary prerequisite of social life and social membership. And I showed how, for Goffman, our sense of self is always tied into the rule-bound contexts of social interaction. The task in the next chapter will be to say something more substantial about this social structuring and to consider how it squares with the account that I have outlined hitherto.

4

Concrete Intersubjectivity and the Lifeworld: On Alfred Schutz

In this chapter I expand my focus to consider, firstly, the practical construction of intersubjective relations in the concrete contexts of everyday life and, secondly, the intersubjective bases of the socio-cultural world ('the lifeworld' hereafter). As the sub-title of the chapter makes clear, the thinker mainly considered in this context is Alfred Schutz. The chapter begins, however, with a discussion and critique of Mead and Merleau-Ponty's respective analyses of the social world. Schutz, I will argue, is useful and important to the extent that his approach allows us to overcome certain problems in their respective approaches.

Beyond Mead and Merleau-Ponty

In his sociological and political writings, Merleau-Ponty (1964a, 1969, 1973) projects his understanding of intersubjectivity onto the social macrocosm, understood both as an interlocking structure of social institutions and as a historical process; that is, as a social system (Crossley 1994). This projection has three effects. In the first instance, it modifies his understanding of intersubjectivity. Intersubjectivity is now understood in its modes of concretisation; that is, in terms of the specific roles and relations that it involves (e.g. capitalist–worker, father–daughter), the ritual and institutional mediation of those relations (e.g. through law) and the place of material objects and resources in those relations and that mediation (e.g. objects are variously defined, valued, possessed, exchanged). Moreover, it thereby integrates into an account of the symbolic reproduction of social life an account of its material constitution and reproduction. Merleau-Ponty's theory of intersubjectivity consistently maintains that symbols and their meanings are inseparable from the material forms (e.g. spoken words, rituals, books) which embody them, but it is only in his theory of the social system that he considers the circulation and reproduction of those material forms (principally the reproduction of the human body and the raw materials required to service it). Secondly, following on from this, Merleau-Ponty turns his attention from hypothetical examples of inter-action towards actual concrete societies (specifically post-war France). His sociology is an attempt to understand his own world, in its particularity. Thirdly, the projection serves to establish a philosophy of the social which transcends the dualism of subjectivism and objectivism, which has been identified and much criticised, as the key faultline of traditional approaches to social theory (Bourdieu 1977, 1992; Crossley 1994; Giddens 1984). This transcendence works at both an ontological and an epistemological level. I will discuss the ontological dimension first.

For both objectivists and subjectivists society is an object. The latter maintain that it is an object in the consciousness, thought or discourse of the human subject. The former, by contrast, maintain that humans too are objects and are placed in it as objects in a box, where it can variously determine their actions from without. Neither of these approaches is sufficient. In subjectivism, society qua object is reduced to the thought of the individual and it thus loses the trans-individual character that is precisely definitive of social phenomena. Objectivism, by contrast, posits a supra-individual conception of the social, but this is equally as problematic and is, in any case, a product of faulty reasoning. Objectivists abstract a structure out of the messiness of empirically available praxes (e.g. language from speech or the economy from processes of exchange), which they then, committing a category error, assume to be both distinct from those praxes and determinate of them (Merleau-Ponty 1964b). Objectivists, in other words, both reify their abstract model of social reality and assume it to be determinate of that reality. Moreover, objectivists presuppose themselves to be exceptions to the rules which they claim to discover in the social world – thereby casting doubt on the very existence of those rules. They fail to consider both that they too belong to that world and that it is made an object of study only by means of their situated intellectual praxis. This is a considerable error (Sandywell et al. 1975).

The key to both of these sets of problems, according to Merleau-Ponty, is the incorrect assumption that society is an object. Society is not an object, he maintains. It is a between world or interworld, in the sense discussed in Chapter 2, an interval. It is neither 'inside' subjects nor 'outside' them. It is the fabric which connects them and to which they belong. Society is the culmination of intersubjective praxes, of action and interaction, and of the instituted and shared praxial and material resources which are mobilised in this process. It is the shared rules and resources which are activated in the production of meaning and the modes of 'being-with' which institute encounters and sustain relations. It is not thought about, at least in the first instance, but participated in. Moreover, thoughts and reflections cannot stand outside of it. They take place within it, assuming its embodied forms (e.g. language) and contributing to its continuation and change. Society, at its most fundamental level, is based in interaction, according to this view, and, accordingly, in agreement in 'forms of life' (see Chapter 2). It is a process which unfolds, through time, in the intersubjective spaces between human beings.

The second aspect of the objectivism/subjectivism debate concerns the epistemological question of how one can know society. For objectivists, the inclination is towards 'scientific' methods. The problems with this approach are well documented. At the very least, as Merleau-Ponty, Schutz and the Wittgensteinian philosopher Peter Winch (1958) maintain, these methods ignore the fact that the social world is meaningful to those who live in it, and they (the methods) impose their own, seemingly arbitrary meanings onto it. Winch provides a good example of this when he notes that soldiers involved in a war, unlike molecules involved in a thunderstorm, have a conception of the process in which they are involved and use that conception in the organisation of their activities. This makes wars very different from thunderstorms, he argues, and it demands that we study them differently. It is important, moreover, that it is the meanings and understandings of the group being studied which are considered and not those of the group who are studying them. This has been a matter of great concern in hermeneutic philosophy and the human science projects informed by it(Gadamer 1989; Merleau-Ponty 1973, 1964b).

The subjectivist, in contrast to the objectivist, is concerned with social agents' own representations of their circumstances, but in a problematic way. Subjectivism focuses exclusively upon the contents of representations and understanding, taking these as an index of the reality of the subject's world. It thereby fails either to situate representation or to consider its role in a more general structure of action. Representations do not stand outside of the social, as a picture of it. They are within the social. They are one of a number of active, practical forces which combine in the constitution of the social. Moreover, subjects do not only 'represent' the social to themselves. They act in it and participate in it.

The intersubjectivist position precisely grasps this. It is concerned with the participative and communicative actions of the subject. It examines the way in which the social world, as a phenomenon that is meaningful to its own members, is produced through their interactions – though it is forced to objectify that intersubjective matrix in order to do this. Interaction, moreover, is understood as an irreducible structure.

A final point about subjectivism, objectivism and intersubjectivism concerns the relation of the investigator to the investigated. Neither subjectivists nor objectivists recognise an affinity between themselves and those whom they study. Objectivists constitute themselves as subjects before objects. Subjectivists, by contrast, subordinate their own position to that of their other. They want to capture the other's view of the world. The intersubjectivist position, as represented by Merleau-Ponty (1964b, 1973), takes a different stance. In the first instance, he notes that he must use his own social belongingness to understand the world of his other. He cannot assume a 'view from nowhere' and must attempt to understand his other through a merging of their perspectives (see also Gadamer 1989). As a creature of meaning, he must penetrate their meaning structure. Secondly, although he understands the social world as an intersubjective site of meaning and action, he recognises that he must objectify it, to some extent, if he is to study it. It must become an object of his reflection. Moreover, he recognises that others lose their individuality and subjectivity in this process.

They are absorbed in generalities and impersonal processes. Finally, however, upon completion of his analysis, Merleau-Ponty returns to take a stance next to his others. He presents them with his interpretation, which he hopes they will respond to and perhaps act upon, and which, he maintains, they must be persuaded to agree with if he is to be taken to be right. At this point he ceases to represent and interpret his other and begins to engage in dialogue with them, challenging and criticising them and inviting their retort (see also Habermas 1988b, 1989, 1991a).

I have discussed the value of this position elsewhere and I have identified the problems of the specific descriptions of the social formation which Merleau-Ponty, drawing upon Marx, Weber and Lévi-Strauss, amongst others, aligns with it (Crossley 1994). Merleau-Pontyian intersubjectivism is the correct philosophical position for social theory to begin from, I argued, but Merleau-Ponty does not provide adequate conceptual tools to develop it into an effective schema of social theory, research and critique.

In addition to these criticisms I now add that Merleau-Ponty's projection of 'intersubjectivity' onto the social macrocosm was too hasty and insufficiently accounted for. He moves straight from an abstract discussion of face-to-face encounters to a concrete account of historical social systems without any consideration of the field of social interaction and the world of culture which binds these extremes; that is, without any consideration of the shared social lifeworld and its significance. In neglecting this domain, at least at the concrete level, Merleau-Ponty fails to consider the diversity in forms and intensities which different social relations involve (e.g. between a friend, a stranger and a lover), and he fails to consider the microcosmic technicalities and conditions for the reproduction and transformation of the social world, with the exigent for further complexity which that places on our understanding of intersubjectivity. He assumes that social life and interaction are unproblematically achieved, failing to address the problems and resolutions which they may entail. Indeed, one might argue that he overlooks the whole problem of social integration.

This criticism applies equally to Mead. Mead's view of intersubjectivity is, as I have shown, largely complementary to that of Merleau-Ponty (cf. also Rosenthal and Bourgeois 1991). He has a very similar view of things and his work can be used to modify and strengthen the intersubjectivist case that Merleau-Ponty presents. Moreover, his account of the assumption of the attitude of 'the generalised other' does provide some indication of how social integration is achieved (see Chapter 3). This account is not completely sufficient, however, as it is too abstract. It fails to address the concrete particularities which must be negotiated in social interaction. Like Merleau-Ponty, Mead is insufficiently aware of the effect of different interaction contexts upon interaction. Moreover, Mead's view of significant symbols glosses over the rather more messy process by which sense is intersubjectively achieved. He tends to assume that utterances will always mean the same thing to both speaker and listener, when clearly this is not so. It is these problems which are resolved in the work of Schutz.

Schutz and Husserl

Schutz was a student of Husserl (see Chapter 1) and the influence of Husserl's work upon his is considerable. In particular he maintains a commitment to phenomenological analysis and he maintains that such analysis depends upon a reduction to the sphere of the transcendental, constituting ego. Importantly, however, this position breaks down for Schutz in relation to the question of intersubjectivity. In the context of his earliest major work, *The Phenomenology of the Social World* (1972), this breakdown is pragmatically determined. Husserl's major attempt at accounting for intersubjectivity, *Cartesian Meditations* (1991), Schutz explains, was published too late for him to be able to consider it. Thus his account of intersubjectivity and of social relations, in that book, is conducted from outside of the phenomenological reduction, with the caveat that the question of the transcendental constitution of the other still remains to be answered and that in all probability it is answered in *Cartesian Meditations*. In his later work, however, Schutz (1970) wrote a powerful critique of *Cartesian Meditations*, arguing that the latter did not provide a transcendental theory of intersubjectivity and suggesting that such a theory may indeed be impossible. This conclusion is rejoined in essays on other phenomenologies of intersubjectivity (Schutz 1973: 150–203). Phenomenology has produced interesting accounts of 'mundane intersubjectivity', Schutz argues; that is, of relations and interactions between concrete psycho-physical egos. But it has never reconciled intersubjectivity with an account of the transcendental ego.

The implication of Schutz's reflections is that a philosophy which wishes to maintain a coherent notion of intersubjectivity must give up its commitment to a transcendental ego. And this he does. All of his discussions and analyses of intersubjective relations effectively bracket out transcendental considerations. They focus instead upon the mundane actor and their lifeworld; that is to say, in his examination of intersubjectivity, Schutz conceptualises the human subject as an embodied being whose actions draw upon a stock of shared social resources and know-how or 'common-sense knowledge' and who is always already situated amongst other similarly embodied and situated beings. This 'stock of common-sense knowledge', Schutz maintains, is in part derived from accidental experience, but it is also stored and transmitted institutionally within the lifeworld, by (amongst others) the family unit and the education system.

This position is clearly similar to and commensurate with the other positions hitherto introduced in the book and I intend to treat it as such in my discussion of it. There is room in Schutz's work for a more mentalistic and transcendentalist reading, but this is not the reading that I will adopt. I will be using Schutz to develop the more basic understanding of human subjectivity and behaviour that I have discussed hitherto.

Action, Interaction and Relationship

Schutz's theory involves many ideal conceptual distinctions. I will begin by introducing some of these and discussing their general significance for our understanding of intersubjectivity.

The first distinction to consider is that between action and behaviour. The former, Schutz maintains, involves prior projection or planning, whilst the latter is spontaneous. Furthermore, both are distinguished from an 'act', in that they signify ongoing, unfolding processes which the actor is not necessarily aware of at the time of performing them, whilst 'acts' are reflective objectifications of actions, viewed by the actor, from the point of view of completion, at some time before, after or (at a pause) during their performance. This compares to Mead's notion of the 'I' and the 'me'; actions and behaviour unfold with the 'I' and are then represented, as 'me', in the form of 'acts'. Actors do not and cannot reflect upon and represent their actions to themselves in the process of actually acting, Schutz maintains, because reflections and representations are actions in their own right and one can only do one thing at one time. Furthermore, the attention of the actor must be occupied with the exigencies thrown up by the action and not by the action itself. Reflection and representation on action can only either interrupt an action or punctuate its beginning or end.

The meaning of action is determined, for Schutz, by the project of the actor; that is, by their conscious plans and the acts and 'in order to motives' which figure in those plans. In order to motives consist in the (prior) discursive stipulation by the actor of what they aim to achieve and what they must do *in order to* achieve it. They are future-oriented, discursively formulated motives and, as such, contrast with what Schutz refers to as 'because motives'. Because motives are ascribed and formulated only after the event. Actors are not discursively aware of them prior to their identified effect. They involve the reactive components of an action (e.g. 'I screeched *because* you kicked me) and those aspects which are reducible to past experience and conditioning (e.g. tradition and habit). In contrast to in order to motives, they do not feature in the plans of the actor.

Already we can begin to see the emergence of concepts which are important to the question of intersubjectivity. The meaning of certain actions is identified with the plan of the actor, which may well be unavailable to the other. Or rather, the act may have different meanings for the actor and their other, respectively, because only the actor has access to the plan behind their own action. A simple example of this, taken from Schutz, is that what appears to an observer to be 'cutting firewood' may, to the actor, be 'earning a living as a lumberjack' or 'letting off steam after an argument'. Both parties may have quite a different conception of the behaviour of the actor because they frame it in a different way. They do not share in a meaning. Their interworld is structured through cross-purposes. Such misunderstandings may be identified and resolved through dialogue, of course. Nevertheless, as we will see, dialogue too rests upon a background which may not be shared.

Having defined behaviour and action, Schutz next defines social action and social behaviour. The adverb 'social' is added when either action or behaviour is 'other-oriented'; that is, when it consciously intends (in the phenomenological sense discussed in Chapter 1) the other as a conscious, intelligent being. Social action and social behaviour are differentiated, as are action and behaviour, in terms of the former's being accounted for in a plan or project.

Next Schutz differentiates other-orientation from affecting-the-other. It is possible, he maintains, to orient to the other without affecting them. If I pull in at a traffic lights in the car, for example, I orient to other drivers as conscious beings, guessing their next move, but I do not wish to affect them in any way. Notwithstanding this, however, oriented action may be motivated to affect the other, and Schutz devises the category 'affecting-the-other' to account for this. This entails acting upon either the action or the person of the other so as to elicit responses from them and thus to affect their future actions in some way. One's in order to motives intend certain because motives for the other and there is, thereby, an intertwining of motives. For Schutz, moreover, affecting-the-other can only be achieved through social action, since it must embody the intention to affect the other.

The primary example of affecting-the-other for Schutz, as for Merleau-Ponty and Mead, is conversation. In conversation, he maintains, we take up the communicative resources of our culture, resources which are shared throughout our culture, and we address ourselves to our other, with the expectation that they will reciprocate. Speech always addresses someone and always expects a response, for Schutz. We might add here, drawing upon Austin's (1971) theory of speech acts, that the type of response expected will depend upon the action performed; for example, a question expects an answer, an order expects compliance, etc.

Breaking his category down further, Schutz refers to those modes of affecting-the-other which aim to elicit a response from the other which is oriented back to the self (i.e. asking a question usually demands an answer directed back upon oneself), which is a properly communicative action, and to those other-oriented actions which are reciprocated. When an other-orientation is reciprocated, that is, when both parties are oriented towards each other, Schutz refers to this as a 'social relationship'. When the actions of each elicit other-oriented reactions, he refers to 'social interaction'. He consistently maintains, however, that affecting-the-other, even when intended to elicit an other-oriented response from the other, need not be reciprocated.

Having outlined the first tier of Schutz's conceptual frame, a few comments and criticisms are necessary. In the first instance it is important to recognise the extent to which these concepts shed further light upon intersubjectivity. Schutz draws our attention to the manner in which actions are oriented towards others, who are recognised as others, and he draws important distinctions within that category of actions; for example, those which are reciprocated, those which aim to affect and those which aim to elicit a reciprocal orientation. This allows us to develop a much more complex and differentiated mapping of the structuring of intersubjectivity than is provided for by Mead or Merleau-Ponty. It breaks down, analytically, the other-orientation that their theories recognise and thus allows for a more sensitive description of such orientation(s).

Some of Schutz's distinctions are problematic, however. My main objection is directed at his claim that affecting-the-other (and its derivatives) is necessarily a social action and is, therefore, necessarily dependent upon prior projection or planning. This is wrong. Consider, for example, the act of asking a question. Clearly this involves the presupposition and the expectation of an answer and it thus intends to affect the other in such a way that they become oriented to one, such that social interaction and a social relationship are intitiated. But it need not involve prior planning or forethought. We do ask questions without planning to or thinking about it. In such cases the 'intention', 'expectation' and 'presupposition' are embodied in the language game of questioning and not in any individual plan. They are instituted, intersubjective expectations rather than individual ones. The actor 'knows' them in the sense that they passed into the structure of their conduct when they learned the language game of questioning, and they may refer to them (tacitly) if their question is not responded to appropriately ('I asked you a question!'), but no planning is required.

The conclusion of this could be that social behaviour as well as social action can affect-the-other, intitiate social interactions and social relationships, etc. I suggest that we take the criticism a step further, however, and eliminate any hard and fast distinction between action and behaviour. In principle this distinction, based as it is on the presence of a plan or project, seems fine. Experience teaches that some of the things we do in life are planned and some aren't. The distinction is difficult to sustain, however, for two reasons. Firstly, plans relate to acts (in Schutz's sense) rather than actions. They deal with ends rather than means and means can't be completely planned for. They are spontaneously produced as a response to conditions of execution and exigencies which cannot be forseen. Plans lay out landmarks but they leave the navigation between those landmarks to spontaneous innovation (Suchman 1987). Whatever action one plans, it is always composed of behaviours which are not planned. When I plan to drive, for example, I do not plan to get into the car, change the gears, etc., and if I do plan to change the gear, I do not plan to move my hands towards the stick, put my foot on the clutch, etc. Furthermore, whilst I do it and whilst it is necessary to the successful completion of my journey, I do not plan to slam on my brakes because the driver in front of me has done so. The point here is that plans do not provide us with criteria by which to distinguish between action and behaviour, because they do not stipulate how an act is to be realised, what will and will not count as integral to its realisation, and, given that they are the sole criteria which Schutz stipulates for this differentiation, we cannot therefore distinguish them. Thus the distinction collapses.

This problem is, to an extent, hinted at by Schutz himself, and he adds the important point that much of the ad hoc management of our actions amounts to intersubjective adjustment; that is, we have to rely upon spontaneity because we can't predict the actions of others in any given situation. He fails to contemplate its implications for the distinction between action and behaviour, however.

The second problem is an intensification of the first, which is also anticipated by Schutz:

> The meaning attributed to an experience varies according to one's whole attitude at the moment of reflection. When an action is completed, its original meaning as given in the project will be modified in light of what has actually been carried out, and it is then open to an indefinite number of reflections which can ascribe meaning to it in the past tense. (1964: 11)

If we may take by this, amongst other things, that plans change midway in their execution or are even generated out of actions as a consequence of the direction manifest in those actions (as Merleau-Ponty and Mead both maintain), and that the 'plannedness' of a behaviour, which grants it its status as an action, can be bestowed retrospectively, then the difference between action and behaviour is finally lost. What is behaviour now may be action later and vice versa. Moreover, if the subject gives two different accounts of the same action, then even this temporal distinction is eroded. What is an action under one description is, at the same time, behaviour under another. This clearly erodes the (mutually exclusive) boundary that Schutz erects.

It is important to add here that, as Schutz himself recognised, plans are not necessarily the properties of individuals. They can be formed between individuals, as an irreducible property of a couple, at least in the types of radically intersubjective conversation discussed in relation to Merleau-Ponty and Gadamer in Chapter 2. In these situations it is not I who decide what to do, nor you. It is we who decide. This possibility amplifies the problems with the behaviour/action distinction because it constitutes a complex interactive situation, which cannot have been planned as such by either side, but within which a plan is formulated.

This critique does not imply that we should ignore human plans or accounting strategies. Quite the contrary. They are very important. What I would suggest, however, is that we reject the distinction between actions and behaviours (for the reasons just stated) and draw a distinction between two forms of behaviour: that which plans or accounts for action and that which either executes plans and is accounted for or which simply copes and gets on with it. Our task should be to examine the numerous forms which the relationship between these behaviours can take: how plans are generated out of actions and vice versa. In this respect, moreover, we should note that Schutz refers to hierarchies of interlocking plans and subplans. The organisation of such plans would be an important focus for a study of planning behaviour.

Social Regions: The Face-to-Face

The next move in Schutz's conceptual schema involves a further subdivision of social relations, according to spatio-temporal factors. He draws up four types of possible relationship, or, rather, four types of possible other, all of which are said to be on a continuum with the first (which is primordial).

The first is the face-to-face relation in which we have immediate access to the other. Schutz refers to others as 'consociates' in this context. Second is the world of 'contemporaries' (including those we know personally and those we don't). These are others who exist at the same time as us but are spatially distant from us – even if we are thinking of them. The third and fourth possibilities involve temporal distancing in the past and the future, respectively; there are 'predecessors' who lived before we were born (i.e. before me personally or you personally), and 'successors' who will live after we have died. Our relations with each of these types of others, whilst they may share some similarities, are quite different for Schutz. Intersubjectivity is a differentiated phenomenon.

This is an important point because it problematises the simple trans-position of the notion of intersubjectivity from the face-to-face to the macrocosm which I identified in the work of Merleau-Ponty at the beginning of the chapter. Later in this chapter I will discuss Schutz's own, more sophisticated version of this transposition. Firstly, however, we must consider the sophistication which his analysis lends to our understanding of the face-to-face.

Schutz recognises in the face-to-face the possibility for what we have referred to as radical intersubjectivity; that is, a situation in which space and time (including lived time) are shared, where each person speaks for themselves and where the intentions, thoughts and feelings of the one unfold before the other, calling forth responses from that other. It is a situation, he maintains, where people can be in their unique individuality for each other, where they see and are seen in the flesh and can correct misconceptions which may arise about themselves. Indeed, in such situations, he maintains, the other is clearer to me than I am to myself, since they stand before me in an unmediated fashion. Moreover, this is the only situation in which the other exists (for me) in this way.

This is similar to the situation described in Chapter 2. Schutz adds to our understanding, however, by considering an issue that was only hinted at in that chapter; namely, the manner in which mutual understanding and agreement is achieved. A consideration of his account of this issue will force us to revise certain aspects of our notion of radical intersubjectivity. In particular we will see that mutual understanding is not guaranteed by virtue of significant symbols, but must be achieved through the work of interlo-cutors. This is a fact attested to in many studies of conversation (Heritage 1984). They show how meaning is actively sustained, lost and regained in conversations, by means of the 'artful practices' (Garfinkel 1967) of their participants.

In the face-to-face, Schutz observes, meanings unfold in a common spatio-temporal horizon. The full meaning of an action, which may be a speech act but not necessarily, is not achieved until its final moment. But the person to whom it is directed is present from its start. The positive side of this situation is that, assuming the fusing of temporal horizons discussed in Chapter 2, the listener grasps the meaning in its immediacy. They are present at its birth and may respond to it directly. The negative side, however, is that misunderstanding is possible if the final moment of the communication is misperceived (which is possible since the only sure clue to the temporal punctuation of the action or utterance is its meaning but one precisely needs to know the former in order to grasp the latter). Schutz offers no account of how this problem is resolved. The work of conversation analysts has provided some insight, however. They have shown how, in different situations, we 'do' the opening and closing of a conversation or utterance by, for example, a gesture (Heritage 1984), so that it is apparent to others where our utterance begins and ends and how it is punctuated.

The articulation of lived time horizons is not the only determinant of meaning in the face-to-face, however. I noted in Chapter 2, with reference to Wittgenstein, that linguistic meaning depends upon certain uses of language which are rooted in common forms of life but which are not explicated, as such, in the words spoken. A listener picks up the way in which a word is being used from what they understand of its context. As Schutz notes, however, that context is never crystal clear to the listener and their understanding of it is itself based in unexplicated forms of life. Indeed the context may involve the imaginary life of the speaker, some aspect of their culture (which may be different to that of the listener) or their personal biography, none of which is necessarily available to the listener. Schutz elaborates this point by considering the problems of linguistic understanding encountered by strangers in a community. Such strangers, he observes, may have a perfect technical understanding of the language of the community in which they have arrived and yet still fail to understand. Not only are accents and local dialects sometimes hard to grasp, but communities (ranging from families and peer groups to societies) have particular ways of saying things, including jargon and technical terms, which take form around and acquire significance from group activities and particularly literature, traditions and belief systems. To fully understand the language one would have to have lived the life that it emerges out of. This is even more so the case, Schutz maintains, in relation to the 'halo of emotional values and irrational implications' that manifest in all languages. These are literally untranslatable aspects of a form of life, known only by those who live it. Who, for example, could explain the feeling which 'Britain' has for the patriot or which 'Holocaust' has for the Jew?

In addition to these general cultural factors, understanding and mutual understanding are structured, according to Schutz, by 'structures of relevance'. Any situation or context can be construed in any number of ways, he maintains, and construal depends upon what is relevant to the actor, which is, in turn, shaped by their motivations or what they are doing ('motivational relevancy'), by the problems or issues that arise in the course of them doing so ('thematic relevancy') and by their selection of common-sense resources to help them overcome such problems ('interpretive relevancy'). The horizons of actors could be fused at each of these levels but each level constitutes a possibility for a different construal of situations by interlocutors and thus for misunderstanding or non-understanding between them.

The work of conversation analysts is useful in showing how these possibilities for misunderstanding are accounted for and managed in communicative praxes (Heritage 1984). Without thinking, these studies illustrate, the communicative agent actively prevents or corrects misunderstanding. Their talk is organised to compensate for the potential gulf of culture and relevancy between their self and their other – though this compensation isn't always successful.

It should be added here that the overlap of relevancies is not always a harmonious process. We do not completely determine our own sets of relevancies, according to Schutz. Some, given our own framework, are imposed upon us and, amongst these, are the relevancies of others:

> Insofar as Peter is the object of Paul's action and has to take into account Paul's specific goals which he, Peter, does not share, Paul's intrinisic relevances are to Peter imposed relevances and vice versa. (Schutz 1964: 128)

In such cases there may well be a battle to determine whose interests and whose relevancies win out.

The process of interrogating a meaning, Schutz observes, is potentially infinite. Any meaning could be checked and any contextual condition explicated, but the process of complete clarification is impossible because every utterance of clarification or explication would stand in need of its own clarification ad infinitum. Meaning always rests upon unexplicated conditions or presuppositions. There is, however, a 'pragmatic determination of meaning' which short-circuits regress such that, as Wittgenstein (1953) observes, we 'just do it'; that is, words elicit the responses that their speakers require and no problem is experienced. This pragmatic determination is possible because of the sharing of forms of life and traditions, with their shared presuppositions and the mutual participation of interlocutors in common projects and the structures of relevancy that issue from them.

The level of pragmatic determination has been identified by the breaching experiments of Garfinkel (1967), where experimenters broke the rules of the pragmatic determination of meaning by constantly asking for clarification of points. This situation created considerable problems and anxiety for participants. Situations did not break down, however, and Garfinkel used the experiments to demonstrate the multitude of techniques available to the agent for restoring and maintaining pragmatic sense in a situation, against the odds. We have, he showed, clear ways of foreclosing the potential infinity of interpretation and ambiguity.

In order that the collective sense-making process is successful, Schutz maintains, communicating agents must be aware of the discrepancies in perspective or background knowledge between themselves and their interlocutors, and they must act to fill in the gaps created by those discrepancies. An obvious example would be explaining who named persons are when referring to them; for example, 'Diane's husband, Mark, says'. In order to work in this way, however, Schutz (1973) maintains, two presuppositions must be made concerning the 'reciprocity of perspectives' between participants. He refers to these as 'the idealisation of the interchangeability of standpoints' and 'the idealisation of the congruency of the system of relevances'.

The 'idealisation of the interchangeability of standpoints' implies that each agent recognises (and assumes that their other recognises) that their 'here' is the other's 'there' and vice versa, and assumes (and assumes that their other assumes) that if they changed places then they would see the same things in the same way, be at the same distance from things as the other is currently, etc. In other words, it involves the presupposition, on behalf of agents, that it is only their different positions in the world that might lead them to experience it differently. Moreover, it entails that the world is experienced as one experienced by others. This presupposition is evident in interaction when we instruct our other to turn to look at something. In this case we experience the thing as potentially experienceable by them. The idealisation of the interchangeability of standpoints is important, according to Schutz, given that most of the 'knowledge' that we use in our action is not derived from direct experience and innovation but is acquired from others on trust. We must presuppose the interchangeability of standpoints if this important pedagogic infrastructure is to be maintained.

The 'idealisation of the congruency of the system of relevances' adds to this that agents assume (and assume that their other assumes) that perspectival differences arising out of their different social situation and biography are irrelevant to the purpose at hand between them and have not affected the manner in which they have understood the situation that they are in. They assume, in other words, that their systems of relevance do overlap and that 'for all practical purposes' they understand a situation in the same way. This includes, moreover, a presupposition that words and phrases have the same significance for the other as for self. Both this and the 'idealisation of the interchangeability of standpoints' are revisable presuppositions for Schutz, but they are our initial presuppositions in situations. We assume a stable, given world which is intersubjectively available.

The 'presuppositions' which Schutz refers to in this context need not and should not be understood in terms of individual psychology. There is no mental process of presupposing that occurs in our heads each and every time we interact. Rather, they are 'taken for granted' in our forms of behaviour. Indeed, they are precisely what we don't think about. Nevertheless, as research by Pollner (1974, 1975) and Coulter (1975) reveals, they are important to our collective construction of an intersubjectively meaningful social world, and not only for the pedagogic reasons already stated.

It is not uncommon, these researchers argue, particularly in legal and psychiatric contexts, for discrepant and conflicting accounts of states of affairs to be offered by different interlocutors, or for a single individual to experience something which prior knowledge and 'common sense' inform them could not be right. Either there is a disagreement over the manner in which a given state of affairs is to be interpreted and accounted for (what Coulter calls an 'interpretive asymmetry') or there is a disagreement over such states of affairs themselves (what both Coulter and Pollner call a 'reality disjuncture'). In such instances, both observe, interlocutors respond to the discrepancy as a puzzle to be resolved. This, for Pollner, is the first key effect of the (Schutzian) presuppositions. It is only in light of these presuppositions that discrepant accounts are experienced as requiring resolution. Moreover, he observes, the presupposition is preserved and protected in the resolution of the puzzle. Rather than question the presuppositions, interlocutors introduce an 'all things being equal' clause into it – i.e. all things being equal the world is intersubjectively available – and then attempt to account for discrepancies by identifying external contingencies which violate that clause. Technical faults might be invoked in cases where they are applicable, for example, or it will be decided that the individuals involved 'must have been' observing events at a different time.

For Coulter, the resolution of such discrepancies is morally structured. For Pollner, it is politically structured. And for both it is structured around certain cultural understandings of particular 'types' of people. The moral structuration of the situation revolves around the preference that interlocutors exhibit, in their interactions, for preserving the integrity of their other. They do not ordinarily find fault with their other, where alternative sources of fault can be found, unless that other belongs to a group who are ordinarily attributed such a fault. One might readily attribute a hallucination to a psychiatric patient, for example, but one would not readily do so for one who is not predefined in that way. Moreover, some groups may claim privileges in relation to some issues if they can lay a claim to expertise. If a psychiatric patient hears a voice and a psychiatrist does not, for example, then this is less likely to be accounted for in terms of the psychiatrist's hardness of hearing or inattentiveness, more likely to be accounted for in terms of the patient's hallucinations, than if two other 'types' were interacting. The struggles and strategies which may be invoked in such cases, by either side against the other, constitute what Pollner identifies as their political dimension. In his discussion of this 'politics of experience', furthermore, Pollner observes the manifold ways in which different social groups (particularly those involved in certain branches of social science) have been quite willing to ironise the experience of their others in order to affirm their own version of the reality of a situation.

Types

The (Schutzian) notion of 'types', which is introduced in this discussion, challenges our concept of radical intersubjectivity. It suggests that, at least in some situations, the other is not opened out towards in their individuality and otherness, but is, rather, typified according to the subject's structures of relevance. For Schutz, such typification is not always necessary. He maintains that it is possible to have a relation of radical openness and sharing such as we have described in this book. He also argues, however, that in many situations, even face-to-face situations, we rely upon typifications of others in our interactions. Social life is, for Schutz, routinised life. We do not approach each situation anew. We rely upon sedimented habits, pre-judgements and know-how. And this applies to our interactions with others. When we want to buy food, for example, we deal with a shop assistant, not the particular individual who is a shop assistant. We have more or less routinised ways of interacting with the shopkeeper and of acting in the shop more generally. Furthermore, types both belong to a system or family group of typifications and involve an expectation of reciprocal tying (again, expectation is not an active mental process here, but a feature of our behaviour); for example, we do not expect shopkeepers to be any more or less than shopkeepers and we do not expect them to expect us to be any more than customers. This affects both our action and the pragmatic determination of meaning in situations. We act towards the shopkeeper as a shopkeeper, assuming that they are oriented towards us as a customer, and we interpret the significance of their actions and remarks in terms appropriate to that situation. Questions, for example, are heard in a passing-the-time-of-day way and not in an intimate-confessions way.

This is not to say that such situations are inflexible. Garfinkel's (1967) breaching experiments demonstrated the durability and flexibility of such ordinary situations as shopping, when confronted with the threat of an intransigent social experimenter. Even here, however, typifications and conventions were the means by which actors attempted to restore order. Participants appealed to the experimenters' sense of common standards and conventions.

The situation described by Schutz may sound like the rationalised world described and criticised by Max Weber and by the Frankfurt School (Habermas 1991a); that is, an impersonal, standardised world where aesthetic and ethical components of interaction have been ejected to leave a narowly instrumental core. Schutz (1964: 65–88, 129) recognises this. He acknowledges that the world which he is describing is the modern, rationalised Weberian world. He rightly maintains, however, that all societies must rely upon habitual routines of interaction and typifications, and he rightly refuses the tendency to criticise that state of affairs in itself. Along with both Merleau-Ponty (1962) and Mead (1967), he maintains that habits and typifications are a pragmatic necessity both for the freedom and intelligence of individuals and for the preservation of any effective level of social organisation (cf. Crossley 1994).

Where typifications are less necessary, from Schutz's point of view, is in the space of intimate relations. Such relations may take many forms, according to Schutz, from sitting opposite someone on a train, to making love or engaging in detailed debate. They are not to be confused with familiar relations. Deep mutual understanding may be enhanced through familiarity if this brings with it a sharing of biographical–cultural frames and structures of relevancy. But a stranger can be opened onto in a radically intersubjective manner, particularly when no type seems suitable to them. Moreover, familiarity can breed typification, albeit of a personalised kind. Those who are close to us are often quite predictable to us and we take them for granted.

Typifications also enter into intimate and open relations in the form of symbols. Symbols, for Schutz (1973: 287–356), signify phenomena which transcend the world of everyday experience, and transcendence is a feature of all situations. In the face-to-face, for example, the experience of each interlocutor transcends the experience of his/her other, since each can see things that the other cannot; for example, what is behind the other's back. In this case, assuming the presupposition of the two idealisations mentioned earlier, transcendence can be accounted for by ordinary signs. Each fills in the gaps for the other. Notwithstanding this, however, nobody sees the whole situation. Nobody in a 'we' has a total experience of that 'we', since they are in it and part of it. The word 'we', in this sense, is a symbol. It signifies, within intersubjective relations and experience, that which transcends intersubjective experience. Schutz emphasises the important function which such symbols play in intersubjective relations of various types and sizes. He notes, for example, that symbols of 'home and hearth' play an important role in the organisation of the network of intersubjective relations which constitute the family. Similarly flags, anthems and 'society' function to bind social relations in wider society. It is important in this respect that Schutz regards each of our social groups (however large or small) as having its own self-interpretive 'central myth' (1964: 245). Symbols, as signifiers of the transcendent group, form the core around which such myths can be articulated. They are the 'we' in the myth of the we.

Social Regions: Contemporaries, Predecessors, Successors

Typified relations at the face-to-face level straddle the categories of radical intersubjectivity and egological intersubjectivity that I described in Chapters 1, 2 and 3. The other is engaged with in this situation, rather than thought about. They are interlocutors rather than objects of thought, fantasy or reflection. We both affect and are affected by them. Our actions interlock. But they are not strictly engaged with in their otherness. They are engaged with according to the role or type which they occupy. There is thus a tacit element of objectification in the engagement and a balance between the radical and egological modes.

As we move away from face-to-face relations, towards our other possible social relations, this balance begins to shift towards the egological pole. The fleshy expressiveness of the other is concealed through distance and they recede further into the one-dimensional existence of the type. Relations are less direct and the possibilities for affecting and being affected are altered. Others are, at least at times, objects of reflective thought rather than subjects in a dialogue or encounter. Agents don't mutually engage; their actions don't interlock. Schutz divides this realm into three regions: the world of contemporaries, the world of predecessors and the world of successors.

The world of our contemporaries is composed of individuals, groups and more abstract social entities (e.g. the law or 'society') who exist at the same time as us and with whom we may therefore engage, but whom we are not encountering at any given time on a face-to-face level. It includes people whom we know, people whom we don't, people whom we have known and people whom we might know later but don't at the moment. There is obviously much variation in the types of relation that may hold here. My relation to a distant friend, for example, is different to that with 'the tax office'. Moreover, Schutz is quite clear that there is no sharp dividing line where the face-to-face ends and this world begins. How far down the road does a friend have to walk, he rhetorically asks, before they cease to be in contact and become part of the anonymous world of contemporaries? Nevertheless, this world has specifiable characteristic features.

It is characteristic of the world of contemporaries that self and other are still able to mutually affect one another. Both are active agents in a relation. The form which this takes is less direct than in the face-to-face, however, allowing the typification of the other to dominate much more. Moreover, interaction may be much more routinised and rationalised. Indeed it may be institutionalised and/or codified in law. One's relation to a big bureaucracy such as the tax office, for example, is mutually affecting. There is an other-orientation. Most of the time this orientation and affecting is more or less automatic, however. They take money. I pay money. Insofar as they are concerned I am a payroll number, a typical taxpayer. Insofar as I am aware of my interactions with them, it is only through either the words 'tax deducted' on my pay slip or through a Kafkaesque fantasy image of 'them'. Nevertheless, I have many of these relations and they are important to my life and, on a wider scale, to the life of society. The economy, the polity and our various systems of cultural reproduction rely precisely upon a multiplicity of such relations.

This notion of the typification of contemporaries knits in closely to Mead's understanding of the composition and functioning of the 'me'. Typified contemporaries are, in effect, varieties of the 'generalised other'. Moreover, Schutz, like Mead, argues that when we interact with contemporaries we view ourselves as contemporaries for them; when we view them as a tax inspector, for example, we equally view ourselves as a taxpayer. What Schutz adds to Mead's account is a clearer understanding of the typifications by which the other and particularly generalised others are grasped, and thus of how the 'me' is constituted in concrete situations. Mead also adds to Schutz's conception, however, through his notion of the dialogue between the 'I' and the 'me'. This allows us to see the dynamic nature of the structure into which typifications function and thus the possibilities that exist for a reflective and self-critical attitude towards typification and/or particular types.

Schutz outlines two conditions which allow for the existence of the world of contemporaries: media technologies and symbols. The importance of media technologies to such relations, assuming those relations to be relations of communicative interaction, is obvious. If relations can't be immediate, then they are mediated, and if they are mediated, then we require media of some description. For Schutz, this mediation was straightforward and theoretically uninteresting in itself. Subsequent theorists, however, have pointed to the transformation in social relations which particular forms of mediation, from the spoken word, through the written word and video links to the Internet, have brought about (Giddens 1979, 1981, 1984; Poster 1990; Stevenson 1995). These tranformations are important because they create situations which are unforseen by and cannot be accommodated in Schutz's typology. Video links, for example, blur the boundaries between the face-to-face and the world of contemporaries by enabling long-distance intimacy. Similarly, as Habermas (1987a: 390) notes, the introduction of mass media has created the possibility of an interactive and effective 'public sphere' in our societies, where questions of politics can be openly discussed and decided. Finally, recent technological changes have opened up a whole new world of interaction with machines, which do not fit anywhere in the Schutzian schema (Suchman 1987).

Symbols, as defined earlier, contribute to the construction of the world of contemporaries because they allow us to coordinate our relations with transcendent phenomena such as 'society' and 'the law'. They represent the most abstract and generalised of generalised others. This is an important notion and it complements Mead's view of relations with a generalised other (which, at its most abstract, is represented by 'society' and 'law'). Symbols are the means by which we relate to such transcendent others. There is a problem regarding this issue, however, in that Schutz, following Weber, assumes that all 'agents' other than human agents are abstractions which are reducible to individuals insofar as they are effective. That is, they are only symbols. They have no agentic properties. As Hindess (1988) argues, this is not necessarily so. Agency, for Hindess, consists in the means of making a decision and acting upon it, and, he maintains, many organisations (e.g. some trade unions and parliament) do this in a manner that is strictly irreducible to the human beings that are involved in them. Moreover, such organisations are recognised and constituted as agents in law. This is not to say that all transcendent phenomena actually constitute agents. Most do not. Furthermore, it is clear that human agency differs from non-human agency. Nevertheless, Schutz is wrong to reduce all agency to human agency.

In addition to the world of contemporaries, Schutz identifies the world of predecessors. Again this world is on a continuum with the world of contemporaries and the face-to-face. Possibilities for relations in this world are different to those in the previous two, however. One's predecessors, Schutz notes, do affect one indirectly. They have contributed to the creation of one's world of contemporaries and to the tools which one may use to both re-create and change that world. They cannot directly affect one, however, since their existence does not coincide, temporally, with one's own. Moreover, one cannot affect them in return. There can be no genuine social relation because predecessors no longer exist and there can therefore be no mutual orientation or mutual affecting. Predecessors' actions do not unfold in the same open future as my own and they can therefore never be changed or affected and can never interlock with my own.

Because predecessors' actions are completed and no longer temporally unfold towards an open future, they lack the unpredictability of contemporaries' actions. Their meaning is not underdetermined as it is in the lived time of contemporaries. Understanding and interpreting predecessors is difficult, however, Schutz maintains, because of the cultural changes which have passed between the time of the act and the time of interpretation. Like Gadamer (1989), he observes that the difference in traditions and systems of relevances between times makes a total fusion of horizons with predecessors impossible. Words, phrases and other signs all change meaning along with their infrastructural forms of life. Thus, whilst we can orient to predecessors, in a fashion, that orientation (in addition to lacking in mutuality) is always imperfect.

What is missing in this account is a consideration of the technologies of communication which make access to the past possible and of the effect of such technologies. Giddens (1979), for example, has noted that societal shifts from pre-literacy to mass literacy make a considerable impact upon the relations of agents to their predecessors. Prior to literacy, he notes, views of the past were limited and uncontested. Agents relied upon story-tellers for their views and they had no independent evidence with which to confront those story-tellers. In literate societies, however, where records remain, the past is open to more interpretation and debate. The actions of predecessors have an actual trace in the present. That this situation is again transformed with video and television technology should be apparent.

The final intersubjective world that Schutz considers is the world of our successors. He has little to say regarding this group. They do not affect us, he maintains, because they do not yet exist, and though we affect them, in the sense that we create the world that they must contend with and some of the tools that they will use, we cannot even orient to them because we do not know what they will be like. We have no knowledge of them, as we do with our predecessors. They belong to the future, which is always indeterminate.

And this disjuncture in our time horizons again makes an interlocking of actions impossible.

Whilst Schutz seems largely right in this respect and whilst I agree that the future is both intangible and indeterminate, I would suggest that his position fails to account for the moral relation which we take in relation to our successors in such contexts as ecological debates and projects or in parenting. In such cases we do assume that our successors will be similar to us and we are affected, in the egological mode, by our representations of them and the sense of responsibility that we feel towards them. Indeed, insofar as our action is always future-oriented, it is always also oriented to our successors.

On Community

What begins to emerge in the account of our contemporaries, predecessors and successors is a sense of different cultures and of group life. The concept of intersubjectivity merges into that of community or, more precisely, of communities in the plural. Schutz (1964) explores this issue in a number of essays. The groups or communities referred to in these essays include whole societies, towns and villages, families and clubs. What Schutz demonstrates, primarily by considering the position of outsiders to them, is the different worlds of meaning that manifest within them, and the sense of identity, belonging and orientation that members variously have and feel towards them.

Groups or communities, whether families or societies, manifest distinct cultural forms, for Schutz. He refers to this as a common stock of knowledge. Whilst this includes propositional knowledge, he tends to mean know-how, rules of thumb, forms of familiarity and habits. His 'knowledge' is equivalent to the practical compentencies of what we have referred to elsewhere as the habitus. These competencies, he maintains, are in part acquired through trial and error in personal acquaintance and experience. Much is acquired, however, in education of both a formal and an informal form. We grow up and live in communities and those communities both structure our learning experiences and teach us about life and how to live it. This ensures that assumptions are shared and thus that the symbolic cement of the lifeworld is reproduced through both time and space. Having said this, common-sense assumptions are not static. They change as the structure of communal life changes. Furthermore, they differ between communities. This is why we sometimes experience a disorientation and anxiety when visiting alien cultures; what we take for granted isn't, whilst others take for granted what we don't.

The habitual form of these competencies is conveyed in Schutz's various descriptions of them. He refers to them as 'and so forth', 'I can do it again' and 'of course' assumptions, thus suggesting their unreflective nature. Or again, he refers to them as 'thinking as usual'. Moreover, he suggests that as long as everything is as normal (including usual problems and crises), they remain both unchallenged and unnoticed. They are not what we think about or understand but are rather what we assume, our pre-understanding and pre-judgement, the very ground on which we think or understand. They are the necessary prejudices which make our thought and expression possible but which, for that reason, remain largely unthought about. Furthermore, they are grounds which cannot themselves be grounded. Like Wittgenstein and Gadamer, who express very similar views on tacit knowledge in *On Certainty* (1969) and *Truth and Method* (1989), respectively, Schutz maintains that there is no justifiable basis for such assumptions and knowledge. They are simply a part of our cultural tradition, of our ways of acting and interacting.

Such 'common-sense' features of the lifeworld include the 'central myths' of self-interpretation referred to earlier. And they also involve typification of outside groups and worlds. This knowledge functions only within the group and for the group, according to Schutz, however. It is too distant and rigid to function in outside groups. This is why, he maintains, strangers have difficulties adjusting to new communities. Their knowledge of these communities breaks down on close inspection. The rolling of time and the breadth and diversity of individuals and events crashes through the static and narrow typifications of the stranger. At least, this occurs if those typifications admit friendly contact. The difference between cultures and the lack of understanding between them can breed aversion and hostility which is sufficiently strong, Schutz maintains, to motivate conflictual encounters and a self-perpetuating negative view of the other. Typifications, in this instance, carry strong negative evaluations, and whilst they may still function to coordinate social activity, they do so in a manner which is either hostile or detrimental to an outside group. Moreover, the imposition of relevances between individuals and groups, as discussed earlier, may take an institutionalised and overtly political form. Schutz (1964: 260) refers to the manner, for example, in which one group 'constructs' the other and then institutes and enforces an identity upon that group and a partitioning and differential treatment of them. His example of this is racist ideology, an example which is borne out in Said's (1978) account of the invention of the Orient, in Sartre's (1948) account of the imposition of Jewish identity and relevances upon Jewish people by anti-semites, and in the many other accounts of racial hatred, conflict and discrimination in its various personal and institutional guises (e.g. Gilroy 1992; Goldberg 1993).

The other side of these hatred ideologies is the feeling of belonging which members of a community enjoy in relation to that community, particularly when away from it. This results, for Schutz, from a range of factors. In the first instance, the group's central myths and symbols, which I have discussed in this chapter, tend to be woven into the personal narratives (see Chapter 3) of its members because their personal history coincides with that of the group. Thus their sense of self is bound to a sense of the group. Secondly, their 'thinking as usual' is the style of thinking which is accepted, valued and which works in those groups, since it is from those groups that this thinking (largely) derives. They thus find that they 'fit' in this group more easily than in others. Thirdly, they have an identified place in the group, a status. They are recognised.

A further factor contributing to the opacity of the community to the outsider, for Schutz, is that its stocks of knowledge are socially distributed and tied to particular roles in the community, such that they do not assume a general form which would be accessible to an outsider and such that they could not function for an outsider in any case. There are a number of issues here.

Firstly, Schutz maintains that different members of a community, assuming a relatively complex division of labour and social differentiation, have different practical knowledge. Their knowledge relates to their own specific position or role within the community. This may be spatial in the sense that they have a geographical orientation based around their own home and the various landmarks of their life (workplace etc.), but it will also be social. They will have their own areas of expertise and will know who, what and where to contact for goods and services that they cannot provide for themselves. Moreover, Schutz emphasises the role of hierarchy and status in this equation. Different ranks in the social order are permitted different forms of knowledge. This oriented and hierarchised knowledge cannot be applied to the outsider since they are not part of the community and have no place within it from which to be oriented. Even if they have a social 'map' of the community, they have no place on that map and thus cannot use it. Moreover, communal culture defies external observation and knowledge because it is a way of seeing and understanding rather than something to be seen and understood and because what is seen is variable according to one's location. Culture is not a homogeneous, uniform, universally distributed phenomenon, for Schutz, but an interlocking plurality of skills and beliefs, whose structure involves stratification and inequality and whose value is only realised in relation to one's own location within it. Finally, and related to this, the knowledge of the community is practical knowledge. It is thereby tied to the specific relevances of the tasks and interests of specific community members. But the outsider, by definition, does not have participatory tasks in the community. Therefore the knowledge does not work for them. Not only can they not find themselves on the map, they have nowhere to go either.

Any member of a community will, of course, occupy a number of different roles related to the different domains of their life. They will consequently have different structures of relevance and different forms of knowledge to go with them. Indeed, Schutz maintains that they will have different and incompatible views in each of their roles:

> As a father, a citizen, an employee, and a member of his church he may have the most different and the least congruent opinions on moral, political, or economic matters. (1964: 94)

This doesn't create problems, providing that these roles don't clash and the groups to which they are appropriate are kept separate. Opinions and concepts, Schutz maintains, are always relative to particular domains. The extreme example of this is the structure of 'multiple realities' referred to in the previous chapter. Schutz adds to this, moreover, that the informed and expert opinion that may develop in relation to specific areas must exert itself in appropriate contexts. As citizens, he argues, we have a duty to stand against general opinion in matters that we are particularly well informed about or involved in.

Schutz's final point concerning group life centres upon their institutional-isation. Within any group, he maintains, relations extend intermittently through time, in a structured fashion, such that they may be picked up and left off on a regular and frequent basis. Goffman (1981) describes one dimension of this in the form of conversations between relatives which go on for years, picking up and dropping off at regular and frequent intervals. The interactions of the workplace, school or family provide rather more general examples, however. These 'primary groups' meet more or less regularly to act out the specific roles that they have developed in relation to each other. Each day they pick up where they left off.

Concrete Intersubjectivity

Schutz's work clearly marks an advance over that of Merleau-Ponty in relation to the issue of the relations between the face-to-face level and the wider social formation. His discussion of the world of contemporaries, predecessors and successors, and of community reveals intersubjectivity as a more differentiated phenomenon than Merleau-Ponty suggests and it fills the gap left by the latter's leap from the face-to-face to the social macrocosm. In doing this, moreover, it facilitates considerable sophisti-cation of Mead's understanding of the citizen-self, the generalised other and community membership. Schutz gives a much clearer idea of what it is to be and to feel part of a group and of what it is for a group or community to be a community. We see clearly in his work that a community is more than a mere population of people in a space; that it is constituted through interlocking systems of roles and taken-for-granted assumptions, which are activated in and through interactive praxes.

There are a number of problems with Schutz's position, however. In the first instance, in contrast to Merleau-Ponty's 'concrete intersubjectivity', Schutz fails to consider actual concrete empirical communities. He still works at a high level of abstraction. Secondly, he presents a very 'small' world and his view on social integration (i.e. that it is achieved by way of shared schemas of understanding) is more appropriate to such a world than to the 'big' worlds of industrial and post-industrial nations. The very earliest sociologists, such as Durkheim, recognised that a large society could not be integrated by way of common agreement as such, and that further mechanisms of integration were required. Moreover, the suggestion of much subsequent sociological work is that large-scale Western societies have undergone a prolonged period of 'rationalisation' which has effectively routinised and instrumentalised many social spheres, not to mention globalised and standardised most cultural forms, to the point where the parochial intimacies observed by Schutz no longer apply (see Chapter 5). The social world, according to this view, is regulated by large impersonal bureaucracies whose modus operandi negates the significance of particularistic cultural norms and values.

A further point related to this concerns Schutz's apparent tendency to equate community with a specific geographical location. He doesn't actually state this but it is the impression he gives. The communities which he describes sound like small towns. This is a common association in the social sciences but it is one which is quite outdated. In the past communities have, by necessity, been tied to particular locations. This necessity has now been removed, however, by a two-pronged process. Societies have become more diversified and pluralised, without ensuring that like-minded people are geographically close and new communication and transport technologies (and the accessibility of them) have facilitated long-distance associations. The ultimate contemporary expression of this is Internet technology and the cyberspace it has given rise to. Already there are thousands of communities for people to join in cyberspace, catering for remarkably specific interests. A user of the Internet might well commune with people all over the world, whilst they remain quite anonymous in their neighbourhood. Another example might be a sporting community or an academic community. In both cases the keen communard will spend so much time engaged in their chosen community (reading its magazines, attending its various events at different locations, watching its TV programmes and engaging in its other activities) that they do not have the time to form any sort of community with the people around them. This is not necessarily a bad thing but it does preclude any inevitable association of community with space.

The third problem with Schutz's account is that it ignores all but the most basic interdependencies which function within and bind groups of various sorts. Schutz fails to consider emotional dependencies, physical dependencies and financial dependencies, for example, all of which have been shown to be central to the construction of solidarity and dynamism of social life by writers such as Elias (1978b). It is such interdependencies, Elias argues, which ensure that no one person in a group can act without affecting all of the others.

The fourth omission in Schutz's work concerns questions of power, control, law and the state. The social formation, for Schutz, it would seem, is constituted exclusively through relations of meaning and agreement, rather than those of legislation, control and force. There is no recognition or account, for example, of the role of war and violent revolution in the construction of social order, nor, for that matter, of the legitimated violence of such institutions as the penal system. Even his discussion of racism is principally a discussion of cultural misunderstanding and typification, which fails to consider the broader issues of the colonial relations out of which much racism springs. This is a regressive step when compared with Merleau-Ponty's account of concrete intersubjectivity, which included reference to both understanding and violence when describing the integration of the social world.

Fifthly, with the exception of an occasional elliptical reference to 'hierarchies', Schutz fails to consider the place of inequality and exchange in social relations. This, I would suggest, is a consequence of his failure to discuss value and its intersubjective base. And it has the consequence of preventing his understanding of macrocosmic intersubjectivity from ever quite reaching the stages of concretisation which I mentioned in relation to Merleau-Ponty at the beginning of this chapter. Merleau-Ponty's 'concrete intersubjectivity' was a capitalist economy in which relations between persons are mediated by their relations to things and, principally, by the ownership and control of the means of material production by one group (bourgeoisie) who can use this position to advantage in relation to those who own nothing and must sell their labour to the former in return for a subsistence wage (Crossley 1994). A number of related points and criticisms can be drawn from this account.

The first point is that intersubjective relations are conducted in and by way of a physical environment. Schutz, to be fair, does recognise this point. He maintains that human beings transform their physical environment, in the form of tools and material culture, and that these environmental materials, in turn, both extend their capacities and potentials and exude the meaning and humanity of their creators. He recognises, in other words, that the embodiment of human intersubjectivity extends beyond the expressiveness of the human body into its transformed physical environments, that we engage with the meanings of our contemporaries and predecessors every time we walk into a house or drink from a cup. What is missing in this respect, however (which is present in Merleau-Ponty's understanding of concrete intersubjectivity), is a recognition of the necessity of the reproduction of this material aspect of the social formation and, importantly, of human beings themselves. Social life, by any description, must facilitate this material reproduction.

This issue raises the question of human need and the manner in which needs are either met or not met in the context of social organisation. Schutz neglects to consider that within the context of the lifeworld that he describes needs must be met or the system will not sustain itself. Moreover, beyond need there is the question of value and desire and of the struggles and social relationships that form around that which is valuable and desirable. This is Kojève's point, as discussed in Chapter 1. Human beings don't just seek out what they need, Kojève argued; they seek out recognition from each other. They desire to be desired and this desire is often mediated through things, which in turn become valuable or precious. Objects are desirable because they represent the desire of others. The introduction of the question of need, value and desire in human life sheds a whole different light upon the character of social relations than that outlined in Schutz. It suggests that human relations are not just about mutual understanding but that they can be and are often about exchange. Moreover, it begs the question of the social organisation of the 'market conditions' under which such exchanges are conducted and the structuring effect which those conditions have upon the outcome of the exchange. This is an issue which was touched upon in Merleau-Ponty's understanding of concrete intersubjectivity, but his account, whilst better than that of Schutz, is still unable to account for it – at least in the context of the contemporary social world (Crossley 1994). I will discuss it in more detail in the next chapter.

Finally, what the notion of concrete intersubjectivity involves but Schutz fails to account for is the notion of a social system. Schutz tends to stick to the sorts of relationship which an individual takes to other individuals or groups at the expense of a consideration of relationships, practices and processes viewed from the trans-individual position of the systems which they form; for example, the economy, law and national and international social systems more generally. Furthermore, insofar as he refers to the community, he concentrates upon the place of the individual in it and not on its own mode of social organisation qua trans-individual social unit. He describes the integration problems posed by and for 'strangers' and 'homecomers' in a community, for example, but gives little to no account of how the community itself functions as a system, perpetuating itself through space and time.

Social systems of the type I am referring to here are, in the final instance, produced and reproduced through the actions and interactions of human beings. We must not make the objectivist error, noted above, of viewing social systems as structures over and above agents, which contain or act upon those agents. To theorise thus is to commit a category error. Notwithstanding this, however, social systems as levels of social organisation have properties and produce effects which are strictly irreducible to the individuals they implicate. Moreover, as we consider more macrocosmic structures (such as national and international economies), we find that we adopt a manner of description in which we cease to refer to individuals and perhaps also to social roles. Rather we refer to units and subsystems within a system. These descriptions do not negate anything that we have said about individuals, groups or social relations. They indicate that we have shifted to a new level of description. These are issues that I will deal with in the next chapter, with reference to the work of Jürgen Habermas.

5
System, Lifeworld and Communicative Action

At the end of the previous chapter I criticised Schutz's understanding of society qua social lifeworld for its failure to consider exchange relations in contemporary society, for its failure to deal with issues of interdependence, power and inequality, for its failure to consider the systemic aspects of the social world, and for its failure to engage with the specific concrete features of a social system (such as our own) in its proper historical context. Each of these features is, as I noted in my discussion, a feature of Merleau-Ponty's notion of 'concrete intersubjectivity'. As I have argued elsewhere, however, Merleau-Ponty's understanding of the (concrete-intersubjective) social world is both theoretically flawed and empirically outdated (Crossley 1994). Moreover, these are not issues which the other intersubjectivists hitherto discussed in this book have considered. Whilst Mead is concerned with the nature of liberal democracies, neither he nor Wittgenstein provides us with the tools by which to understand contemporary social systems. The intersubjectivist paradigm does not run out of steam here, however. It changes gear. We must consider the work of writers whose work is intersubjectivist but who are more concerned both with the concrete particularities and with the systemic features of the intersubjective fabric qua social structure. This is the purpose of this present chapter.

The major (though not exclusive) focus of the chapter will be the work of Jürgen Habermas. Intersubjectivity and the lifeworld are primordial for Habermas. They are the basic starting point for social theory and, indeed, for social life itself. The earliest and most basic societies, he argues, were exclusively constituted in the form of the lifeworld. According to Habermas, however, the evolution of societies has seen the emergence of systemic features, and the lifeworld has been relegated to the position of a subsystem within a system. Modern social scientists and social theorists must address this systemic level, he argues. They must study the social system qua system, as it perpetuates itself and realises goals, in relation to the exigencies imposed upon it both from within and from its external environment (which is composed of other systems and of the natural world). This does not lead Habermas to abandon or subordinate the notion of the lifeworld, however. On the contrary. He maintains that systems are always necessarily anchored in the lifeworld, such that the lifeworld remains the primordial societal constituent and such that hermeneutic explication of the lifeworld remains a central task for social scientists and philosophers, even those who are primarily concerned with systems analysis (e.g. he maintains that the goals of a social system, in contrast to a natural system, cannot be identified independently of the definitions and aspirations which prevail in the lifeworld belonging to that system, and thus that there can be no proper systems analysis that does not determine the goals of the system by way of lifeworld analysis). Furthermore, he outlines a critical research programme focused upon the interrelation between system and lifeworld and, in particular, upon the infringement of imperatives of the former upon the latter. For Habermas, modern societies must necessarily be studied both from the perspective of the lifeworld and system and from a perspective which will study the relation between the two. These ideas will be central to my discussion in this chapter because, as I will show, they provide a coherently intersubjectivist paradigm for the analysis and critique of social systems.

In addition to his discourse on the relations of system and lifeworld, Habermas adds two further important ingredients to our discussion. He constructs a theory of communicative action and its evolution, which forms the basis both for an important political intervention in the theory of intersubjectivity and for a considerable development of our notion of the lifeworld. These modifications to the notion of the lifeworld are my starting point in this chapter.

Communicative Action and the Lifeworld

Habermas derives his understanding of the lifeworld from three philosophical sources, all of which have been central to this study: phenomenology (particularly the later Husserl and Schutz, but not Merleau-Ponty), the pragmatism of Mead and the linguistic philosophy of Wittgenstein and Austin. Of these, Mead is most important to Habermas. Mead provides him with a model of the social actor as a communicative and communicatively engaged being and provides the outline of a theory of communicative action which Habermas takes as the basis for his own. Three aspects of Mead's theory, all already discussed in this book, are particularly important here. First, Habermas takes the notion that entrance into the symbolic order of language fundamentally changes the human organism's relation both to itself and to its environment, by mediating those relations and constituting them as relations of meaning. A social theory of human behaviour must base itself at this symbolic level, according to Habermas. Secondly, he takes the notion that human beings can stand in communicative (and thus non-instrumental/non-objectifying) relations to each other. Thirdly, he takes the notion that dialogue and (linguistic) communicative processes more generally are irreducible. These notions revolutionise social theory, he argues, by initiating a relocation of the locus of action and of rationality (both of which are central notions in social theory) away from individual consciousness, towards the communicative interworld. It is these communicative inter-worlds and the action and rationality that manifest within them that provide the key focus in Habermas's theory.

The linguistic theory of Wittgenstein and Austin serves to elaborate this communicative paradigm by providing a philosophy of language and meaning which is consistent with Mead's work but surpasses it. Witt-genstein's use theory of meaning provides Habermas with a theory of linguistic meaning which rests on the idea of the speech community rather than individual consciousness, thus further allowing him to prioritise communication over individual consciousness. And Austin's account of speech acts and their felicity conditions allows him both to rethink the notion of social action and to identify the institutional conditions for the effec-tiveness of such actions. This again prioritises the interworld over conscious-ness. Furthermore, the understanding of 'forms of life' (in which linguistic meaning rests) is understood as a useful formulation of and contribution to the concept of the lifeworld.

The position of phenomenology in this theory is more ambiguous. Habermas uses many concepts and ideas which are borrowed from the work of Husserl and Schutz, including the very concept of the lifeworld itself. He discusses the role of taken for granted assumptions, of shared horizons of meaning, of problems of relevance and their relation to plans, etc., and he outlines a notion of the pre-interpreted world. Notwithstanding this, however, Habermas identifies phenomenology with the philosophy of consciousness, which, for reasons which compare directly with my critique of Husserl in Chapter 1, he is very critical of. Thus, he offers his work as a communicative critique of phenomenology, rather than an embrace. Furthermore, he identifies the need to go beyond a phenomenological explication of the lifeworld. We must understand the lifeworld as a cultural system, he maintains, with its own conditions of reproduction and oper-ation. And this entails that we objectify the lifeworld, casting aside some of our more phenomenological sensibilities. Thus, whilst phenomenological concepts are borrowed in Habermas's theory of the lifeworld, phenomen-ology itself is displaced. In this respect his position is very similar to the one I have developed hitherto in this study.

What Habermas adds to this combination is an understanding of the validity claims which are integral to our communicative interactions. When agents interact communicatively, he argues, they simultaneously make claims regarding their own subjectivity as speakers (e.g. their sincerity), the objectivity or verifiablity of particular circumstances referred to or implied in what is said, and the normative role-and-rule structure of their social world (e.g. their social and moral right to say whatever it is that they have said). Each of these types of claim is intersubjectively defeasible, with the important consequence that every genuinely communicative interaction is potentially contestable. We can contest the claims of the bogus and the insincere and we can point to facts in the intersubjectively experienced world to counter the assumptions or claims that others might make about it. Even when we contest the claims of others, however, insofar as our interaction is based in communicative action, we still recognise them as speakers. Indeed, in disagreeing with them we are precisely recognising them as serious interlocutors. A successful communicative action, for Habermas, is one in which such disagreement is worked out by the force of argument, where the best argument wins out and consensus is achieved. He refers to these as 'ideal speech situations'.

Not all action and interaction is communicative action. It is central to Habermas's social theory that there are both instrumental and strategic modalities of interaction, to contrast with communicative action. Both strategic and instrumental action may involve communication but they do not rely upon agreement for their success and they are not oriented in the same way. Instrumental action is means–end action, on behalf of an atomised agency, which is judged soley on the basis of its success in realising the 'end' to which it is oriented. Usually Habermas understands by this the sort of physical labour required to transform material nature and to provide for our material needs for food and other goods. It is 'production', and Habermas tends to identify it with the work sphere. Strategic action, by contrast, is interaction with others, which relies upon given institutional-intersubjective norms or resources (money or power), rather than agreement, for its effectiveness as action. For example, a teacher doesn't need the agreement of a child in order to exclude the child. Their institutional authority will suffice. In cases of strategic action the process of argument is short-circuited by an economic or political intervention.

These claims are some of the most hotly contested by Habermas's critics and interpreters. Four criticisms in particular have been made. Firstly, it is argued that the distinction between communicative action and instrumental action is somewhat artificial since the two modes of action will tend to be bound together in any concrete situation (Giddens 1982; Joas 1988). This point is particularly aimed at the claim that specific spheres of social life, such as work, rely upon specific modes of action, such as instrumental action. Secondly, it is argued that there are many forms of human interaction, such as joking and playing, which do not raise the validity claims that Habermas describes (Joas 1988; Thompson 1983). Thirdly, it has been argued that the 'ideal speech situation' is an under-theorised notion because Habermas fails to specify the conditions under which it is possible (Thompson 1983). Finally, it has been argued that the possibility of reaching consensus in language is undermined both by the heterogeneity of language games in contemporary society and by an apparent tendency to paralogy in linguistic contexts; that is, consensus, even in language games of science, is only a stage in a process in which it is always eventually challenged and overturned (Lyotard 1984).

The second of these criticisms is the least problematic. It is certainly true that some language games (such as joking) don't involve the validity claims that Habermas has identified and he can be criticised for not having recognised this. This has no shattering consequences for his theory as a whole, however. As long as interlocutors are able to distinguish occasions where claims are raised and the types of claims raised, which they should be able to do as competent language users, then there is no problem. A similar retort applies to the second part of the fourth objection. There is no ruling in Habermas's argument that consensus must be final, as long as the break-up and reconsolidation of consensus is an orderly process – which it is in the case of the studies of science identified by Lyotard.

The first objection is more complex. As it stands it has no great consequences for Habermas's theory. Following our above line of retort we can argue that Habermas's theorisation is secure so long as speakers are able to identify those actions (or aspects of action) which are communicative and thus require a response, and again I would suggest that a competent language user ought to be able to do so. As we will see later, however, this objection reoccurs in a different context where it is not so easy to dismiss.

The third criticism is more contentious. On the one hand, contra his critics, Habermas does suggest the conditions for an ideal speech situation, insofar as he differentiates communicative from strategic action. An ideal speech situation is one in which each of the validity claims of participants is met and the process of argument is allowed to unfold without being short-circuited through economic and political interventions. On the other hand, there is a considerable question concerning the manner in which any such situation could be instituted at the level where important economic and political decisions are to be made. This is a problem but it isn't Habermas's problem. It is a problem which he allows us to identify, which must be resolved through political praxis.

The first part of the fourth objection (by Lyotard) is badly put and seemingly based upon a misunderstanding of Wittgenstein's concept of a language game. The beauty of the language games idea is that although such games are heterogeneous and changing, we are still able to understand each other and reach some sort of agreement. To suggest otherwise is to substitute the idea of language games with the more rigid and deterministic notions of language that the idea seeks to oppose.

Rationalisation of the Lifeworld

Communicative action in the lifeworld, as Habermas defines it, is oriented in three directions: towards mutual understanding, towards the coordination of action and towards socialisation. Moreover, it is mutually oriented and mutually negotiated. As such, he argues, it serves to transmit and renew cultural knowledge, to achieve and maintain social integration and to form and sustain personal identities. Each of these three functions refers to a distinct structure of the lifeworld: culture, society and the person. Culture, according to this schema, is the stock of knowledge that a society possesses and transmits. Society is 'the legitimate orders through which participants regulate their membership in social groups and thereby secure social solidarity' (1987a: 138). It is the structure of normative frameworks which social members abide by and refer to and which thus regulates their behaviour. The person or personality is 'the competences that make a subject capable of speaking and acting, that put him in a position to take part in processes of reaching understanding and thereby to assert his own identity' (ibid.). Effectively then, the lifeworld is said to be (symbolically) reproduced through mutually oriented, mutually negotiated communicative action, and it is identified as consisting in a tripartite structure. Habermas is clear that communicative action is the only means by which the lifeworld, qua symbolic order, is reproduced. He adds, however, that the account of symbolic reproduction must be integrated with an account of material reproduction. The material substratum of the lifeworld, which includes the (speaking/symbol forming) bodies of symbolic interlocutors, needs to be maintained and reproduced. Moreover, it is mainly instrumental labour of the sort discussed above which will achieve this reproduction. This material/instrumental dimension, which I discuss later, is central to the lifeworld/system distinction.

Social theorists hitherto, Habermas observes, have tended to be focused upon only one of the three symbolic structures that he identifies. Phenomenologists, who follow Schutz, have been narrowly concerned with social knowledge, Durkheimians with questions of social integration, and symbolic interactionists, who follow Mead, with questions of socialisation, of roles and self-formation. By contrast, Habermas's social theory deals with all three structures.

In effect this amounts to a demonstration of the interdependency of the three structures. This is demonstrated through a consideration of the problems or pathologies which can be triggered at any one individual level but which have effects at each level. A disturbance in socialisation, for example, may lead to psychopathology at the personal level, withdrawal of motivation at the societal level (and consequent social disintegration) and a rupture of tradition at the cultural level. Alternatively, a disturbance at the level of social integration may have the effect of unsettling group identity at the cultural level, creating anomie at the societal level and alienation at the personal level. This interdependency should be fairly evident. Indeed, given what we have discussed so far, the separation of lifeworld structures appears only as the product of theoretical abstractions, with no actual separation in practice. Each structure is a moment in the reproductive cycle of communicative action. There is a separation in practice, however, which Habermas discusses under the rubric of the rationalisation of the lifeworld.

The idea of rationalisation is an enduring theme of social theory which Habermas discusses in relation to a great variety of writers. All of these writers have attempted to use the notion of rationalisation to explain the differences between traditional and modern societies and to outline the relative opportunities and constraints afforded by the transition from one to the other. In this context 'rationalisation' becomes an index for a multitude of (lifeworld) evolutionary processes, ranging from the Enlightenment displacement of religion by science and the separation of aesthetic and moral judgements from each other and from knowledge claims about the world (i.e. facts from values), to the displacement of absolutist monarchies by democratic parliamentary systems. Habermas's aim in *The Theory of Communicative Action* (1987a, 1991a) is to show that and how traditional approaches to rationalisation have failed, because of their rootedness in an (atomistic) philosophy of consciousness, and to reconstruct the theory of rationalisation in a communicative and intersubjectivist mode. This reconstruction involves a number of key claims.

In the first instance, he maintains that there has been a structural differentiation of the lifeworld, in which culture, society and personality have developed a relative differentiation and autonomy from each other. At one level, the institutional structure of society has been gradually uncoupled from the ideas, knowledge and worldviews belonging to the common cultural sphere, through a differentiation of functional institutional units, the rise of formal bureaucracies and the emergence of specialised forms of knowledge (e.g. the professionalisation and institutionalisation of separate educational and health provision). Formal organisations and professions function through impersonal rules/roles and procedures, Habermas maintains, which are relatively disconnected from and indifferent to the beliefs and initiatives of those who staff them or of the wider cultural sphere. Similarly, the scope for the development of personal relations and identity has become more contingent and less embedded in ascribed cultural patterns or social institutions, and the relations between culture and personality have loosened and changed, such that 'the renewal of traditions depends more and more upon individuals' readiness to criticise and their ability to innovate' (1987a: 146). Individuals are able to think *about* their culture, in other words, as well as *by means* of it. The central and important point in this, for Habermas, is that social order and interaction are determined less by a blind adherence to lifeworld traditions and more by open communicative agreement. The differentiation of structures is a distantiation which provides for the possibility of discussion and agreement between communicative agents. Each structure provides a viewpoint from which the others can be viewed, discussed and legislated for.

Secondly, Habermas identifies a differentiation of form and content in each of the three structures. At the cultural level, for example, the substantive content of beliefs has been dissociated from formal communicative devices, such as 'communicative presuppositions, argumentation procedures, abstract basic values'. This is evidenced in our ability to argue about beliefs: we have different beliefs but we agree (in forms of life) about how to argue about them and are thus able to do so meaningfully. At the societal level, differentiation manifests in the formation of more abstracted legal and moral codifications, which are not tied to the contextual particularities of concrete forms of life. In particular Habermas argues that law has been divorced from morality. It has become a bureaucratised, codified system with its own mechanisms of enforcement (e.g. police and judiciary), whilst morality has been privatised and relocated in the personal sphere. He adds to this that morality itself has become more formalised and abstract in this process and that this has led to a greater potentiality for discussion and debate of moral principles. Finally, at the level of personality, the cognitive structures acquired by way of socialisation are less tied to specific cultural knowledge and locations. Agents are able to reason in a fashion which is largely freed of contextual particularities. They are able to assume and compare different perspectives on the world. These processes are essential to the institution and separation of the three validity claims which Habermas identifies in contemporary communicative action. We can contest each of these claims because they have been separated and differentiated through the process of rationalisation.

Finally, Habermas refers to a functional specialisation of social reproduction. In the cultural structure this involves the institutionalisation of art, law and science as discrete, organised social fields. In the societal structure, it involves the emergence and institutionalisation of large, formalised bureaucracies and organisations, of the democratic mechanisms for the selection of government and the cultural forms appropriate to the functioning of democracy. In the personality structure it involves the emergence of specific pedagogic institutions and practices for the correct upbringing of the child. What is important with respect to each of these changes, for Habermas, is not simply that societies have specialised functions of reproduction, but that in each case the mechanism of reproduction is made visible and thus open to debate. We don't just bring up children, for example; we have an accountable institution to do so and we debate and discuss the correct goals and functioning of that institution. It is important, moreover, that specific institutions assume responsibilities for specific social functions. This entails a functional specialisation which sharply contrasts with the situation in traditional societies, where the family unit in particular was the agent which provided for most social and personal needs.

In each of these points there is a stress on the potential for discussion and open argument (and thus democracy) opened up by the rationalisation process. Rationalisation is identified as having liberated us from the ties of tradition and potentiated the possibility of a dialogical negotiation of our ways of life. It has, to reiterate, opened discourse to the test of the three validity claims of (contemporary) communicative action. This point is clearly illustrated by Habermas through a comparison of Western communicative reason with that of so-called 'primitive' societies. In such societies, he argues, the three validity claims of communicative action (subjectivity of speaker, truth of circumstance and role/rule structure of social world) are not differentiated, with the consequence that claims cannot be contested and debated in the same way. Indeed, he argues, such societies do not even distinguish interpretations from the interpreted world. This is not to say that the modern lifeworld is or could be completely transparent to its members. It couldn't. Meaning and decision, for Habermas, will always rest in unexplicated background structures of pre-judgement and pre-understanding.

Nevertheless, rationalisation brings with it the potential for much greater reflexivity and for a democratic contestation of ways of life.

Rationalisation only creates the potential for democracy, however. There is no guarantee that it will be realised. Rationalisation unfolds within a context and it can be, and for Habermas has been, steered in a quite contrary direction; that is, it can unfold and has unfolded as a rational domination (of nature and people), an 'iron cage' of control and bureaucracy. This more pessimistic vision of rationalisation is by no means new in social theory. Habermas himself identifies it with Weber, the French post-structuralists and earlier writers in his own German tradition of Critical Theory. Where Habermas differs from these earlier writers, however, is in his insistence that this potential for domination is not immanent in rationality itself but is the effect of the circumstances of rationalisation. Rationalisation becomes rational domination only when realised in the context of specific economic and political systems. Furthermore, as such, rationalisation remains a double-edged sword. It potentiates domination but it equally potentiates communicative critique and transformation. To pursue this further we must consider the relations of the lifeworld to the social system and the definition which Habermas gives of the latter.

Lifeworld and System

Habermas considers the differentiation and interrelation of system and lifeworld at two distinct levels: the methodological level and the social-evolutionary level. At the methodological level his demarcation criteria for lifeworld processes and mechanisms is that they can be inferred from the knowledge, goals and orientations of the actor and, more importantly, from communicative negotiations between actors. The lifeworld is that dimension of society whose mechanism for social organisation, integration and reproduction is communicative interaction and the mutual orientations of actors to each other and to shared conventions. It is a communicatively established order. The system level, by contrast, is the structure of impersonal interconnections which mediate and coordinate actions, functioning beyond the level of the immediate awareness of the actor and integrating and coordinating the unintended consequences of that action. It refers to those purposes of both communicative and instrumental action which transcend the individual goals of the actor who performs them, and it refers to the mechanisms which link such purposes. Principally, it concerns those actions which are structured through their situation in an institution, bureaucracy or formal organisation and which are largely shaped (in their possible consequences) by way of that situation; that is, routinised and stabilised patterns of acting. Moreover, it is matters principally relating to the material (as opposed to symbolic) reproduction of the lifeworld which Habermas identifies with this level. Symbolic reproduction is effectively controlled at the level of communicative action, he maintains, but this is not so for the mechanisms of material reproduction (and, principally, of the economy). The mechanisms of material reproduction and maintenance are not of 'surveyable dimensions'. They cannot be forseen and controlled at the level of individual interactions and will.

Analysis of both lifeworld and system must rest in an understanding of 'insider knowledge', Habermas observes. The former remains in this sphere, however, whilst the latter, in the final instance, involves taking an outsider's perspective. That is to say, the lifeworld perspective begins and ends with an explication of the know-how of the members of a community, where the system perspective (whilst it must be hermeneutically sound; not importing distinctions which prevail in one system into another) involves reference to mechanisms not inferred in that know-how. Systems analysis involves an objectification of the lifeworld, which renders it analysable as a system. This is not to say, as Joas (1988) takes Habermas to be saying, that systems theorists make any claim to literally disconnect themselves from their lifeworld situation. This would, as Joas notes, be a totally unacceptable move, given the hermeneutic grounding of Habermas's ideas. What it does suggest, however, is that theorists take a different, more objectifying attitude towards their social situation.

As we transcend the lifeworld perspective of communicative action, Habermas argues, we are prompted to identify new methods and means of societal integration. The 'social integration' (as he now calls it) achieved by way of the organisational properties of communicative action is supplemented by 'systems integration'; that is, mechanisms of integration which coordinate the lifeworld, economy and polity, and which enable their survival in an environment which is never completely under their control (a 'hypercomplex' environment). This is achieved by way of new 'mediatisations' of social relations which function to provide 'feedback loops' for the stabilisation and organisation of the system (see below).

Habermas's evolutionary argument effectively grounds this methodological argument, fills in its substantive content and provides a justification for moving between the system and lifeworld perspectives. The argument is that, along with the rationalisation and differentiation of the structures of the lifeworld, the transition from traditional societies to modern societies, following a continuum developed in the transition from tribal societies to traditional societies, has involved a differentiation of lifeworld from system:

> . . . the lifeworld, which is at first coextensive with a scarcely differentiated social system [i.e. in tribal society], gets cut down more and more to one subsystem amongst others. In the process, system mechanisms get further and further detached from the social structures through which social integration takes place. (Habermas 1987a: 154)

He is clear, moreover, that it is specifically economic structures and mechanisms, alongside political structures and mechanisms, which have become differentiated in this way. The significance of the economy and polity is that they both involve 'mediatisations' of interaction which can bypass communicative negotiation. The economy organises interaction by way of money and the administration organises it by way of power. Whilst economic and political exchanges may involve some talk, money and power override the need for linguistic agreement and negotiation. They instrumentalise and rationalise situations, freeing interactants from obligations to accord with communicative validity claims. They allow for and involve instrumental and strategic action.

The essential point that Habermas is making is that societies, as they have developed, have burst the banks of what is able to be achieved through direct coordination of interaction. In this context, self-regulating mechanisms have emerged, within which instrumental behaviours which are free of 'norm-conformative attitudes and identity-forming social memberships' (1987a: 154), are facilitated and expected. Behaviour and interaction patterns are stabilised and regulated in the context of bureaucracies and formal organisations. They are rationalised, subsumed under formalised orders, roles and routines, such that they are indifferent to the private attitudes of their incumbents and even to particular worldviews. The relation and regulation of such rationalised organisations is mediated by money flow and/or power rather than communicative action.

These structures must rest in the lifeworld. They depend upon the intersubjective maintenance and recognition of economic and political institutions, such as the monetary system and the democratic process, for their continued existence. But they are nevertheless 'uncoupled' from the lifeworld insofar as they are freed from its normative constraints and, as such, constitute the basic framework of the systemic level of the social formation.

We will get a clearer understanding of this uncoupling of system and lifeworld if we consider it in its proper social-evolutionary context. This will take us back to Habermas's understanding of the rationalisation of the lifeworld.

In tribal societies, Habermas observes, lifeworld and system are inseparably bound. Whilst such societies are more complex and differentiated than much sociology and anthropology have suggested, they are nevertheless strongly bound by shared mythologies and normative frameworks, concretised in religious and kinship systems, which structure all situations. This binding through shared belief is usually referred to, following Durkheim, as 'mechanistic solidarity'. Moreover, like Durkheim, most social theorists, including Habermas, maintain that mechanistic solidarity can only be sustained in relatively small-scale societies, where it is feasible that a high level of conformity to central beliefs can be sustained and where the communicative initiatives of agents are sufficient to coordinate activities.

For Habermas, it is particularly important that, in tribal societies, (economic) exchange and power are interwoven with lifeworld norms and conventions to the point where it is hardly possible to establish any distinction between economic and non-economic value or between authority and family authority. All 'economic' actions have a religious or kinship significance and, more importantly, are regulated by the normative framework of the religious and kinship systems. This indicates that exchange and power still remain inseparable from the lifeworld, that '[s]ystemic mechanisms have not yet become detached from institutions effective for social integration' (1987a: 163).

The first step away from the lifeworld-system integration of the tribal society comes about through the hierarchisation of tribal societies, leading to the formation of a new political structure: the state. Societies in this condition are 'politically dominated', which means, amongst other things, that tradition is, to a degree, undermined as the basis for the legitimacy of action and replaced by political authority. There is a new regulation of action, over and above mutual agreement, based in law and state power. Moreover, social stratification is relocated away from the family-role system, and on to the political apparatus. Social position is now determined by relations to that apparatus rather than by position in the kinship system. At this stage, for the first time, society becomes an organisation with official membership, that is, citizenship. All members of society, by virtue of their relation to the state, are now citizens. This is significant because citizenship is a more flexible status than family membership. It can be alienated, appropriated and negotiated.

In these societies, economics is enveloped in the state. Political power leads the society and controls the economic function. The next step, however, is the birth of money and the marketplace (at least in the case of capitalist society). This involves, amongst other things, a further differentiation and displacement of the centralisation of social organisation through the state. Society is now organised by means of monetary exchange and the market mechanism. Bureaucratisation and the rise of large, formal organisations is important too, since this provides the institutionalisation of action orientations required for an economic society. Furthermore, social position becomes connected less to one's relation to the political apparatus (the state) and more to money and other capital assets. Tradition and its normative framework no longer drives society. Neither does the power of the state. Rather, the relatively unconstrained process of financial exchange constitutes the engine of social change. This process divides the lifeworld according to economic classes. Different classes, with different experiences and life conditions, form different ways of understanding and making sense of the world – a point excellently illustrated in Pierre Bourdieu's (1984) discussion of class habitus.

It is central to this case that the economic system does not form a self-contained and sealed unit. If the economy is to function as a 'steering mechanism', that is, if it is to function in relation to other subsystems and to drive or organise those subsystems, then those subsystems must involve money. The economy will only influence those aspects of life which are, however indirectly, interwoven into it by way of the monetary system.

Such structural-evolutionary changes, Habermas observes, must be prefigured by facilitating changes in (i.e. rationalisation of) the lifeworld. New mechanisms are nested in the lifeworld by means of processes of institutionalisation and bureaucratisation which regulate and facilitate them. The institutionalisation of money and the market mechanism, on the one hand, and of the financial and administrative bureaucracies, on the other, are obviously important here. The aforementioned changes in law and morality are also important both for upholding these changes and for facilitating the emergence of a (morally) unfettered market and a sovereign (consuming) individual (see also Abercrombie et al. 1986). Pluralised individual preferences and choices replace collective moral strictures and thus free the market.

The important implication of this point is that the systemic aspect of society is created out of the rationalisation of the lifeworld. Shortly I will be considering how, for Habermas, this process works the other way round: how system imperatives and processes impinge upon the lifeworld. Before doing this, however, it is instructive to consider in more detail the system that Habermas identifies with modern Western societies.

The System (1): Marx's Capitalism

Habermas understands the contemporary system as welfare capitalism, the model for which he derives from Marx. It is with Marx, therefore, that I begin.

For Marx, capitalism is a 'mode of production', consisting both of means or forces of (material) production and (social) relations to those means of production. In early capitalism, when Marx formulated his theory, the dominant means of production were industrial technologies (factories, systems of primary extraction of natural resources) and society was principally divided into two groups whose (objective) identity was determined by their relations to those means of production. There was a small class of capitalists, the bourgeoisie, who owned and controlled the means of production (i.e. owned the factories and the mines), and there was a large group of labourers, the proletariat, who owned nothing (in terms of the production process) but their own labour power (which itself constitutes part of the forces of production). Relations between the bourgeoisie and the proletariat were mediated through the forces of production. The bourgeoisie required the labour power of the proletariat to work their factories and produce material goods, whilst the proletariat, in order to survive, had to sell their labour power to the bourgeoisie to earn a wage – which they would then use to buy the necessities of material reproduction (e.g. food and clothes) from the bourgeoisie or from 'petit bourgeois' shop-owners who, in turn, had bought them from the bourgeoise.

Described in this way, capitalism sounds quite functional. Marx posits a political critique of it, however, defining it as a system of exploitation. Moreover, he argues that it manifests crisis tendencies which will eventually lead to its downfall.

The thesis of exploitation is based in Marx's understanding of 'surplus value' and, ultimately, in his understanding of value. Value, for Marx, has two components. Things are valuable to the extent that we can use them for some purpose ('use value') and that we can exchange them ('exchange value'). All things that have an exchange value, in this account, have a use value. Nobody wants to purchase what is useless. But not all things that have a use value necessarily have an exchange value. Moreover, in contrast to use value, exchange value is dependent upon specific social conditions. It demands a social division of labour, such that people each possess different things and have a need and a purpose to exchange. And it requires a system of equivalences whereby relative values of objects can be determined and exchanges thus facilitated. Money is the obvious example of such a system of equivalences but it is not the only one and it is a particularly rationalised form in comparison to others. In societies which meet these conditions, producers must produce specifically to exchange, in order that they can purchase those things which they do not directly produce themselves. These things or objects which are produced for the purpose of exchange are referred to as 'commodities' and capitalist societies are the prime example of a system of commodity production and exchange.

The value of objects, for Marx, is determined by active human manipulation or labour. It is labour which appropriates and transforms its environment, such that parts of that environment acquire a use (e.g. transforming animals into 'food' or trees into 'weapons' and 'tools'). Moreover, it is labour which constitutes exchange value, insofar as the exchange value of objects is proportional to the amount of labour time required to produce them. That which requires more labour has more exchange value. Labour value, it should be added, is not determined by individual labour time – such that the products of a slow worker are worth more. It is determined by the average time/effort requirement of a society ('socially necessary labour'). Furthermore, it is not just immediate production time that is accounted for in this equation. The skill level and more particularly the training time required to acquire that skill level is also included in exchange value.

In capitalism, as I noted above, the proletariat sell their labour to the bourgeoisie in return for a wage. Labour is a commodity in the capitalist system. It is exchanged on a labour market. This is where exploitation emerges, according to Marx, because, he argues, the wage which the proletariat receives is worth considerably less than the value which their labour produces and the difference, the 'surplus value', is kept and accumulated by the bourgeoisie. In the early capitalism that Marx analysed, for example, workers received a wage which was sufficient only to reproduce themselves and their family (a subsistence wage) and thus to maintain the labour force, whereas the value produced through their labour was considerably in excess of this wage.

This exploitation constitutes a conflict of interests at the very heart of capitalism. What is beneficial to the proletariat (such as an increase in wages) will tend to be bad for the bourgeoisie (because it will be deducted from their profit margin) and vice versa. And, as we have shown, it is the bourgeoisie who benefit in capitalism, insofar as it is the proletariat who are exploited. This conflict makes the system unstable, according to Marx, and it constitutes the proletariat as potential agents of (revolutionary) change. When their wage only suffices to provide the basics, they have everything to gain by attempting to transform the system and nothing to lose but their 'chains'. This conflict of interests is not the only structural problem of capitalist societies, however. Marx identifies two further structural problems: the tendency for the rate of profit to decline and the tendency towards overproduction crises.

To understand these two tendencies it must be understood that the bourgeoisie, whilst they may be said to have certain interests in common, are nevertheless in competition. Capitalism is based upon the competition to sell goods in the market. It is this competition which keeps the system alive and which has motivated some of the immense technical transformations that the history of capitalism entails. For Marx, however, it is equally this competition which will destroy the system from within.

Capitalist competition is based around the attempt, given maximum extraction of surplus value, to realise surplus value in the form of profit. The capitalist wants to recover what a commodity is worth (and more) on the market. If an enterprise is producing at a rate equivalent to socially necessary labour, then this realisation is usually achieved. The commodity is being produced at a competitive rate and can be sold at a competitive price. This harmony is constantly threatened for the capitalist, however, by transformations achieved in the rate of socially necessary labour by way of technical innovations. Capitalists compete to produce new technologies (first industrial, next automated, now information technology) which will enhance labour power, reducing the time and effort required to produce, thus allowing products to be produced more cheaply, prices to be undercut and markets to be dominated. This is why products which were once expensive to produce and were exclusive are now cheap and commonplace. Such innovation is very expensive, however, and it contributes nothing to the production of value (since labour produces value). Furthermore, it needs to be constant if each individual capitalist is to keep up with the competition. Consequently there is a tendency for profit to fall.

Marxists express this tendency in the equation: profit = $S/C + V$, where S = surplus value, C = the cost of technologies and raw materials ('constant capital') and V = the cost of labour power ('variable capital'). With this equation it is possible to demonstrate the tendency quite clearly: assuming $C = 3$, $V = 5$ and $S = 10$, the rate of profit = $10/3 + 5 = 1.25$; and if constant capital is increased to 5 without a change in the other values, then profit = $10/5 + 5 = 1$. There is a drop from 1.25 to 1.

This tendency can be avoided if surplus value can be increased, which in turn means cutting costs on labour. There is a finite limit on the extent to which wages can be cut, however, whilst there is no necessary limit on technological expansion. Furthermore, there is a further contradiction in the sense that capitalism requires more than just production from the proletariat. It requires them as consumers and it thus requires that they have sufficient spending power to be consumers.

One of the consequences of this tendency is a tendency towards the concentration of capital and monopolisation. Some firms withstand the losses and win out, others can't withstand them and they lose. And those which win get bigger, buying out the losers at cheap prices, thereby putting themselves in a position where they can eliminate competition from new, smaller firms. The paradox of this is that capitalism effectively destroys the situation of market competition that constitutes it. It outgrows itself. Some Marxists have argued that this outgrowing manifests in considerable economic problems, not to mention social problems (Harman 1989).

There is a further possibility for crisis in capitalism, which again eliminates competition by progressively wiping out small fry and consolidating the large firm: overproduction crises. These periodic crises stem from the combination of a number of factors. Firstly, that the realisation of surplus value is dependent upon sales and thus upon the linking of supply and demand. Secondly, that capitalism, in order to survive, must seek out ever more demand and thus expand its markets. Thirdly, that the role of supplier has to be competed for. Finally, that the linking of supply and demand in the market is an anarchic rather than a planned process. The consequence of these factors, particularly the latter, is that supply periodically exceeds demand and there is overproduction. Capitalists cannot sell their goods, therefore cannot realise their surplus value, therefore lose money and in some cases 'go to the wall'. This process can escalate in a downward spiral in the sense that the result of an overproduction crisis (or indeed of a falling profit rate) will be the laying off of workers, which reduces demand for goods and thereby either causes a further overproduction crisis or at least reduces the demand for labour in further firms, leading to further lay-offs, etc.

In short, for Marx, capitalism contains the seeds of its own destruction. It is composed of classes whose interests are structurally antagonistic, and it is prone to tendencies both for the rate of profit to decline and towards overproduction crises. It is important to add here, moreover, that the only way in which the bourgeoisie can hope to offset the costs of crisis is to further depress the wages of the proletariat, a process which cannot but fuel the possibility that the structural antagonism between classes will be realised in the lifeworld in the form of class consciousness and struggle. The logical outcome of this, for Marx, was revolution. The proletariat would rise and overthrow capitalism.

For Habermas, the rise of the labour and trade union movements in the earlier part of the twentieth century is clear evidence of the beginnings of the realisation of such conflict. Like many other contemporary writers, however, he has a different story to tell about capitalist evolution and crisis.

The System (2): Habermas's Welfare Capitalism

Habermas is critically appreciative of Marx's position. In essence he accepts that the original configuration of capitalist economic forces was prone to crisis in the manner that Marx argued. But in contrast to those Marxists who argue that these tendencies can still be shown to prevail (Harman 1989; Mandel 1970, 1980), he maintains that the structure of capitalist societies has adjusted so as to contain these crisis tendencies, or rather to shift the potential for crisis into other areas. In particular he is concerned with the rise of the democratic and interventionist state, which has effectively taken responsibility for the smooth running of the economy and for welfare and which, in doing this, has made itself partly accountable to the citizens of the lifeworld to which it belongs. For Habermas, this rise is in part accounted for by the class-based movements mentioned above (cf. also Hall 1984). It is the outcome of a class compromise and to this extent it conforms to the picture that Marx painted. However, the interventionist state transforms capitalism in a manner which Marx neither predicts nor accounts for.

Underlying this point there is a sharp theoretical departure from Marxism. Habermas argues that we cannot take the logic of economic exchange as an autonomous, exclusive or primary motor force in social development (as Marx presupposed and as subsequent Marxists argued). He shows how the course of economic development is affected by political processes. Furthermore, he is equally clear that economic and political processes are engaged with socio-cultural lifeworld processes (of symbolic reproduction) which are essential to their survival. Taking each of these components (economy, polity and lifeworld) and their respective interfaces into account, Habermas opposes the (monadic) Marxist model of social systems and crises with a four-tier model. This involves a neo-Marxist model of the economic system and crises (which modifies the Marxist model in accordance with changes in the nature of capitalism) and it adds to it and integrates with it an account of rationality, legitimation and motivation systems and crises.

The rationality system corresponds to the state's role and means (qua administrative agent) of managing the economy. The modern state, Habermas observes, would seem to have lightened the burden of the tendency for the rate of profit to decline, by taking scientific–technical development into its remit (e.g. financed research in the university). The tendency towards overproduction has also been offset, moreover, by careful consumer analysis and by the provision of (state) welfare services which considerably reduce the drop in consumption rates potentiated by redundancies. In addition to this the state has become an effective economic agent with a limited planning and managing capacity. It has appropriated and monopolised certain utilities, creating a stable public sector. And it has developed the mechanisms of taxation, national insurance and controls over banking and interest rates, all of which are levers for steering and managing the economy.

Economic management and the systemic imperatives of the economic subsystem are not the only involvements and imperatives of the administration, however. As a democratic state, which has pacified the possibility of class conflict and revolution through a system of welfare provision and has thereby assumed the responsibility for the well-being of its citizens, it must maintain its legitimacy in the eyes of those citizens. Democratic government finds its 'necessary limitations' in 'available legitimations'. This is a problem because state provision, of whatever kind, costs, so what is gained through democracy must be lost from the economy, and vice versa. Thus, the class conflicts of capitalism are not eliminated. They are recoded as an internal conflict of the administrative system, between its economic imperatives and its democratic and welfare imperatives. Both, moreover, are central to its functioning. The administration will collapse if the economy collapses, just as surely as it will collapse if its legitimacy is withdrawn.

If the administration fails in its management of economic exigencies, then Habermas refers to a 'rationality crisis'. If it fails in its accountability to the populace, then he refers to a 'legitimation crisis'. Legitimation crises differ from rationality crises in that they are simultaneously system crises and lifeworld crises. They threaten both system integration and social integration. In the first case, this is because they involve a withdrawal of the mass loyalty required by the administration for its effective legitimation. They threaten social integration, by contrast, because they entail popular unrest.

Drawing on the work of the German sociologist Claus Offe, Habermas identifies the probable causes of rationality crisis in the emergence of sectors of the population whose action cannot be directly controlled through standard monetary controls; for example, professionals whose work is not directly related to the operation of the market, the unemployed and the aged, and large monopolies that tend to work according to their own plans rather than being immediately responsive to market conditions and changes in fiscal policy. To control the economy is to control action, he argues, and the only 'legitimate' way to control economic action is by means of economic intervention. Groups not directly involved in the wax and wane of the economic market cannot be controlled in this way, however. They put elements of the economy beyond control. And this potentiates rationality crisis.

The other side of this, as I have noted, is the possibility of a legitimation crisis. In averting rationality crisis the state may threaten its own legitimacy. This too must be avoided. Managing legitimacy is not a straightforward process, however, since it must bridge the administration and the lifeworld (as the rationality system mediates the economy and the administration), without disturbing 'motivation orientations' rooted in the lifeworld (e.g. the work ethic), which are required by both the economic and administrative systems. It must interfere with the lifeworld without disturbing it too much. The potential for legitimation crisis, then, is balanced between a potential for both rationality and motivation crises. The administration must secure its own legitimacy without threatening either the stability of the economic subsystem, with its imperatives, or the motivation tendencies of the lifeworld (qua subsystem), with its imperatives (i.e. the reproductive imperative serviced, ordinarily, by communicative action). It is the crucial link which holds the total social system together.

The legitimation function which the state assumes is, Habermas notes, a difficult one to fulfil. The cultural traditions of the lifeworld, in which legitimations must be rooted, have their own means of reproduction, but these means are 'nature-like' and cannot be either 'objectivistically prepared' or 'strategically employed' without being destroyed:

> . . . traditions can retain legitimizing force only so long as they are not torn out of interpretive systems that guarantee continuity and identity. (1988a: 71)

Traditions and meaning systems evolve, in other words, but they cannot be consciously created: 'There is no administrative production of meaning' (1988a: 70). This is a problem because, according to Habermas, the system is creating an ever greater need for legitimation. This need, he maintains, has a double source. First, the expansion of the administrative system, which has gone hand in hand with capitalist development as a means of pacifying its potential for economic conflict and crisis, has created ever new functions for that administration and thus new needs for mass loyalty in relation to the execution of those functions. Secondly, administrative expansion has entailed a shift in the boundaries between the lifeworld and the state, which has effectively undermined many of the taken-for-granted assumptions of that lifeworld, so that they are no longer taken for granted and are now open to critique and discussion. Each new area of the lifeworld that the administrative system encroaches upon becomes a contested area. The details of socialisation, education, health, regional and city planning are all now open to (often fierce) debate, where once they were taken for granted. This has an additional effect insofar as it politicises ever greater areas of life and thereby threatens 'motivation crisis' in the form of a rescinding of 'civil privatism' (see below).

Given that the state, as noted above, cannot create meaning or traditional legitimation, the struggle for legitimacy that this creates is one based on 'use values'; that is, upon the success of the state to satisfy the demands and needs of the now more self-reflective populace, who themselves are oriented to their own success:

> The fiscally siphoned-off [by means of taxes] resource 'value' must take the place of the scanty resource 'meaning'. Missing legitimation must be offset by rewards conforming to the system. (1988a: 73)

And legitimation crises arise

> . . . as soon as the demands for such rewards rise faster than the available quantity of value, or when expectations arise that cannot be satisfied with such rewards. (ibid.)

Having said this, Habermas maintains that legitimation crises are not inevitable. It is possible, he argues, that civil demands, providing they are pursued in a privatised fashion, remain within the bounds of what the system can provide and thus do not threaten legitimation – even if competition between parties does raise people's expectations higher. Moreover, he is clear that the administration is able to protect itself by limiting access to and limiting the agendas for debate in the public sphere. The more control is asserted over the public sphere, the less opportunity for the diminution of mass loyalty and legitimation crisis.

If the states of Western Europe face legitimation problems, then, it is for reasons beyond those outlined. In his relatively early study *Legitimation Crisis* (1988a), Habermas believes that they do and that these reasons relate to the potential within the system for 'motivation crises'; that is, a discrepancy between the motivations and orientations demanded by the state, occupational structure and education system, and those actually produced by the socio-cultural lifeworld (i.e. by means of communicative action). Or, to emphasise the other side of the coin, changes in the lifeworld which are 'dysfunctional for the state and for the system of social labor' (1988a: 75).

The concept, 'motivation crisis', and Habermas's argument for it, are based in four basic claims. Firstly, any social system is dependent upon particular motivations and these motivations are, in turn, based in culture and tradition. Secondly, capitalism has tended to rely upon individuals who are (a) motivated to contribute to and be concerned for reproduction of the administration but who are not concerned with issues of legitimation ('civic privatism'), and (b) individuals who enjoy and invest in a privatised family life and who are concerned to advance themselves at work in order to sustain that life ('family–vocational privatism'). This is a pre-capitalist orientation, like civic privatism, which is mixed with a capitalist ethos (derived largely from the Protestant work ethic) to produce possessive individualism and achievement orientation. Thirdly, capitalist development is unable to secure these motivations because it is unable to generate culture and tradition and it is actually eroding those conditions, listed above, which are necessary to its own reproduction. Finally, there is nothing to take the place of these motivations which would secure the survival of the system. Thus, the system is said to be heading for crisis because its basic lifeworld conditions are being undermined.

Habermas's discussion of the factors likely to precipitate motivation crisis are too far removed from our central concerns to discuss here. Suffice to say that, in his later work, he tends not to understand the undermining of the lifeworld in terms of 'motivation crisis', but rather to understand it in terms of a 'colonisation of the lifeworld' and a 'cultural impoverishment'. This redescription, as we shall see, does not exclude the possibility of change or of the emergence of agencies of change, but it suggests a more durable capitalism; one capable of (possibly) accommodating even its tendency towards motivation crisis.

The Relation of System to Lifeworld

Habermas begins his discussion of the colonisation of the lifeworld (in *The Theory of Communicative Action*) by formulating, formally, his argument for the uncoupling of the system from the lifeworld and his account of the relations between the two. As I have already noted, his account of the uncoupling relies upon an understanding of the rise of the independent nation state, on the one hand, and the rationalised economy, on the other. And it particularly rests upon the fact that both of these 'subsystems' replace communicative action, as their medium and vehicle, with an alternative. The alternative, in the case of the economy, is money. In the case of the state it is power. Carrying this argument forward, Habermas identifies two distinct spheres within the lifeworld, each of which corresponds or relates to one of the other two subsystems. There is a private sphere which corresponds and relates to the economic (sub)system, and there is a public sphere which relates to the administrative (sub)system. Furthermore, each of these two spheres can be further divided into two roles which individuals occupy and which are 'mediatised', in the sense that they rely upon money or power for their organisation, rather than communicative action. Within the private sphere, individuals play the role of employee, where they sell their labour power and receive a wage; power is expended and money received. They also play the role of a consumer, in which they constitute an economic demand and purchase goods and services, both actions being mediated by money. In the public sphere individuals play the role of client, in which they pay taxes, which is mediated by money, and they benefit from organisational achievements, which are the result of an expenditure of administrative power. They also play the role of citizen, in which power is exercised upon them, in the form of political decisions, and in which they exercise power in the form of their political/national loyalty, voting behaviour, etc. The family forms the core of the private sphere, according to this schema, at least insofar as it is the chief site of consumption. And the mass media, as the agency of opinion and will formation, form the core of the public sphere.

This is the way in which the lifeworld is integrated into the system, as a subsystem, along with the other two. The flow of money and power in this schema serve as 'feedback loops' which coordinate the system, providing checks and balances against total crisis. As we saw in the discussion of the various crisis tendencies, problems in one subsystem or domain are either displaced or communicated to the others by way of the channels of money and power (e.g. citizens withdraw their loyalty [power] because political decisions [power] are unacceptable to them). Furthermore, each system relies upon each of the others working and interacting in specific ways. Importantly, moreover, each stage in this systemic process can be registered at the level of the lifeworld. Public opinion formation is an ongoing, communicative praxis, for example, but it is equally 'mass loyalty', a systemic property. It secures social integration, on the one hand, and systemic integration, on the other. Similarly with labour. It is a 'concrete action', formed in a communicative context and contributing to social integration. And it is an 'abstract performance' which secures systemic (economic) needs for material reproduction.

It is important for Habermas that this system/lifeworld equivalence is maintained. This is what allows us to register the effects of systemic changes and logics upon concrete lives. Moreover, it allows us to see how systems evolve and change. We have a sense of the dynamic and interactive processes which underpin it. It is in this vein, moreover, that Habermas strongly resists the tendency to convert completely and exclusively to a systems perspective. To do this, for him, is to suggest that human intersubjectivity has been totally eclipsed by the processes of routinisation, rationalisation and bureaucratisation that he and others have identified with the formation of the system. And this has not happened.

A positive consequence of Habermas's approach is that he is still able to maintain an ethical stance. Systems are related to persons and therefore their development can be judged good or bad. In some respects Habermas is prepared to say that systematisation is good, that it has achieved a more advanced potential for human survival. At another level, however, he maintains that systemic developments have led to a colonisation of the lifeworld which is certainly not desirable; indeed, which is 'pathological' and which needs to be stopped.

Colonisation of the Lifeworld

The colonisation of the lifeworld is said to occur when the 'mediatisation' of relations, by money and power, extends into the core processes of symbolic reproduction, thereby displacing the role which communicative action would ordinarily play in those processes; that is, when money and power mediatise the processes of socialisation, social integration and cultural transmission. Moreover, Habermas maintains that this colonisation is occurring, has been occurring for some time and is motivated by the necessity to avoid economic crisis; that is, it is part and parcel of the administrative and economic expansion that I have already mentioned, whereby traditions are undermined and state- or market-regulated mechanisms fill in the breach.

It is of considerable importance to Habermas that it is the roles of 'client' and 'consumer' in particular which are expanding under this process and that the public sphere, where the individual assumes the role of citizen, is shrinking. There is less opportunity for public participation and debate in political processes, whilst leisure, sexual relationships, family life and even self-hood and psychological predisposition are increasingly incorporated into both the administrative gaze and the marketplace. The chief dangers of this process, for Habermas, are increasing intrusion of outside agencies into the private lives of individuals and growing dependency of individuals upon managers and service providers. In both of these cases the autonomy of individuals is undermined. He adds, moreover, that this colonisation involves an increasing tendency for social organisation to be steered by money and power, at the expense of 'consensus formation in language', with the potential for rational argument and the requirement for validity claims that the latter involves. The crux of the colonisation argument is thus that once negotiable and contestable areas of life are increasingly being eroded and overtaken by the logic of the economic market and the exercise of administrative power. Communicative action is replaced by 'strategic action'; action which appeals to a source other than rational consensus and defeasible validity claims (e.g. power) to achieve its intersubjective ends. Social integration is achieved less by consensus, more by definite strategies and techniques of control. That this is a further erosion of local autonomy should be evident.

In addition to the notion of colonisation, Habermas adds a notion of cultural impoverishment. Stephen White summarises this second process as follows:

> . . . increasingly specialised forms of argumentation become the guarded preserve of experts and therefore lose contact with the understanding processes of the majority of individuals. . . . the process . . . has a deforming effect on everyday life, for now that participation in the transference of validity which a rationalised lifeworld opened up to all competent speakers is increasingly short circuited. (1988: 116)

These 'experts' are tied in to the administrative and economic systems. This is the link between the colonisation and impoverishment theses. Moreover, the result of the latter appears to be a disempowerment of social subjects in relation to the former. The practices of the experts, Habermas notes, are not comprehensible to the ordinary citizen and they cannot, for this reason, be opened up to public argument and thereby made publicly accountable. This prevents citizens from being able to think critically.

Habermas refers to this as a 'fragmentation of consciousness' and he compares it with the 'false consciousness' of traditional Marxist theory. Contemporary citizens are pacified not by a false or inverted picture of the world, he argues, but rather by their inability to formulate a coherent worldview. They are not so much duped as cognitively overpowered or overloaded. Their world exceeds their comprehension. Such a process must surely hold the potential for legitimation crisis at bay, and indeed encourage civic and familial privatism. The public sphere is effectively eclipsed and only the private sphere holds out any hope for meaning. This, to return to my earlier point, is rationalisation in a capitalist context. This is the considerable down-side to rationalisation as it has evolved in Western Europe.

This 'fragmentation' thesis is open to some objection. Thompson (1983), who otherwise praises the thesis, has argued that it must not mislead us into thinking that ideological uses of language and symbols are of no relevance in contemporary political life. This is a criticism which I would support. Furthermore, I would suggest that it also points to problems in relation to

Habermas's claim that there is no administrative production of meaning. Whilst this is strictly true, at least in the sense that the administration cannot create the traditions which form the bedrock of meaning, nevertheless administrations can, as Gramsci (1982) quite clearly shows, manipulate traditions or align themselves with them as a means of securing their control. In the case of Britain, for example, the success of Thatcherism has been shown to be, in the first instance, an ideological success based in the Thatcher government's ability to identify itself with valued aspects of British culture in the popular imagination (cf. Hall 1987). Whilst we might be persuaded to follow Habermas's idea of fragmentation, then, we must not allow this to pre-empt our understanding of the manner in which political leadership or control is secured.

The conclusion to *The Theory of Communicative Action* is not wholly pessimistic. On the one hand, the systems dimension of Habermas's theory itself is said to provide for a more coherent vision of the operation of the system. On the other hand, and better still, Habermas identifies a twofold catalyst for change within the lifeworld. In the first instance, his account of the rationalisation of the lifeworld, as discussed above, identifies the emergence of a new reflexivity with the erosion and eradication of tradition which is a permanent potential source of criticism and agitation. More specifically, however, he points to the emergence of (so-called) 'New Social Movements' as evidence of a resistance to the colonisation and impoverishment of the lifeworld. Such movements aren't formed in relation to questions of distribution, as used to be the case (e.g. with trade union and socialist resistance), he argues. Their concerns arise out of the 'grammar of forms of life'. They want either to defend threatened traditions or to change (now unsettled) cultural forms for the better. Or again, they aim to achieve some form of local democracy and accountability.

Habermas Assessed

Although *Legitimation Crisis* was only published (originally) in 1973 and *The Theory of Communicative Action* in 1981, there have been quite considerable social transformations since their publication. Political and economic globalisation, for example, have undermined some of the sovereignty of the administrative subsystem qua nation state. The emergence of international economic and political agencies and the influence which each is able to assert within the boundaries of national states have effectively undermined the sovereignty of such states as economic and political actors. The nation state is now one agent amongst others (albeit a powerful one) even in relation to events in its own territory. The effectiveness of its political and fiscal interventions is dependent upon the international flow of capital and policy – though, of course, it has some say in international politics by virtue of its participation in the decision-making bodies and processes of international political agencies. Moreover, political changes within national politics have considerably changed the direction of the trends identified by Habermas. The rise of the New Right has involved a shift in the rationality systems of certain national administrations, which has involved a 'rolling back' of the welfare state and a re-marketisation or privatisation of once public sector domains. Furthermore, this decentralisation has been matched by a new ethos of decentralisation within organisational and management philosophies (Lash and Urry 1988).

At the level of concrete description, these changes obviously date some of the substantive content of Habermas's ideas. His general model can be preserved, however, if we allow for the existence of new economic and political agencies, for the integration of national systems into international systems and for the potential crisis possibilities which they bring with them (e.g. the potential for crisis provoked by perceived/actual loss of sovereignty). Indeed, whilst globalisation brings a host of new issues with it, it nevertheless represents a further advance of the mediation of social relations by power and money. There is now more money, more administration and less room for talk. Moreover, some of the changes can be accounted for partly in the terms of Habermas's dynamic model. The rise of Thatcherism in Britain, for example, can be identified as a response to the (rationality) crisis of Keynsian welfarism at the end of the 1970s and the legitimation (even motivation) crises which this brought with it. Thatcherism is, in many respects, a response to some of the sorts of problems that Habermas identifies. On the whole, then, I would contend that recent social changes, whilst they shake up some of Habermas's categories, do not undermine the potential of his perspective to provide a concrete description of actual social systems.

At the more abstract level, he allows us to make significant advances with regard to the theoretical position that we are developing. His account of the tripartite structure of the lifeworld and of its reproduction through communicative action advances our understanding of the lifeworld quite considerably, as does the account of the validity claims raised in communicative action and the consequent claim concerning the contestable nature of symbolic reproduction. We still need Schutz here, I would contend, to account for the different time/space structuration that communicative praxes can assume. This is noticeably absent from Habermas's account and constitutes a limitation of his work. Nevertheless his innovations are very important.

Equally as important is the introduction of an account of material reproduction and of social systems. That Habermas is able to introduce these notions in a cogent manner and still remain faithful to an intersubjectivist position is one of his most valuable contributions to social theory and certainly to intersubjectivist social theory. It is also historically important in the light of recent post-Marxist thinking. As Harland (1987) has noted, the collapse of Marxism has given rise to a range of social theories which all but ignore the role of state and economy in social life – which is a considerable shortcoming. Habermas restores an economic and political angle to social theorising, without sacrificing the possibility of detailed and sophisticated lifeworld analysis.

There are problems with Habermas's account, however. Some of these have been introduced in the course of this chapter but others must be dealt with here.

The first problem concerns Habermas's tendency to equate intersubjectivity with linguistic communication, in a narrowly cognitivist sense, and to ignore the embodiment of intersubjectivity. Habermas says nothing about human embodiment, emotion, perception or imagination. He even suggests that we must avoid consideration of perception because that returns us to a philosophy of consciousness. This neglect is problematic on three grounds.

In the first instance it appears that Habermas is only able to sustain his particular vision of human relations by excluding a large sector of human experience from consideration. This suggests, in turn, that his theory is vulnerable to the extent that this sector can be invoked in argument. This vulnerability, as it happens, is more apparent than real. My analysis of embodiment, perception, etc., in Chapters 2 and 3 suggested that they do not tear the intersubjective fabric, but are woven into it. Habermas is therefore saved. Nevertheless he is only saved by going beyond his own narrow system, to consider the wider perspective which we considered earlier in this book. Indeed, there are conceptions of perception, emotion, etc., which are quite opposed to his intersubjective view of human beings and he would therefore be advised to subscribe to the view that we have developed.

Secondly, Habermas's failure to theorise the body is problematic because of the pivotal role which the human body plays (albeit implicitly) in his system. The body is pivotal for Habermas because it lies at the centre of material reproduction. Material reproduction is primarily the reproduction of healthy human bodies and it lies at the heart of the account of social systems. A more adequate account of human embodiment, therefore, would amount to a more adequate account of material reproduction. It is not just material reproduction which is of concern here, however. If we follow the Merleau-Pontyian route outlined in Chapter 2, then the human body is equally the agent of symbolisation and language; that is, of communicative praxis. In this sense both material and symbolic reproduction find their locus in the communicative body, and so too therefore do system and lifeworld (Crossley 1995c).

Finally, Habermas's narrowly linguistic account is problematic because it doesn't provide a convincing description of intersubjectivity. Our experience of being-with-others simply is an embodied experience; an experience of gazes which overlap, of feelings and shared fears and fantasies. This needs to be captured in a theory of intersubjectivity.

This doesn't negate the positive aspects of Habermas's theory of communicative action. It does suggest, however, that we need to blend Habermas's account with the account that we have already developed. There is no problem with such synthesis because Habermas and the writers whom I discussed in earlier chapters are working within (broadly) the same paradigm with certain of the same goals (cf. also Crossley 1995c).

A further problem with Habermas concerns his understanding of behaviour in formal organisations, particularly his tendency to suggest that behaviour in formal organisations is systemically (rather than socially) integrated. This is said to lead to a portrayal of the social agent as a 'cultural dope'. McCarthy (1991) is the key advocate of this point. There is a difference, McCarthy concedes, between behaviour in organisations and that outside of them, and this is partly due to the lack of autonomy and creative expression in formal organisations. Nevertheless, key studies of organisations suggest that communicative negotiation is far more important to them than one might expect. Indeed they are very much constituted through communicative action and are therefore socially integrated. Consequently, McCarthy suggests, organisations must involve an overlap of social and system integration. This point rejoins the early criticism, attributed to Joas and Giddens, that social spheres cannot be neatly divided between those involving instrumental action and those involving communicative action.

My view of this criticism is mixed. On the one hand, as a view of the ethnography of bureaucracies and formal organisations it would seem correct. Anybody working in a formal institution can recognise the pull between system imperatives (money- and power-driven requirements on action) and communicative negotiation. Moreover, to return to my earlier point, one can recognise the extent to which such institutions have an affective structure. Indeed, insofar as work is a central source of male (in particular) identity, one might argue that work organisations are central sites for the communicative reproduction of symbolic identities (Fraser 1989). Nevertheless, it is not clear that what Habermas is necessarily interested in is this 'internal' perspective. What he is more concerned about is that the output (and external input) of such organisations, in the final instance, is either economic or political, that they trade in money and power and that they respond to economic and political conditions.

A more convincing criticism, in my view, is the other side of this one; namely, that supposed lifeworld relations are and always have been regulated through micro-economies of money and power. Nancy Fraser (1989) provides a powerful formulation of this point. Habermas artificially consigns material reproduction to the sphere of paid work, she argues, and he thus ignores the unpaid domestic and mothering work of women, work which is central to the material reproduction of the species. Furthermore, as numerous analyses show, control is often achieved in both families and the public sphere by means of power, violence and money, as much as by means of communicative action. This isn't colonisation of the lifeworld, Fraser argues. It is a form of control which predates the system and which is constituted squarely within the lifeworld. Moreover, insofar as it extends to control over opportunities in the labour market and the means of political expression, it has major structure-forming effects. The consequence of this, for Fraser, is that we need a much more 'multidirectional' conception of system–lifeworld relations. Furthermore it suggests that the action of some of the groups we refer to as 'New Social Movements' may not be fully captured by Habermas's account. Whilst feminism may be resisting a colonisation of the lifeworld, for example, it is equally resisting inequalities within the lifeworld itself.

This point is very important and links in to the questions of racism and gender inequality that I have touched upon at several places so far in the book. Space will not permit me to do justice to them here but it is clear that their importance should not be underestimated in relation to the question of intersubjectivity. What can be studied more closely in this book, however, is the issue of micro-powers within the lifeworld and of the multidirectional relations which Fraser identifies between system and lifeworld. That will be the topic for the next chapter.

6

Intersubjectivity and Power

Habermas introduces the concept of power squarely into our debate. Power is, for him, a means of system integration which short-circuits the (more democratic) process of communicative action and the social integration achieved by means of this. As such it is an integral constituent of social relations in modern complex societies. Furthermore, he argues that the lifeworld is undergoing a process of colonisation, whereby once consensually governed areas of life are increasingly governed by strategic (rather than communicative) actions and are thus increasingly subjected to money- and power-based directives and imperatives. The grip of power is extending, or rather over-extending, through the social formation. This is an important theoretical step which some intersubjectivists, particularly Schutz, fail to take, and which others, such as Mead and Merleau-Ponty, fail to treat systematically. There are problems with Habermas's approach to the power question, however.

In this chapter I identify these problems and consider how they can be rectified. This involves a consideration of the definition of power and the work of some key thinkers in this area, most notably Foucault. I will not be introducing this new work uncritically and without caution, however. I will be drawing upon some of the criticisms of Foucault that I have developed in previous work and I will be expanding on my previous attempts to reconstruct Foucault's ideas on power in a more intersubjectivist fashion (Crossley 1993, 1994, 1996). I find many aspects of Foucault's work problematic but, in particular, I object to the view (at least associated with Foucault) that subjectivity and intersubjectivity are effects of power. This is, as I have argued (ibid.), an unsustainable notion. Indeed, power in Foucault's sense can be shown to be precisely the effect of a particular configuration of intersubjective relations and practices (ibid.). My view is that power is parasitic upon intersubjectivity, that it needs intersubjectivity and draws upon intersubjectivity to create its effects. This is not to say that all intersubjective relations are relations of power. But it is to say that power relations are always intersubjective. This latter point is the thesis that I particularly focus upon and aim to establish in this chapter. I argue that a perspective which takes power seriously must necessarily take intersubjectivity seriously, and vice versa. I arrive at this argument by way of a discussion of Foucault and Habermas, beginning with the latter.

Habermas and the State

Habermas's account of power, at least in *The Theory of Communicative Action*, is centred upon the state. He argues that power is granted to the state by its citizens, through the election process, and that this power then flows back into the polity in the form of political decisions, legislation, policy, etc., and through welfare and policing functions. The limit of this power for Habermas, as we have seen, is determined by the need for legitimacy. The administration has power only insofar as citizens exercise their power to support it.

Lest this sound too uncritical, it is important to reiterate a number of points from the previous chapter. Firstly, Habermas understands this process to be situated in (unequal) capitalist class relations, where it functions as a means of dissipating the conflict that could stem from those relations. Secondly, he is concerned about the over-extension of the administration into areas of social life which could be regulated through communicative action and agreement. Thirdly, he is particularly concerned that the public sphere of the lifeworld, which is where questions of politics and policy are publicly debated and decided (in part), is shrinking and being made ever less effective. The mass media and new communications technologies do potentiate the existence of an effective public sphere, he argues, but this potential is not actualised in many cases (Stevenson 1995). Information flow and open debate are considerably limited. In effect, then, Habermas argues that citizens are being doubly disempowered: firstly, through a colonisation of social spheres which were once communicatively negotiated, and, secondly, through a shrinking in the place afforded them in political debate and decision-making.

This view is an important one which is both empirically and theoretically cogent. Moreover, it is a view which many perspectives in social theory, including that of Foucault, are incapable of producing because they lack both the conceptual tools and the theoretical breadth. It is only from the point of view of a wide-ranging systems analysis, such as that of Habermas, that one can identify problems of this sort and understand them in a coherent and cogent fashion. Having said this, there are problems with Habermas's view. Most of these can be drawn out through a comparison of his work with that of Foucault, but there are some more general points which need to be considered.

The first problem is that Habermas appears to subscribe to the 'capacity–outcome' model of power, which has been strongly criticised in contemporary sociology; (Hindess 1982; Weights 1981). What this model entails, and what Habermas's view appears to entail, is that a given agency, in this case the state, is said to have power to the extent that it has the capacity (a presumably relatively fixed capacity) to secure certain definite outcomes, even against the will of other agents. This view has been criticised because, it is argued, concrete social/political outcomes (of the sort associated with 'power') are never the result of the capacities or actions of a single agent but rather of a struggle between agents, a dia-logical engagement in conditions which present definite obstacles (including the action of third agents) to those agents and which must be negotiated (ibid.). Outcomes, in this sense, are contingent and cannot be predicted upon the basis of identifiable capacities of the agents involved – as is shown by the fact that they don't always go the way that we expect them to. Power is irreducible to the agent. The agent does not 'have' power. Moreover, the resources which any agent may draw upon in any concrete struggle always have a value relative to a particular social arena (an 'arena of struggle', as Weights and Hindess call it) and to certain functions in that arena, such that they may be regarded as properties of the field and the location occupied by the agent in it, rather than of the agent itself; for example, a lecturer may be in a position to demand an essay from a student but this is about the only thing that they can demand, and even then they can only demand it insofar as they remain lecturers and their students remain students.

This critique is of considerable relevance in relation to the nation states which form the centre-piece of Habermas's account of power. As I noted in the previous chapter, the emergence of international political and economic agencies, who are able to act within and between national boundaries, has transformed the role of the nation state. It is no longer a sovereign power. It is a player amongst players (albeit an important one), in a political arena which is beyond its own full control. It cannot guarantee the effectiveness of its own actions within its own territory (or, for that matter, the rather different arena of international relations) because that effectiveness is dependent upon the action of these international agencies. If, for example, a multinational firm transfers its investments out of the national boundary, then economic policies are unforeseeably jeopardised. Moreover, in this international sphere there is no designated sovereign power. To a large extent, I suggest, Habermas realises this. But he still tends, in his more abstract theoretical moments, to lapse into capacity–outcome formulations of power, which reduce it to the capacities of the state.

Having made this criticism it is important to add that it cannot be allowed to completely undermine the case that Habermas is making. There is a vast administrative stratum in contemporary societies which has assumed responsibility for many of the functional requirements of society and which is central to the process of systemic integration for that reason. Habermas is completely right in this respect. Moreover, and most crucially, the state acts towards its citizens in a strategic rather than a communicative manner. It imposes directives upon its citizens and is not oriented towards linguistic consensus and mutual understanding in its interactions with them. Its actions are power-based. This is demonstrated by the fact that it implements laws and policies in a routine manner on a day-to-day basis and fully expects and demands compliance. The reason that the state is able to do this, from a Habermasian point of view, is that the arenas of struggle which potentially bind the state and its citizens have been neutralised in a compromise formation, whereby the state is entitled to act for the population as long as they continue to legitimate it at the ballot box. There are exceptions to this, such as is demonstrated by the history of the poll tax in Great Britain, where decisions of state were directly challenged and defeated; and there is always the possibility of such struggles or indeed the possibility that citizens might overturn a decision of the state by appeal to one of the new international agencies, such as the European Courts; but the compromise formation is the usual case. In this sense, then, the critique of the capacity–outcome model is limited in its relevancy to Habermas's theory. It is overridden in most cases by the compromise formation of democratic politics. Moreover, this same process occurs in microcosm in most areas of life. Relatively fixed hierarchies do exist in many of our institutions. Orders are given and they are obeyed precisely because they are orders. The possibility of mutual consensus is short-circuited by means of strategic, power-based action.

A further objection to Habermas, similar to the first, is that he tends not to consider the internal conflicts of government itself and its own shifting constitution. Government is not the unified agency which he would sometimes seem to suggest that it is. It is composed of a range of different agencies, practices, interests and internal struggles, which are mobilised in different configurations in relation to different issues. Moreover, it is intersected by different lobby groups and external loyalties. Indeed, even individual parties and cabinets (perhaps even individuals) are divided in this way, such that their agency itself is always a result of the containment or resolution of conflict. These internal processes are important because they mediate the authority granted to the state by the voters. They establish political agendas and determine both how those agendas are framed and how the issues raised by them are resolved. There is not a simple and unproblematic transfer of the power of voters into the power of the state. Again, this objection does not negate Habermas's view. In the final instance, decisions and actions come out of the administrative system and are enacted as he says they are. Nevertheless, his view could be more sensitive to these issues.

A final criticism that should be considered is that Habermas tends not to comment upon the 'legitimate violence' exercised by the state and its agencies; for example, the penal and psychiatric/psychological services which routinely remove certain (non-conforming) citizens from the general population. The operation of such agencies generally reinforces Habermas's conception of power. Police and other agencies refer directly to their legitimacy when dealing with intransigence. Their action is strategic rather than communicative. It is not open to persuasion by a better argument – indeed violence may be used. There is a problem in Habermas's failing to consider this level of social control, however, because it has direct effects upon social integration and the possibilities of communicative action. The action of such agencies effectively removes from the communicative order of the lifeworld those who are not directly controlled, to a socially acceptable degree, by the exigencies of communicative action. Communicative social possibilities are won, in other words, at the expense of controlling those who will not play this game. Thus, the social integration of the communicative order is not as harmonious and voluntaristic as Habermas's analysis might suggest. It is possible only because those who would make it impossible are removed by other means. This leads us into the next section of criticisms of Habermas: the Foucauldian criticisms.

Foucault and Habermas

Foucault's work differs from Habermas's in the sense that it takes the form of concrete historical studies, which are informed by a distinctive philo-sophical framework but which refuse to engage in the standard philo-sophical/theoretical debates and which resist the temptation to construct totalising theories of the social formation. The aim of these studies is to construct provocative historical analyses of specific social practices, particu-larly discursive practices, whose themes disturb or subvert the self-images of those engaged in such practices and those who support them. Often this involves using history to make philosophical points or rather points about philosophical issues such as reason and human subjectivity. And, in many of his studies, this tended to involve a consideration of the considerable role of power in the organisation of human subjectivity, of discourses and of arenas of social life.

Viewed negatively, the dual concern with philosophy and history could be said to have resulted in work which scores poorly on both registers. Foucault has been criticised as a poor philosopher, because he tends not to present cogent and logical arguments for his views (Dews 1987; Fraser 1989), and a bad historian, because he is sometimes quite inaccurate and does not present his work in the usual historian's way (Merquior 1985). Viewed more positively, however, Foucault's work has captured the imagination of many writers, sparking off philosophical, sociological and historical projects and illuminating the politics and power relations embedded in everyday life. He has provided a different way of looking at the world which has proved both enticing and useful in the problems it has posed and the questions it has asked. It is in this vein that I appropriate him in this chapter.

Before I consider the relation of Foucault and Habermas's respective views of power, a brief note must be made concerning their different modes of working. That Foucault does not engage in grand social theorising of the Habermasian sort and that he may even have opposed such a way of working does not, in my view, prevent us from incorporating the results of his historical and (non-grand) theoretical work into such a work. There is no compelling reason given by Foucault why we shouldn't theorise in this way and there is no good reason why the insights of his (genealogical) histories cannot be reframed. I will proceed, then, on the assumption that we can do this, and, moreover, on the assumption that there is much to be gained by a cross-fertilisation of Foucault's ideas with those of Habermas.

Many of Foucault's studies and subsequent studies by his followers (e.g.

Dean 1991; Donzelot 1980; Nettleton 1992; Rose 1985, 1989) paint a similar, though empirically richer and more nuanced picture to Habermas's account of the rationalisation and later colonisation of the lifeworld. Tracing our transition into the modern era, Foucault examines the numerous techniques, practices and ensembles by which human life has been made governable, and he considers how these modes differ from those of earlier eras. He examines the techniques of discipline which manifest in the workings of schools, prisons, factories, etc.; that is, ways of organising and coordinating bodies through time and space, and of making them more docile and efficient. Such micro-technologies of power invest all of our chief institutions, he argues, and they form a web of control which spans the entire social formation, transforming human beings into calculable and manageable subjects. Alongside this microcosmic web of power, moreover, he traces the formation of 'bio-power', a welfare-based macrocosmic 'power over life', which has replaced the 'power over death' (i.e. the power of execution and torture) which was so central to the state of the *ancien régime*. This form of power consists in the numerous administrative techniques for making populations knowable and controllable, and a variety of expert systems and agencies which enable this to function. In his later work, on 'governmentality', moreover, Foucault provides an empirical analysis of the administrative rationality systems which were so central to Habermas's account of the crisis tendencies of welfare capitalism (see Chapter 5). He and his followers trace the emergence of the various understandings of government and its limits, which have informed government practice, and of the mechanisms (such as national insurance and taxation) which have functioned therein.

In addition, in a theoretical move which brings his account close to Habermas's understanding of the role of power in system integration, Foucault stresses both that power is positive in its effects, that it produces 'socially desired' or normal states of affairs rather than simply repressing undesirable tendencies, and that this facilitates the effective functioning of the state and other hegemonic blocs. Power in the modern world is integrative for Foucault, not prohibitive. Indeed, for some writers who have developed Foucault's position (Clegg 1989), disciplinary power, as a routine feature of everyday life, is precisely a requirement for the social organisation and integration of modern complex societies and their institutional forms. It is, to use Habermas's terms, necessary to contemporary system integration. Following on from this, Foucault shares the Habermasian notion that power need not be 'bad'. Like Habermas, he assumes that certain forms of power are 'pathological' (Foucault 1982: 209), but he is equally clear that all societies necessarily involve power (ibid.: 223).

There are several crucial ways, however, in which Foucault has a different understanding to Habermas of what he studies. These differences revolve around Foucault's concern with technologies of power, rather than the agency which it serves, with his tendency to see the state qua socially administrative apparatus as historically dependent upon such technologies, and with his understanding of power as an 'ascending' rather than a 'descending' force; that is, as something constituted in the periphery which sustains the centre, rather than as something which emanates from the centre. Many aspects of the disciplinary web have been colonised by the state and centralised through it, Foucault argues. But the state is very much the dependent term in relation to this web. The modern state is an effect of administrative discipline (and bio-power) as much as it is its nerve centre. For Foucault, therefore, the power derived through democratic legitimacy (which is the centre-piece of Habermas's account) is a secondary power based upon a more fundamental political infrastructure:

> . . . although, in a formal way, the representative regime makes it possible, directly or indirectly, with or without relays, for the will of all to form the authority of sovereignty, the disciplines provide, at the base, a guarantee of the submission of forces and bodies. (1979: 222)

Beneath the formal rights of citizenship and supporting them, he continues, there are 'non-egalitarian and asymmetrical' practices of discipline. Democratic power, such as Habermas describes, is parasitic upon a more fundamental, disciplinary power. Moreover, Foucault argues that such techniques have migrated into wider aspects of culture, such that they now form part of the repertoire of our voluntary actions.

I will deal with the points raised here separately and assess their implications and cogency in relation to both Habermas's work and the intersubjectivist approach more generally.

Discipline and the State

The claim that the modern democratic state is subtended by and dependent upon relations of discipline is, at one level, only a reiteration of Habermas's claim that the rise of the modern administration and systemic mechanisms of societal integration was dependent upon a rationalisation of the lifeworld. Foucault himself avoided referring to a global process of rationalisation but many of his studies can be read in this way. Moreover, the process of rationalisation does entail an understanding of the emergence of disciplinary forms. To this extent, Habermas's position is not challenged by that of Foucault. It is empirically substantiated and confirmed. Furthermore, the further criticism that would appear to follow from Foucault's analysis, that power is not centralised in the state but is constituted through localised practices, is in fact largely negated through Foucault's own (afore-mentioned) conclusions to his study of discipline; namely, that discipline has been largely colonised within apparatuses of the state. This twist in Foucault's argument is effectively similar to the twist that Habermas makes in his own account from the rationalisation of the lifeworld, which gives rise to the modern state, to the colonisation of the lifeworld by the state. It is certainly consonant with this account. In both cases the possibility of centralised state control and thus of liberal democracy is said to lie in the prior rationalisation of specific arenas of social life and the concomitant introduction of certain control technologies, and it is then argued that the centralised state has appropriated these technologies and established its hegemony over them.

Foucault might be said to be superior to Habermas in relation to this issue, because he gives us a clearer idea of the ways in which attempts are made to achieve control. But this does not raise any serious problems for the Habermasian position. Habermasians may regard these Foucauldian insights as useful additions to their own position. Furthermore, Habermas's perspective has an advantage over that of Foucault in that it thematises and theorises the formal democratic political system that is constituted by way of rationalisation and control processes. Foucault's analysis of the polity stops at the explication of the techniques whereby populations are made governable or where discipline constitutes the conditions for the possibility of democracy. This limits what his perspective is able to say about the organisation and operation of parliamentary politics in either concrete or abstract terms. The 'politics' of which he speaks is not and cannot be the big 'P' politics of mainstream political theory and analysis (Walzer 1986). Habermas, by contrast, provides us with a clear sense of the functioning of the democratic system which the rationalisation/disciplining of social relations gives rise to, and of its shortcomings. As such he allows us to conceive of the manner in which disciplinary mechanisms, having constituted a precondition of democratic government, are then subject to transformation by those same governments. For example, education policy in Britain has had a direct effect upon the use of disciplinary techniques, such as examination. It has both removed exams (11+) and introduced them (national testing). In addition, educational policy has legislated for the types of punishments (what Foucault [1979] calls 'micro-penalties') which can and cannot be used in schools. This is significant because it adds a further dimension to the Foucauldian schema and illustrates the two-way movement between formalised democratic power and disciplinary power. Furthermore, it introduces for us the possibility of a further system crisis. We can see that the administration must balance the need for legitimacy with the need for control. Control effectively creates the basis for democracy and thus legitimacy, but control must itself be legitimated and, in the final instance, the democratic state is the linchpin of legitimation.

If we accept this account, then we must admit of at least two different modalities of power: firstly, that which is appropriate to direct forms of control, such as discipline; secondly, electoral power, the power connected to the vote and to the mandate it bestows upon government. My main concern in this chapter will be with the former, but it is important to bear their interrelationship in mind throughout. With this said, we can return to the next key point of contrast between Foucault and Habermas: the question of technique.

Power Relations, Technique and Intersubjectivity

In contrast to Habermas, whose major concerns regarding power are that it exists, that it must be legitimated and that it is exercised by either the state or the expert agencies who work on its behalf, Foucault is more concerned with the question of *how* power is constituted and exercised. He is concerned with the technique of power. Moreover, the implication of his work is that this question is more primordial than the Habermasian type of questions, particularly if Habermasian approaches tacitly reify power as, for example, a fixed capacity of a social agent. To ask how power is constituted is, for Foucault, a way of moving beyond the naïve view that power is a capacity or possession of a given social agent.

I have already partly discussed this objection to 'capacity–outcome' models in relation to Habermas above. Furthermore, the distinction which I established above, between disciplinary and electoral power, bolsters this defence by suggesting that there may be two forms of power and two ways, therefore, of conceptualising and analysing it. I now add to this defence that Habermas's concept of 'strategic action' runs counter to a reified account. It points towards an understanding of the constitution of power relations within given social arenas. Strategic action is that mode of action whose efficacy Habermas associates with power (as well as the exchange of money). It is the means of the realisation of power; the manner in which power is exercised. In this sense he at least recognises the 'how?' of power and postulates a form of action to correspond with that 'how?' Notwithstanding this, however, Habermas has relatively little to say about strategic action or its power-based efficacy, and to this extent his account would benefit from an engagement with Foucault's analysis of the 'how?' question.

In his early studies of power, such as *Discipline and Punish* (1979), Foucault answers the 'how?' question of power empirically, with reference to the emergence of specific configurations of technologies of social control which begin to appear in the practical discourses (e.g. architectural blueprints, policy documents, training, pedagogic and management manuals, etc.) of late eighteenth-, nineteenth- and early twentieth-century European society. These documents reveal a particular rationale of disciplinary control, he maintains, and they reveal a particular logic of power.

In his later work, however, Foucault's answer to the 'how?' question of power assumes more the form of a definition of power or a methodology of power analysis. Effectively, he asks the question prompted by his earlier work: what constitutes a form of social organisation as a technology of power? This is an important question, not least because of the tendency afforded by some of Foucault's work to see everything as either a form of power or an effect of power, a tendency which sees power everywhere and therefore nowhere.

The first important step in Foucault's definition is to suggest that power is a feature of interhuman relations:

. . . let us not deceive ourselves; if we speak of the structures or the mechanisms of power, it is only insofar as we suppose that certain persons exercise power over others. The term 'power' designates a relationship between partners. (1982: 217)

Furthermore, he adds, power is 'deeply rooted' in 'systems of social networks'. Obvious though it may seem, this is an important step in the development of Foucault's thinking. Earlier work by him had seemed, on occasion, to take the unwarranted step of portraying power as a force external to human relations, which somehow acts upon those relations. This sets the record straight. Power does not exist independently of human relations. It emerges within them. This claim is important, from our viewpoint, because it identifies power with a relationship. Foucault points, in other words, towards intersubjectivity and an intersubjective understanding of power. Power is viewed as existing 'between' people, in an interworld – though Foucault does not have the theoretical tools to fully conceptualise a between or interworld and wouldn't use such terms as 'intersubjectivity'.

This intersubjectivist element is further developed when Foucault argues that there are two elements necessary to a power relation:

[that] the 'other' (the one over whom power is exercised) be thoroughly recognised to the end as a person who acts; and that, faced with a relationship of power, a whole field of responses, reactions, results and possible interventions may open up. (1982: 220)

These may sound more like the requirements for a friendship than a power relationship and it is of course necessary that more criteria are added to our definition, such that we can distinguish the two. What Foucault is doing in this quote, however, is differentiating relations of power from those of violence and physical determinism. Power does not prevent people from acting, he is arguing – though of course one may be prevented from acting. Neither does it act upon people as a physical force or cause. Rather it 'addresses' them as agents of action and acts upon their action, so as to influence it. Moreover, it is central to this contrast that it is actions that are acted upon or potential actions and not the person him- or herself. Violence is an action upon a person (qua object). Power manifests as inter-action:

. . . it is always a way of acting upon an acting subject or acting subjects by virtue of their acting or being capable of action. A set of actions upon other actions. (1982: 221)

This involves no fixed manner of acting: 'it incites, it induces, it seduces, it makes easier or more difficult' (ibid.). What is important is that actions are acted upon as a means of controlling them and that those whose actions are acted upon are always addressed and sustained as agents of action.

This does not mean that violence and power cannot coexist in the same sphere, perhaps even working together. Indeed, as Parsons (1967) has shown, uses of violence can be meaningful communications which effectively act upon the future actions of agents; for example, the slap which communicates disapproval and warns of 'more to come' if intransigent behaviour continues. The point is, however, that power and violence are different forms of social action which need not coincide. Violence will only coincide with power when it is used in a way which acts upon action. This applies equally to another category of action: communication. Though he does not have a theory of either speech or action, Foucault recognises that power is often constituted in communicative situations by way of speech acts. He is clear, however, that we must distinguish the communicative elements of actions and situations, by which he understands the transmission of information, from the power element. Power and communication, on this account, are different elements of action which may or may not coexist in specific actions, such that communication may be a vehicle for relations of power but not necessarily and not always.

An inference which we might draw from this point, which will be developed in more detail later, is that Foucault's theory of power is a 'use theory' of power. That is to say, no action in and of itself constitutes power for Foucault, rather it is the use of particular forms of action which must be considered. In particular, to reiterate, he is concerned whether actions are used as a means of acting upon the actions of others so as to induce particular actions from those others.

This line of inquiry is extremely suggestive to an intersubjectivist perspective. The notion of acting upon action and potential action recalls some of the ideas that I discussed in Chapter 2; for example, Mead's understanding of the conversation of gestures, Schutz's understanding of the fusion of time horizons and acting together, and the irreducibility of conversation as discussed by Merleau-Ponty and Gadamer. We get an impression that the logic of power relations is an intersubjective, dia-logical logic and that, again, power relations qua relations must constitute a 'between' or 'interworld'. Power doesn't belong to a person. It forms at the intersection of actions, as a consequence of the irreducible structure that forms between those actions and the strategic possibilities which this effects. Moreover, given the distinction which Foucault wants to draw between power relations and relations of violence and physical determinism, it becomes clear that power is, for him, constituted through an interworld of thought and meaning; that is, it is effected through the shared significance of actions rather than by means of their physical/causal properties. The force of power is an intersubjective force based in meaning.

Notwithstanding this, however, at this stage Foucault has said too little to differentiate his understanding of power from, for example, that of conversation. Asking a question, we might say, is a way of acting upon another's action so as to affect them in some way, but it is hardly a paradigm case of what we would ordinarily regard as a relation of power (even if questioning may form part of a power situation – e.g. in interrogation situations). So what makes an action which acts upon action a case of power?

Before we answer this question it should be pointed out that Foucault is not necessarily referring to individuated actions when he refers to power; thus the objection that I just raised, concerning questions and answers, is slightly bogus. When referring to power, Foucault tends to refer to ensembles of actions, 'a total structure of actions', which implies a reference to specific contexts of action. Or again, as in his major studies of power, he tends to refer to the historical emergence of specific though broader patterns of action, such as procedures of timetabling, confessional techniques, etc., rather than any concrete action taken out of context and in isolation. The implication of this is that no individual action, in isolation, can be taken to exemplify 'power'. All actions must be considered in contexts, in relation to the actions with which they are combined (both spatially and temporally), and, more particularly, they must be considered from the point of view of the way in which they are used. This reiterates and develops my earlier point concerning Foucault's 'use theory' of power. Nevertheless, this still doesn't answer the question of why some ensembles of inter-action and some uses of action merit the name 'power', whilst others don't.

One of the ways in which Foucault begins to answer this question is by reference to the concepts 'conduct' and 'government'. Conduct has a double meaning, he notes, and both aspects are integral to power. Power is conduct, in the sense that it is behaviour or action, but it equally conducts. It leads or governs other actions. Or again, it structures the possible field of action of others. There is an implicit recognition of asymmetry here. One agent leads another but is not mutually led by the other. Moreover, Foucault adds, although this may involve consensus, power relations are not, in essence, consensual. This latter claim may have a number of implications but what is of particular interest here is the way in which this fits with Habermas's work. Power, Foucault is saying, is based in a situation which is not oriented towards mutual understanding and agreement (consensus), nor can it be meaningfully said to be linked to such consensus, that is, a mutually agreed coordination of action. It is not, in other words, an ideal speech situation. It is a different type of situation, oriented in a different way, though it is probably still a speech situation. This notion is important because it shows us where Foucault and Habermas overlap and mutually reinforce one another. Habermas provides us with an indication of the type of action (communicative action) that is not power, whilst Foucault elaborates upon that which is (and which Habermas refers to as strategic action). Furthermore, and most importantly, they seem to more or less agree in the middle, on the issue of consensus. The presence or absence of consensus is the deciding factor for both. Habermas takes the (argumentative) orientation towards consensus to be central to the ideal speech situation, whilst Foucault takes the absence of such an orientation to be central to power. They are arguing for different sides of the same coin.

It is important to add in here that it is this question of consensus and of the orientation towards consensus that introduces the moral and critical dimension into the power question. It is admitted by both Habermas and Foucault that complex modern societies cannot achieve all that they must to survive on the basis of consensual agreement. Nevertheless, as the notion of the colonisation of the lifeworld suggests, there can be an intrusion of power into areas of life which could be regulated in this way and which might be better for it. An identification of power relations in such cases would be a critique. It would imply a call for communicative action to replace power relations (and strategic action) in that particular domain, and thus for democratisation of the domain.

This takes us much closer to a workable definition of power, but we can sharpen it up further by considering five points which Foucault suggests that an analysis of power should consider. This will give us a clearer idea of how he feels that power manifests and what he considers it to involve. And it will allow us to consider the intersubjectivity of power in more detail.

The first aspect of power relations that Foucault identifies is the '*system of differentiations* which permits one to act upon the actions of others' (1982: 223, original emphasis). Such systems, he argues, may be laws, traditions regarding status, economic differences, differences in competence, etc. Thus, we might say, only the police officer has the power of arrest, the doctor the power of diagnosis, etc. This is interesting from our point of view, since such systems are necessarily intersubjective in nature. They depend upon a mutual, if perhaps only implicit, recognition of different rights of action. They are constituted through 'agreement in forms of life' and exist and have a force precisely to the extent that they are mutually sustained in social encounters. It suggests that power is rooted in the horizons of our lifeworld, in the structuration of our language games.

A good example of this is provided in the work of feminist writers who have suggested that 'speaker positions' are gendered and that the position of women is subordinated. Women, it is argued, are not allowed to do the same things with their words as men are, and the meaning of what they say is sometimes dependent upon the fact that they are a woman saying it. They do not, of course, consent to this, but it is a fact determined in the between and is not in the individual hands of anybody in particular.

This point is more generally developed in relation to speech situations by Pierre Bourdieu (1979, 1992, 1993). In a critical engagement with speech act theory, which was discussed in Chapter 2, Bourdieu discusses the social and institutional mediation of the effectiveness of speech acts. Whether words successfully perform acts, he notes, depends upon the way in which they are received and responded to by others, and this, in turn, can depend upon who is speaking, in what context and in what way (e.g. both their accent and their style). If speech does not conform to the demands of its market, then it will simply not be effective. Either it will not be understood or it will not work. One clear example of this, from Bourdieu's work, concerns the naming of a ship: the words 'I name this ship . . .' are quite sufficient to do the job of naming, he notes, but only if you are the person designated to do that job. Another clear example, which I noted in Chapter 2, would be the dissolving of parliament. This act is constituted by way of a simple linguistic exchange but its necessary participants are rather exclusive.

Having made this point, it should be noted that Foucault actually says very little about such systems of differentiation in his own work (except, perhaps, in relation to the status of some professional groups and the relative statuses of the mad and the sane). In particular he has very little to say about those durable differentiations which cut across many of the social spheres that his particularistic analyses focus upon. There is no account and scarcely any recognition of the class structure in his work, for example, or of gender relations or the relations of different ethnic groups. Perhaps these are not the sorts of differentiations that Foucault has in mind, but if they are not then they should be. To talk of the power of psychiatry as a technique of social control, as Foucault does (1965, 1979, 1987), for example, without discussing the enormous impact of ethnic inequalities on that sphere is seemingly to miss what is most significant about the political operation of that particular social apparatus (Fernando 1988, 1991).

A final observation regarding this point involves the overlapping concerns of Foucault and Habermas with the rise of 'experts' whose expertise serves to authorise them to intervene in and regulate social affairs in a range of different arenas. Foucault is, without doubt, the more empirical of the two writers on this issue. He accounts for the rise of medical, psychiatric, sexological and other such expert systems which, he argues, police public health. Habermas has a very important contribution to make here, however, through his thesis of 'cultural impoverishment'. This notion allows us to overcome an obvious problem in Foucault's work; namely, that it is supposed to be critical but in fact it is not because, as it stands, it (only) describes a state of affairs which many people would regard as both self-evident and politically unproblematic; for example, we all know that doctors enjoy certain epistemological and political privileges over our bodies, but we tend to think that this is a good idea since it will help to alleviate our pain and possibly help us to live longer. The idea of 'cultural impoverishment' allows us to problematise this more deeply by raising questions of accountability, validation, deskilling and disempowerment. We can understand the professional colonisation of particular areas as both a loss to our public skill base and a loss to the range of issues which fall within the arena of public accountability. It may and probably will be, of course, that we still want the doctor. But we at least have a language with which to formulate our concerns, and this could provide the basis for arguing for some changes in practice. It meets trends towards specialisation with a call for democratisation.

Foucault's second point concerns the '*type of objectives* pursued by those who act upon the actions of others' (ibid., original emphasis). This point more or less speaks for itself. It is worth noting, however, that Foucault considers that many of these objectives are not personal but are tied to a specific role that a person occupies in an organisational structure and to the particular function that they serve as such. This ties in to Habermas's understanding of bureaucracies and the systemic mediation of action as discussed in Chapter 5. Functionaries in bureaucracies pursue stipulated objectives whose effects are central to the achievement of system integration.

Thirdly, Foucault identifies the '*means of bringing power relations into being'* (ibid., original emphasis). Amongst the examples cited here are threats of force, economic disparities and relations of surveillance, as well as the incitation, seduction, etc., that was mentioned earlier. This point is of special interest for intersubjectivism because it concerns the logic of the interworld and interaction, or, to talk colloquially, the way in which people go about 'pressing each other's buttons'. How do people incite, seduce, etc.? Certainly, for the moment, we can say that this is based upon mutuality and a set of common understandings about the value, significance and meaning of particular types of events and actions. You can't 'check mate' a person who can't play chess any more than you can effectively 'seduce' an inanimate object. Effects will only flow from one person to another, assuming no violence, by way of shared meanings and understanding. Symbolic actions will only allow one person to control another if the meaning of the symbol is shared by both; that is, if they belong to a common symbolic interworld. Furthermore, it will only be effective if it is effected within a shared system of relevancies and a shared context, within which it is deemed appropriate. Power, in other words, needs a lifeworld.

This is not to say that a shared system of relevancies and a lifeworld will guarantee the effects of power. Nor does it deny Parsons's (1967) observation that symbolic forms of power are often 'guaranteed' by physical force or some similarly more direct sanction in a fashion akin (and similarly indirect) to the manner in which money is guaranteed by gold. The point is, however, that the symbolism of the lifeworld is ordinarily sufficient to secure control.

Two further intersubjectivist points should be added here. Firstly, following Elias (1978b), I contend that human beings are always already involved in networks of interdependency (financial, emotional and practical), and that these networks provide some of the leverage required for power relations. It is because we lean on others, because we depend upon them for being what we are and achieving what we want, that we are open to their influence. If they control the ties that bind us to them, then they have a good chance of controlling us. These ties are our 'buttons', or at least they are the closest thing that we have to buttons. Secondly, integral to this is the desire for the desire of the other that we have discussed at numerous points in this book. We are able to be influenced by others because others matter to us and we are, in a sense, incomplete without them. We can be controlled because we do not want to have our recognition withdrawn, or again because we do not want to be seen in particular ways. This particular tie is very strong as it concerns the constitution of our relationship to our self, our identity.

In this sense we might say that power involves an action upon motivations or value systems, which necessarily channels those motivations in particular ways. Those who have power exercised over them are left with no choice but to act in specific ways if they wish to achieve certain things and to either reach or sustain a particular identity.

It is integral to this discussion of the means by which power is brought into being that power is constituted in a 'between' or 'interval'; that is, that it depends upon the logic of a particular interrelationship, which depends in turn upon the sharing of particular meanings, relevancies, presuppositions and contexts – none of which belong to individual subjects but rather to their interworld. Power is not in the hands of the one who exercises it. It is an effect of the particular structuration of an interworld or between. Indeed, it may even be the case that the power effects of particular actions are unintended, undesired or unknown to the one who exercises them, especially in cases where human relations are structured by organisational hierarchies and roles or by other relatively stable mediating factors. This is illustrated in Foucault's discussion of the Panopticon, an eighteenth-century prison design which involves a central watchtower that cannot be seen into from the outside but from which every part of every cell can be seen. Power in this prison is intersubjectively organised, as I have argued elsewhere (Crossley 1993, 1994). It derives from the fact that the prisoner feels constantly watched by the watchtower occupant and that they are situated as 'an object of information, never a subject in communication' (Foucault 1979: 200). This effect is not dependent upon the intentions or motives of the watchtower occupant, however, and they may even be, oblivious to it. Their occupation of the watchtower alone is what sets in motion the prisoner's 'anxious awareness of being observed' (ibid.) and this is all that is required. Clearly this is not the only such case, however. Any police officer, for example, by virtue of their uniform and its symbolism alone, will create a similar effect. The same is also true in a whole range of cases.

The fourth point that Foucault highlights for power analysis is '*forms of institutionalisation*'. Institutionalisation, in this sense, has a double meaning. It refers to the way in which certain practices become settled and stabilised; that is, in which they become institutions. But it also concerns that way in which they settle in particular forms of social organisations, such as the family and the workplace (which we also refer to as 'institutions'), accommodating and also coming to rely upon specific features of such institutions. This is best illustrated in *Discipline and Punish*, where Foucault traces the emergence of various interlocking disciplinary practices in a range of different institutional settings. Different institutions, he notes, instituted the same practices in different ways.

The general point being made here is that power takes root, it becomes instituted, in institutions. It is paramount to Foucault, however, that this institutionalisation should not mislead us into believing that power can be reduced to the institution (qua organisation) as an effect of it (Crossley 1994). For him, power is the effect of practices (which I take to be intersubjective practices) which may transcend individual institutions. Furthermore, the institution is as much an effect of power as power is an effect of the institution, according to this view. This point is most clearly captured in Clegg's (1989) observation that many of the complex organisational forms which characterise modern societies would simply not be possible without the historically contingent, systematised disciplinary techniques described by Foucault. These techniques, Clegg notes, provide the basis for integration in such organisations (systemic integration) and, as such, provide for their very existence.

Foucault's final point concerns '*the degrees of rationalisation*' manifest in any particular form of power. What he appears to mean by this is that we should study the way in which and the extent to which relations and practices of power accommodate to their circumstances (which will include the resistance of others) and the way in which they are organised. There is a call, in other words, to study the social organisation and adaptability of forms of power.

An additional point, not mentioned in this list but mentioned elsewhere in Foucault's work, is that power is always coupled with resistance. Power, he argues, can always only be exercised over those who are free (not least because it wouldn't be power if its subjects weren't free; it would be physical determinism), but this freedom equally ensures a constant and consistent intransigence in the power relation, an 'agonism', as he calls it. This is an interesting point, in relation to Habermas. On the one hand, it rejoins Habermas's claim that the colonisation of the lifeworld is and has been resisted. Moreover, Foucault refers to some of the same resistance movements that Habermas refers to; for example, the women's movement, struggles against administration, etc. Notwithstanding this, however, Foucault's work also suggests a more immediate sense of resistance than is found in Habermas, such that his portrayal of the administrative/administered world tends less towards a model of cultural dopery.

The Ubiquity of Power

The part-way conclusions to this chapter are twofold. Firstly, power is an irreducibly intersubjective phenomenon. Secondly, the work of Foucault and Habermas can be made quite complementary. In particular, Foucault can help us to develop the Habermasian notion of 'strategic action' through his conception of power, whilst Habermas can bring to Foucault a conception of communicative action which substantiates the notion of consensus in action which Foucault uses as a foil to his understanding of power. This is useful to Foucault because his approach needs a clearer conception of what is not power for both analytical and political reasons; that is, to sustain itself as a reasonable definition of power and to allow it to develop a more positive ethical element in its critique of power.

There is a further aspect of Foucault's work, however, which at least poses an obstacle to Habermas's approach – and which rejoins Fraser's critique of Habermas (discussed in Chapter 5). The crux of this problem revolves around the fact that Habermas seemingly identifies power with the operation of the state and suggests that it is only latterly imposed upon the lifeworld, whereas, for Foucault, power is already embedded in the lifeworld. I have already suggested that, to some extent, this problem is partly offset because Foucault recognises that the state has colonised many

of the apparatuses of power, whilst Habermas identifies the modern state as
an outcome of the process of rationalisation. This does not completely solve
the problem, however, because Foucault suggests that techniques of power
don't just get absorbed into the state mechanism but also seep into the
everyday practices of the lifeworld. In *The History of Sexuality* (1981), for
example, he describes how the concern for sexuality in the Victorian period
restructured a range of both social and personal relations, constituting them
as relays of power or 'spirals of power and pleasure'. Parents and teachers
were encouraged to police the sexuality of their children, for example, and
men were encouraged to police the sexuality of their wives. Everybody was
to observe and police the behaviour of everybody else and the lifeworld was
alive with games of hide and seek and 'capture and seduction'. Moreover,
the ultimate effect of this, for Foucault, is that people assume a self-policing
function. The operation of power invests their very personality structure:

> There is no need for arms, physical violence, material constraints. Just a gaze. An
> inspecting gaze which each individual under its weight will end interiorising to the
> point that he is his own overseer, each individual thus exercising this surveillance
> over, and against himself. (Foucault 1980: 155)

These ideas pose no problem to intersubjectivism. The 'relays' of power that
Foucault identifies passing through the lifeworld and the 'spirals of power
and pleasure' that he suggests issue from the 'games' of 'capture and
seduction' all fit well with the intersubjectivist position (Crossley 1994).
Moreover, the idea of self-policing and its derivation from policing by others
fits identically with Mead's idea of the reflexive relation of 'I' and 'me' and its
role in securing social control (see Chapter 3). For Mead and Foucault alike,
social and self-control are achieved at once in modern societies, through the
self-assumption of the 'attitude' of external authority figures. There is,
however, a difficulty in relation to Habermas (and thus to the position that
we have developed) in the sense that this seems to suggest that the lifeworld
is constructed not so much through relations of communicative action as
through relations of power. Or again, that distortions in communicative
relations in the lifeworld are not reducible to the systemic pressures of an
economically and politically dominated society – as the thesis of the
colonisation of the lifeworld might seem to suggest.

   We can only resolve this problem satisfactorily by compromise. The first
point in this compromise is the claim that Foucault is right to identify
relations of power in the lifeworld. I suggest that Habermas too would
recognise this. He tends, when talking about state power, to be clear that it is
state power in particular that he is talking about, thus leaving open the
question of other forms of power. Whether or not he recognises it, however,
there are relations of power in the lifeworld, such as those in the family, and
these cannot be ignored. Furthermore, these relations function within the
process of the reproduction of the lifeworld. In structuring the relations of
parents to children, for example, they structure the socialisation function.

   The second point of compromise, however, is that not all relations are
(always) relations of power. There is nothing in Foucault's work to suggest

that there cannot be power-free relations or relations of communicative action (where the power of argument is the only power involved). Indeed, his efforts to demarcate and define power precisely indicate that there are relations which are other than power relations. Importantly, moreover, these relations too may be involved in the reproduction of social orders. People can argue freely and act upon this basis. They have democratic as well as power-based ways of resolving their disagreements and each will be appropriate to different circumstances – which is not to say that they will be used appropriately. Furthermore, it may be that the powers which function within the lifeworld are challenged by communicative action in both the public and private spheres and that through this pressures can be effected within the political system which act in turn upon the lifeworld as a means of alleviating such situations. Recent debates on child abuse and domestic violence, as well as more issues of power in the home, provide a very good example of this. They are lifeworld issues which have been pulled into the public sphere and into the political system, where they have been opened up in a communicative situation, resulting in at least some changes.

Integral to this second point is some criticism of the Foucauldian notion that we voluntarily subject ourselves to certain forms of power. There is something quite suggestive about this idea. We get a sense of a subject who is divided (through time) into an I and a me and who actively undertakes to control her- or himself from the point of view of the community. Moreover, as Foucault stresses, those who do not control themselves in this way will be controlled from the outside (by police, psychiatrists, etc.). Having said this, however, as Mead emphasises, the relation of the I and the me is a dialogue in which ideas are exchanged until something is decided. We don't just control ourselves, we debate with ourselves (reasonably). One's relation to oneself, as with one's relations with others (on which the former is based), can be communicative as well as power-based.

Finally, it must be added that relations of power in the lifeworld very often find their support in systemic relations. Power relations in families, for example, which are often understood as relations of power which a father enjoys over both his wife and his children, have traditionally found support in the fact that the father's position has been sustained through law and through his greater access to paid employment and money. This is, of course, part of the objection that Nancy Fraser raises against Habermas. There are, she argues, internal economies within families, whereby men control the money. This point cuts two ways, however. It equally suggests that power in the family is shaped by the mediations that involve it in the process of systemic integration; that is, its relation to the economy and the legal system.

Colonisation?

The implication of these points is that the lifeworld is not and has never been a site of pure communicative action which is corrupted only through state colonisation. The lifeworld too is a site of power relations (as well as communicative action), some of which are not directly joined to the structure of the administration.

A further implication of this could be that the colonisation of the lifeworld by the state may not be so bad and may, in fact, be positive. At least this is so if it entails a replacement of 'unofficial' and irrational forms of power which aren't democratically regulated with official forms that may be open to some sort of democratic accountability. State intervention into family life, for example, may help to topple a political structure which already exists in that unit and may at least be a more empowering system of power, by virtue of the official complaints procedure that it involves. On the other hand, the proper value position for a social critique based upon these notions must surely be for a restoration or construction of the possibility for the self-regulation of at least some social domains by means of communicative action.

Having said this, the identification of forms of power with the lifeworld does not alter the general picture of colonisation that Habermas paints. There can be no doubt, historically, that many areas of the lifeworld have been colonised by relations of state power. Furthermore, it is quite evident that the impact of colonisation has been to introduce inequality and control into the picture.

It is important to emphasise, moreover, that colonisation, for Habermas, entails an extension of market as well as power relations into the lifeworld. This is a highly significant point which sets Habermas aside from many other contemporary social critics and which allows his perspective to account for the enormous differences in social experiences and life opportunities which are determined by the unequal distribution of wealth and income. His theory is still, basically, a theory of capitalist societies (see Chapter 5) and as such it recognises a two-pronged attack upon the lifeworld. The lifeworld is undermined by an overextension of administrative relations, according to this view, but it is equally undermined by a process of commodification, whereby actions and services which were once performed routinely in the lifeworld acquire both a price and a brand name. Moreover, these two prongs are clearly interrelated; that which is on the market is open to administrative control through economic management.

Master and Slave?

As a final point before concluding this chapter I will briefly return to the fable of the struggle for recognition, as outlined in Chapter 1. In this fable two consciousnesses engage in a fight to the death, the aim of each being to achieve self-consciousness. One capitulates and thereby becomes a slave for the other, but this denies both recognition and neither becomes self-conscious. The slave is not recognised because he is a slave. The master is not recognised because the slave is not worthy of recognising him.

Human history is littered with such fights to the death, some of which have resulted in the death that their description alludes to, whilst others, as in the fable, have resulted in slavery or some equivalent form of violent domination or exclusion. The legacy of European colonialism, of the Soviet gulags or of the Nazi concentration camps are all reminders of the systems of violence which have been implicated in the creation of our present. And it continues. Nationalist struggles in the former Yugoslavia and their bloody consequences are only too obvious examples.

In this chapter I have been tracing the path of a rather more subtle, perhaps 'liberal' form of power; one which utilises an intersubjective relationship, sustaining the other as a subject of action rather than attempting to negate them. This form of power works through relations of shared meaning and aims to foster and utilise the other, sustaining their freedom so that it can be put to 'good use'. Rather than negate the social bond of intersubjectivity and the desire for recognition, it uses it. This, I believe, is the common form which power assumes in our societies, with the more violent 'struggles to the death' usually only serving as a back-up for when things go wrong.

This modern form does not involve a perfect mutual recognition, however; this is why we still call it 'power'. It entails a subordination of otherness. Perfect mutual recognition, according to the perspective developed in this book, would involve the ideal speech situation which we have associated with Habermas. It would entail an effort to achieve consensus and mutual understanding by means of argument alone. Such a situation precisely entails that the other is recognised as an independent perspective upon events, equal to one's own. It takes seriously and treats seriously the objections of the interlocutor, where power aims at most to channel the perspective of the other for its own purposes. Power is a distortion of the communicative, mutually recognising relation.

It would not be possible for our modern society to continue in its complex forms without some element of this power structure remaining. If everything had to be decided by open argument, we would get very little done. Sometimes we must just allow ourselves to be subsumed by our roles and our place in hierarchies for purposes of getting on with life. But some areas could be opened, and we should address at least some of the 'systems of differentiation' attached to relations of power. In particular we should consider those differentiations, such as gender and ethnicity, which are reproduced across different social spheres and which are seemingly attached not to roles but to categories of personhood which we take to be fundamental and which we hold constant. In short, we should aim for a society where the mechanism of power is not overextended, so as to preclude the possibility of self-determination, and we should aim for a power which is both just and accountable.

This point returns us to the Habermasian issues discussed at the start of this chapter, in particular the shrinking of the public sphere. The public sphere is precisely the context for making relations of power accountable and it is precisely the site within the lifeworld/system which should allow for open debate. How far it goes in achieving this and how much needs to be done to reform it cannot be fully addressed in this study, however.

Lifeworld, Legitimation and Control

A number of clear conclusions can be drawn from this chapter. Firstly, the study of power can assume two forms. We can study either parliamentary power, that is, the mandate afforded a political party by a majority of voters, or we can study the technical infrastructure of the forms of power which regulate our lives on a more day-to-day basis. The concern of the present chapter has primarily been with the latter of these, but I have emphasised their interrelatedness. The technical infrastructure of power is what makes the liberal state effective, but aspects of it can be problematised within the parliamentary system and changed therein. In this sense, there is a two-way movement between parliament at the centre and the control practices at the 'ground level' of the social world, and there is a balance which needs to be struck between the need for control and the need for legitimacy. Politicians must attempt to utilise the control systems to create and re-create the sort of society they want, but at the same time they must be careful not to jeopardise their legitimacy in so doing.

In exploring the idea of power I have also argued that it is embedded in intersubjective relations and a lifeworld. Power doesn't work by magic and it certainly doesn't explain anything to invoke it. Power works through the logic of human relations, through shared meanings and interdependencies. It is the product of particular properties of intersubjectivity. Furthermore, it rests in the particular ways in which those properties are used and invoked. This is what I have referred to as the use theory of power. From this, it follows that we might do more to investigate the intersubjective pragmatics of power, as writers such as Bourdieu (1977, 1992) have done. We need to see how, in concrete circumstances, interdependencies and symbols are used and invoked to create effects of power.

A further aspect of this intersubjective theory of power is that subjects are not negated by the operation of power, but, rather, their subjectivity and particularly their desire are utilised as a means of controlling their actions. This stands in marked contrast to the Hegelian schema of master and slave – though of course relations of master and slave do persist in our own and other societies.

A final contention of the chapter has been that, although the state does exercise effective possession over many of the major forms of institutional control, this does not apply to all forms. Consequently we must argue, contra Habermas, that power is produced in the lifeworld irrespective of systemic imperatives. Having said this, however, I have argued both that not all relations in the lifeworld are power relations, that some are constituted through genuine communicative action, and that non-systemic forms of power can be made accountable by way of communicative action. This latter process, I added, may result in social agents using more accountable forms of state power to protect themselves against less accountable and less controllable forms of lifeworld power.

7

Citizens of the Lifeworld

In this final chapter I complete my study of intersubjectivity through a consideration of the concept of citizenship. Much has been written about this concept in recent years, in both academic literature and the popular press. Many different perspectives and controversies have emerged. I do not intend to review all of this literature or even the most central contributions here. Sheer volume would make that impossible and it would detract from the purpose of this book. I intend, rather, to examine the relationship between citizenship and intersubjectivity, to consider how and why citizenship is important from the point of view of intersubjectivism, and vice versa. My argument is that the issues and concepts relating to intersubjectivity add a new depth and dimensionality to the question of citizenship and contribute to our understanding of the value and importance of this notion. Moreover, I contend (from the other side of the equation) that the concept of citizenship allows us to think Politically (with big and small 'Ps') about intersubjectivity. Full citizenship, I contend, is the political embodiment of intersubjective possibilities.

Arguing this case will necessarily involve some repetition of material discussed earlier. This is worthwhile because it affords us the opportunity of seeing this (now) familiar material in a different light and therefore of re-evaluating it. Furthermore, it allows us to reveal some of the writers discussed (particularly Mead) as a hidden tradition in the social theory of citizenship. These writers have much to say about citizenship but they are seldom, if ever, acknowledged in debates on the issue.

The chapter begins with a general discussion of the relevance of questions of intersubjectivity to the debate on citizenship, which is then sharpened up through a discussion of some of the central concepts in that debate. Next I consider the type of intersubjective relationship most appropriate to an understanding of citizenship and I discuss the process of becoming a citizen. The work of Mead is central to this part of the chapter. Finally, shifting my attention to the work of the neo-Hegelian Francis Fukuyama (1989, 1992), I consider the extent to which full citizenship, understood as the political form of intersubjectivity, has been realised in Western societies.

Citizenship, System and Lifeworld

Citizenship may seem an inappropriate topic to consider in a study of intersubjectivity because, prima facie, it is a formal political relationship and status and, as such, it belongs to the systemic level of society, not its intersubjective lifeworld. The question of citizenship, it could be argued, is a social-structural question, concerning the formal system of institutional definition, provision and enforcement of rights and duties, of the courts, parliament and the welfare state. This is how the central figure in contemporary citizenship debates, T.H. Marshall (1992), conceives of it. Moreover, the debates which follow from his work, whilst they are often critical of his conception (Roche 1992a; Stewart 1995; Turner 1990), show little signs of shifting from the systemic level. Even if a more local form of citizenship is advocated, it is often still referred to a tier of government. Furthermore, much of what is discussed under the rubric 'citizenship' concerns matters of national or global proportion, and thus seems too far-reaching and abstract to be related to the more intimate and interpersonal matters that are ordinarily associated with the intersubjectivity problematic.

It would be foolish to try to overturn this definition and understanding of citizenship in any substantive way. If citizenship is to have any meaning, this is surely what it means (more or less). I will not, therefore, be introducing intersubjectivity into the debate on citizenship by way of a paradigmatic revolution. Indeed, it will be part of my own argument that citizenship is integral to the process of 'system integration', as this process is defined in the work of Habermas (1987a), and that we must maintain a societal and systemic focus in our analysis of it. Having said this, however, I do intend to deepen and substantiate the formal, systemic definition of citizenship, and in doing this I intend to reveal that it has an intersubjective core.

Citizenship is a systemic property, insofar as it is a political status and an institutional system (an ensemble of relatively stable social practices) which guarantees the rights and enforces the duties appropriate to that status. Citizenship is also a role, however, and, as Habermas notes, as such it involves a mediation between system and lifeworld. Citizens qua citizens translate political views derived through debate and discussion in the lifeworld, specifically the public sphere of that lifeworld, into the systemic currency of votes. And in doing this they partake in the systemic process of legitimation. Moreover, the citizen role must be maintained within the motivation system of contemporary societies, and this system, as Habermas (1987a, 1988a) recognises, is constituted in and through the lifeworld. In order to perform their role, citizens must have a shared sense of that role, a sense of citizenship. And they must have the know-how required to perform that role competently. 'Citizenship' must be meaningful to them as a group. It must be a constitutive feature of their shared interworld and an identity which each assumes therein. It must be embedded in the texture of taken-for-granted assumptions which comprise the meaning horizon of our everyday life; that is, in the (intersubjectively constituted) lifeworld (Roche 1987; Schutz 1964). Moreover, all of these 'musts' must be achieved, in large part, by way of intersubjective–communicative interactions. They are not guaranteed through the action or mechanism of the system (at least if that system is understood to be exclusively mediatised by way of money and power), but only by way of intersubjective praxes which are grounded in the shared horizons of the lifeworld and which place a moral imperative upon citizenship participation. Citizenship, in this sense, is constituted as a form of social identity, through symbols, identifications and action orientations. It has a social–cultural as well as a political–contractual basis.

Whilst the mainstream social theory of citizenship does not use the concepts 'intersubjectivity', 'lifeworld' or 'the citizen role', it clearly has some recognition of the phenomena to which I am referring here, and of their importance. In the final pages of his classic essay *Citizenship and Social Class*, for example, T.H. Marshall bemoans the difficulties involved in sustaining a sense of citizenship and its duties amongst the population:

> A successful appeal to the duties of citizenship can be made in times of emergency, but the Dunkirk spirit cannot be a permanent feature of any civilisation. (1992: 46)

This difficulty, he states, is the reason why many people think that citizenship loyalties are better anchored at a local rather than a national level. People can identify and feel part of a local community, he argues, but this is difficult at the national level. I will return to this problem later. Suffice it to say for present purposes that Marshall is identifying a motivation problem (though not a crisis) in relation to citizenship and that, in doing this, he is conceding that citizenship has a lifeworld basis.

The case that I am making here is not just an abstract theoretical point. It has an important analogue in practical political life because it concerns participation and the motivation and competence required to participate in political processes. As such, it is of considerable importance to the effective functioning of citizenship in any given society (at a national or international level). We worry that election turn-outs are low, for example, because this seems to indicate a failure of citizenship, in spite of formal institutional provision. And we hesitate at regarding the British as European citizens because of their/our low rates of interest and even lower rates of participation in those processes appropriate to European citizenship; the British are not full European citizens, we say, because they do not assume the role of European citizens and because 'Europe', as a symbol, is somehow not properly connected to 'citizen' in the lifeworld(s) of British society. Indeed, because 'citizen', in the horizon of meanings which compose that lifeworld, involves an element of nationalistic and patriotic identification which is not (yet) reconciled with 'Europe' and is perhaps even antagonistic to it.

Our understanding of this intersubjective anchoring of citizenship can be further advanced through consideration of a number of key concepts which are related both to intersubjectivity and to citizenship. In particular we need to consider '*membership* of a *community*', '*duty*' and the notion of '*recognition*' which is intimately bound to the concept of citizenship qua 'status'. Discussing these notions will allow us to discern further how and where 'citizenship' and 'intersubjectivity' overlap and intertwine.

Some Key Conceptual Links

The notion of membership of a community is fundamental to any definition of citizenship. To be a citizen is to be a member of a political community (Marshall 1992; Roche 1987; Stewart 1995). Furthermore, in recent years a more substantive sense of 'community' has been posited, by both left- and right-wing thinkers, as a central mechanism for the establishment of a sound basis for contemporary citizenship. Community, in this view, mediates between the state and the individual, facilitating the correct balance between the two in citizen relations. A centre-left formulation of this view is advocated by the leader of the British Labour Party, Tony Blair. Citizens don't want an overbearing state which intrudes deeply into their lives, Blair argues, but neither do they want to live alone in a social vacuum. They need a third way between these two alternatives and this third way is community. A community is the proper environment for the nurturance of citizenship and, indeed, for the better side of our nature:

> 'Community' implies a recognition of interdependence but not overweening government power. It accepts that we are better equipped to meet the forces of change and insecurity through working together. It provides a basis for the elements of our character that are cooperative as well as competitive, as part of a more enlightened view of self-interest. (Blair 1995: 18)

That this also implies 'intersubjectivity' and that the arguments on intersubjectivity outlined in this book lend some substance to what is said here should be clear. A community, as we have established (see Chapter 5), is more than a mere population in a given space. To be a community, a population, who need not be geographically close, must share in certain understandings of themselves as a group and of their environment. They must derive a common identity from a shared lifeworld and must have shared interests and investments. Their roles must be interdependent and relationally defined and must be mutually recognised as such, and this must both involve them in and derive from mutual interactions. A community is an irreducible structure of interactions, which is both self-defining and self-regulating – or at least relatively so. Furthermore, 'membership' is logically tied in to this. To be a member is to be involved in the shared understandings of the community, to have an interdependent role within it and to be recognised as such.

In other words, a community is necessarily an interworld, an intersubjective space. And the ontology of community and membership, and thus of citizenship, is necessarily an intersubjective ontology. Citizens are intersubjects.

There is an important question which comes out of this idea concerning the extent to which communities, as such, will coincide with 'the Political community' and thus with 'citizenship'. Communities are more or less self-creating phenomena which, in large pluralistic societies, may always remain sectional in relation to 'the Political community'. So how is such a political community to be constituted? Must it be constituted if we are to talk meaningfully of citizenship? I will reserve judgement on this question temporarily and return to it later. For the moment it must suffice to note that the question is central to our understanding of the potential for motivation problems in relation to citizenship, as discussed above. Citizenship will not be sustained without a clear citizen role and identity, and these in turn will not be sustained without a political community. We might add, furthermore, that the evidence for strong communities of any sort is lacking. It is generally considered by social scientists that lifestyles have tended to be increasingly privatised and familiarised (i.e. centred upon the family) through the course of the post-war period.

The second concept to consider is 'duty'. This concept was, until recently, relatively underused in debates on citizenship. It was secondary to rights. Although people generally recognised that rights and duties are two sides of the same coin, that every right presupposes a duty to respect it, they tended to emphasise the former over the latter. They emphasised the right to financial support, for example, over the duty to pay taxes to provide such support. Tides, however, are changing. As Roche (1990, 1992a) notes, a new discourse of duties has been ushered into political culture, by way both of the New Right and of New Social Movements (particularly feminist and ecological movements). In the case of the latter, this discourse on duties has arisen out of a discourse on rights, but in the former duty has been the flagship of arguments on citizenship. Moreover, in both cases the duties identified extend beyond the realm of big 'P' political duties. They involve duties to the environment, to children, to sexual partners, etc. Citizenship is an active relationship to others (including animals and the environment) in this view and one which involves a sense of responsibility and obligation to those others. It is as much secured through our lifeworld interactions with others, as through a system of formal rights and institutions – though, of course, government too has its duties, and these are provided by way of such rights and institutions.

A clear statement of the role of duty, in this case from the New Left, is again provided in the aforementioned speech by Tony Blair. Duty, for Blair, is intimately bound to community, providing us with a way of building a society which does not 'subsume our individuality' but rather allows it to flourish:

> Duty is the cornerstone of a decent society. It recognises more than self. It defines the context in which rights are given. It is personal; but it is also owed to society. Respect for others, responsibility to them, is an essential prerequisite of a strong and active community. (Blair 1995: 18)

This quote almost spells out the intersubjective aspect of duty in itself. Blair mentions a recognition of 'more than self', of interconnectedness. And he discusses respect and responsibility in relation to others. There is, of course, a difference between this political formulation and the various philosophical debates that have been raised in this book. In particular Blair raises an ethical dimension which we have only touched upon and he refers to a very specific form of conduct (dutiful conduct) which we have not yet elaborated. Moreover, I assume that the problems of otherness posed in the work of writers such as Husserl and Hegel do not trouble Blair to any great extent. Nevertheless, there are continuities. Duty does presuppose a subject who can recognise and co-exist, respectfully and responsibly, with others. It presupposes a consciousness which transcends its own particularity in the direction of a communal universality and which thereby recognises itself as a citizen. In short, it presupposes intersubjectivity. The sense of duty and citizenship that is integral to the practical realisation of citizenship relations and the citizen role is an intersubjective sense of belonging to a common world with others.

The final concept to be discussed in this first part of the chapter is 'recognition'. Recognition is implied in the notion of citizenship insofar as citizenship is a status. To be a citizen, to enjoy citizen status, is to be recognised and respected as such. This sense of recognition relates directly to the concepts 'desire for recognition' and 'struggle for recognition' that have been discussed hitherto in this book. For Kojève, for example, full citizenship is the institutional resolution of the struggle for recognition. It satisfies the desire for recognition. It provides institutional confirmation that a subject is a subject by bestowing rights and duties upon them that are only appropriate to a subject (see below).

This position is developed concretely and in relation to recent world history by Fukuyama (1992). Fukuyama argues, firstly, that the citizenship offered by modern Western democracies is as close as we can get, institutionally, to a satisfaction of the desire for recognition. And he adds to this, secondly, that the continuing collapse of totalitarian alternatives to liberal democracy is testament to the historical significance of this desire. No society which denies recognition can exist indefinitely, he argues. History will always make an opportunity for desire to convert to action and overthrow forces which deny it.

Insofar as we can accept this argument, and I think that we must accept it to some extent (see below for my discussion of it), the formal rights of citizenship can be interpreted as an institutional embodiment of an intersubjective relationship of recognition, which is in turn the outcome of an intersubjective struggle. This does not mean that all societies have arrived at citizenship by the same route. They clearly have not (Turner 1990). But it suggests that the same intersubjective dynamic may underlie those different paths. Moreover, as Honneth (1995) argues, it provides some element of explanation for the variety of different citizenship struggles that are currently alive in the lifeworld of our and other societies. According to this view, as long as people are denied the dignity of recognition, at whatever level, but particularly in the institutional form of citizenship, they will always be potentially opposed to their situation, and that situation will consequently be unstable.

The Intersubjective Basis of Citizenship

Having identified these fundamental links between intersubjectivity and citizenship, we can now consider the intersubjective basis of citizenship in more detail. The first point which must be addressed here concerns our distinction between radical and egological modes of intersubjectivity. Which of these two modes of intersubjectivity provides an adequate basis for citizenship? Moreover, which provides for the normative current that necessarily runs through any discussion of citizenship?

The answer to both questions is, I suggest, the egological mode. This mode operates at a level of generality, anonymity and universality which is sufficient for citizenship and for an ethics of citizenship, whereas radical intersubjectivity does not. Radical intersubjectivity is only sustainable at the face-to-face level. And the ethics which is generated from it is, likewise, an ethics of the face-to-face. It is an ethics which shuns any form of objectification or typification and which condemns experiential reduction of the other. An ethics of this sort is advocated by both Buber (see Chapter 1) and Levinas:

> You turn yourself toward the Other as toward an object when you see a nose, eyes, a forehead, a chin, and you can describe them. The best way of encountering the Other is not even to notice the colour of his eyes! When one observes the colour of the eyes one is not in a social [i.e. ethical] relationship with the Other. (Levinas 1985: 85)

This perspective may have much to offer to an ethics of face-to-face encounters. Nevertheless, relations of citizenship can never be ethical from this point of view and they do not conform to the architecture of the radically intersubjective relationship. Fellow citizens are, as Roche (1987) puts it, 'fellow strangers'. They do not meet face-to-face and thus cannot be encountered without (imaginative) objectification. Indeed, each is for the other no more than an abstract category, characterised by certain crucial features but not exceeding a given threshold of anonymity – at which point they cease being citizens and become particular persons. Citizens are, to use Schutz's terms, 'contemporaries' but not intimates or 'consociates'. Or, to be more precise, 'fellow citizens' are a sub-category of contemporaries, since not all of our contemporaries are our fellow citizens (e.g. members of other societies than our own are contemporaries but not fellow citizens). This does not mean that citizenship is not grounded in intersubjectivity; neither does it deny the intersubjective, ethical basis of citizenship. As I have said, it implies that citizenship is grounded in an egological intersubjectivity.

To understand and elaborate this we must turn back to Mead's discussion of the acquisition of 'self' in childhood. Integral to this acquisition, for Mead, is the acquisition of language, the entrance of the child into the symbolic world of a particular language community. In addition to this, however, he stresses the importance of 'taking the attitude of the other'. This (imaginative) process, as I noted in Chapter 3, takes place initially through the child's involvement in play, where it takes different roles and learns to assume the attitude of specific others. It then develops through the child's involvement in games, where it learns to assume the attitude of a 'generalised other', which involves the view of the community as a whole, its rule structure, etc. Through involvement in games the child assumes the attitude of the community and comes to view itself from this position. This particular pathway to self-hood is important, in contrast to other possible pathways (such as Merleau-Ponty's 'mirror stage'), as I argued in Chapter 3, because it explains how a sense of self can involve a sense of belonging to and integration with a community and thus it allows for a 'citizen self'. This is a point which Mead emphasises strongly. To be a self, he argues (1967: 162), one must necessarily be a 'member of a community'. To have self-conscious-ness one must have adopted the views of others and, indeed, the view of the community. Citizenship and self-hood therefore coincide for Mead.

This is not to deny individual differences nor the possibility of a constructive dialogical alteration of viewpoints, Mead continues, but there must be 'a common structure' between selves if there is to be a community. Moreover, rights can only be granted on this basis:

> We cannot be ourselves unless we are also members in whom there is a community of attitudes which control the attitudes of all. We cannot have rights unless we have common attitudes. That which we have acquired as self-conscious persons makes us such members of society and gives us selves. (Mead 1967: 164)

This might be read as a purely analytic statement; that a system of rights is impossible to sustain, socially, without a certain commonality of attitudes (irrespective of a powerful state which might try to enforce them). Nevertheless, it has normative implications and these implications are brought into sharp focus later in Mead's study when he claims that animals, because they do not participate in a community and do not have self-consciousness, cannot take on responsibilities and cannot have rights: 'We are at liberty to cut off their lives; there is no wrong committed when an animal's life is taken away' (1967: 183).

I would suggest that we moderate Mead's position slightly. Whilst the deontological considerations that he raises certainly do underpin much of our moral–political thinking, they do not pre-empt it entirely. Part of our moral thinking is linked to basic utilitarian considerations, which would at least suggest that we should not cause any unnecessary pain to animals. On this basis we might say that there is a case for animals having some form of rights. Or at least our moral theory would be out of step with a large part of our society if we did not make a minimal claim here. Notwithstanding this, however, I agree with Mead that the status of citizenship is and should be founded on intersubjectivity. There would be no point in affording the status of citizenship to a being who was incapable of assuming the 'basic structures' of the community, because they could not act out their own part of that status (the citizen role) and would not therefore be citizens. What use has a donkey for the right to vote? Moreover, such beings could not honour their duties as citizens, and their enjoying such a status would therefore, at the very least, constitute a social injustice at the heart of citizenship, and, at the most, would collapse it from within. They would be a group that had rights without duties. But in not fulfilling their duties they would effectively undermine the rights of everybody else. Nobody would have proper rights because there would be a class of beings at large in the polity that lacked the capacity to respect those rights.

This is why citizenship is and must be a conditional status; that is, conditional upon the capacity to fulfil the obligations associated with it and upon the fact of actually doing so. My argument, following Mead, is that those conditions are bound to the developmentally derived, (egological) intersubjective nature of human beings. We are and can be citizens because we can 'take the attitude of the other', transcending our particularism and assuming a communal view. Selfhood and citizenship coincide, in this view, by virtue of their respective intersubjective natures.

There are of course ambiguous fringes which need to be accounted for in this argument. I have already mentioned that animals might have rights without being citizens, for example. And it is equally clear that within the category of 'human beings' there are groups, such as infants, who don't completely fit with our criteria – since they haven't yet developed the secondary (egological) intersubjectivity that we are referring to here. Even within the adult human population there are groups who may, on occasion, lose their intersubjective citizen-orientation; the symptoms of senile dementia or some cases of schizophrenia, for example, may involve periodic splits from intersubjective reality into realities which are deemed hallucinatory or delusional from the point of view of the community. Furthermore, this is, in some instances, sufficient for us to drop some of the rights and responsibilities of citizenship; for example, as in the insanity plea in law or compulsory detention. Such cases are extremely difficult to think through in terms of intersubjectivity and citizenship, not least because the conditions which they refer to are extremely complex phenomena, which do not fit neatly in terms of our criteria. This is no reason to drop our criteria, however. At least, dropping our criteria would not make the issue any clearer and would lose us all that we have gained from them so far. What we need to do is to work with and around our criteria, to determine the extent to which people can 'measure up' to the requirements of citizenship. This is, of course, something which the law and parliament already claim to do, but their judgements are more or less continually contested in contemporary political life and are likely to remain so.

Community? What Community?

An objection which could be levelled against the Meadian position, at least as it stands, is that it presupposes a homogeneous community life which is unidentifiable in terms of the complexity and plurality of contemporary societies. In Chapter 3, when I first raised this objection, my way round it was to suggest that we can refer, quite coherently from Mead's point of view, to communities and generalised others in the plural. This retort will not suffice in relation to the question of citizenship, however, because citizenship does in fact presuppose some element of homogeneity. Mead's 'community' and 'generalised other' in the singular are necessary to it. Citizenship presupposes 'the Political community' in the singular, and that community must be sustained if citizenship is to be sustained.

This problem is not exclusive to Mead's view of citizenship. It is equally problematic in relation to all views of citizenship, since all views must suppose a singular political community which all citizens are citizens of. This is not just a theoretical problem. It is a practical political problem, a motivation problem such as I have already described. Or, rather, it consists in two practical problems. Firstly, there is the problem of integrating the diverse plurality of socio-cultural communities existing within any given polity. If system integration and the relations of full citizenship which this entails are to be achieved and sustained, then the various communities which make up the system must be bound in to a common political community. Secondly, there is a problem of achieving and sustaining a citizen role and identity in relation to the polity, given the degree of abstraction at which this 'community' exists and its removal from everyday affairs. Local or interest group communities, which are directly participated and invested in and which are tangible to their members, are relatively easily identified with. But, as Peter Saunders (1993) has observed, this is not so easily achieved in relation to the abstract status of citizenship and the socially distant machinery of government to which that status is fixed.

Paradoxically, this second problem, the problem of abstractness and identity, is integral to the resolution of the first problem. Citizenship status can absorb the great and growing diversity of contemporary societies, or at least it could if we adopt the right political tactics, because citizenship is a relatively abstract status. It is able to embody the element of universalism that it does because it is far removed from the particularisms of everyday interaction. Fellow citizens, to reiterate Roche's point, are 'fellow strangers', and they identify with each other as such. They do not need to like each other, know each other or to share the same beliefs and values. They can have different lifestyles and religions and live in distinct communities – whether those communities are geographically based, work-based, computer-based or whatever. Citizenship does not require homogeneity, providing that the basic requirements of social duty are fulfilled and any conflicts of interest are resolved in and through the appropriate legal or political systems.

Citizenship, in this sense (as I said at the outset of this chapter), functions for the social system, not the lifeworld (though it is embedded in the latter). One hopes that citizenship will ensure systemic integration but one never imagines that it will achieve social integration. Smaller communities, which are characterised by greater homogeneity, may achieve social integration.

And such integration is necessary to the achievement of social order as a whole. Small communities (not necessarily geographically based) provide islands of stability and social integration within the social system and for this reason they should be encouraged. But this has nothing to do with citizenship as such. The task of citizenship, as a systemic unit, is to link these islands coherently, without disrupting their stability and the integration it provides. To do this, as I have said, citizenship must remain formal and abstract. It must provide for the plurality and not side with any one community. Moreover, as Parsons (1967: 422–65) emphasises, it must 'include' different groups without trying to assimilate them, since assimilation will necessarily destroy the stability achieved by way of the community's localised solidaristic social integration.

This is not to say that citizenship is a morally and politically neutral category. It is not. Its formality and abstractness embody a liberal preference for plurality and democracy. Moreover, it is the product of a particular process of rationalisation (Habermas 1991a), originating in Europe and the USA and formed in accordance with the evolutionary exigencies of those societies. Furthermore, this view of citizenship requires that its island communities stay within the law and fulfil their citizen duties. It is not an 'anything goes' citizenship but an 'anything goes so long as . . .' citizenship.

But what then of a citizen role and a feeling of citizenship? What community is there to be and feel a part of? There is plenty. To see this we must accept Habermas's distinction (one he takes to be real, concrete and historical) between the public and private spheres of the lifeworld, and we must identify the island communities that we have been discussing with the private sphere. Within this private sphere we may occupy a plurality of particular relationally defined roles. We may play the role of citizen in this sphere, particularly if we are concerning ourselves with an issue of duty, but the citizen role has no particular privilege at this level, other than by way of the duties we fulfil. Moreover, those duties will often lose their specific 'citizen' tag, as the duties of citizens are ordinarily devolved into more specific roles; for example, one of the duties of a citizen, if s/he is a parent, will be to be a good parent and to provide for what his/her child might need in order to grow into a good citizen. One assumes the duties of a citizen, in this case, by performing well in one's parent role, and one may do this without any particular sense of citizenship. There is a sense, then, at the level of the private sphere, that one can fulfil one's citizen role without having to identify with an abstract political community or with a citizen identity tag. This, I would suggest, is where the arguments of the New Social Movements referred to earlier, regarding decentralised rights and duties, are of importance. The citizen role is, at one level, a second-order role which involves the proper performance of a range of other roles that one might occupy. Notwithstanding this, however, the citizen role is not just a cumulation of subordinate roles. It equally involves a higher level of activity.

The site of this higher level of activity is the public sphere. This is the sphere of the lifeworld which transcends its pluralism. It is the site of political debate and discussion and, according to Arendt, it exists only in and through such discussion (Passerin d'Entrèves 1992). It is an 'artificial community' (ibid.) based not in mutual attraction or shared attitudes, beliefs and values, but in issues of common concern; that is, political issues. Citizens don't come together and discuss because they want to but because they must, because their existence is inseparably tied up with others and with common resources, and because the terms of these ties must be negotiated. Parliaments are the obvious forum for such debates, at their highest level, but as Habermas (1987a) and Stevenson (1995) emphasise, the mass media constitute its necessary environment in contemporary societies – even if they do not perform this function in a manner that is wholly desirable. The mass media create the shared space within which common issues are debated.

It is important to add here that it is specifically debate which constitutes the public sphere; that is, communicative praxis. This presupposes that disagreement in opinion, at this level, is underwritten by an agreement in forms of life and by a discursive structure of argument, such as is identified in Habermas's (1987a, 1991a, 1991b) formal pragmatics. The public sphere disintegrates if and to the extent that communicative action is undermined by the intrusion of the systemic mediums of power or money, or, indeed, if serious argument is undermined by defensive rhetoric. In this sense it is perhaps best considered as an ideal which is approximated in contemporary social life, rather than being fully realised. Moreover, as Habermas (1987a) observes, it is a sphere which is apparently shrinking because of the colonisation of the lifeworld.

To refer to the artificiality of the public sphere, as I have, is in no way to undermine its importance nor to suggest that strong identities cannot be bound to it. Given the systemic integration of contemporary societies, by way of both the economy and the political system (including the welfare system), there are many pathways of interdependency to link citizens. They have many common concerns, even if their interests are opposed. What happens in the economic, legal, welfare and control systems affects all of them, if not always in the same way and to the same degree. Thus they have a shared interest in debating such matters and in attempting to exert influence over them. Furthermore, these interdependencies are made available to them both by way of their participation in the practices and rituals which they involve (e.g. voting, following political life in the media, paying taxes) and by way of the political discourses that are enmeshed in those activities. Moreover, there are many 'symbols', in the Schutzian sense (i.e. signifiers of transcendent phenomena, including all memberships – see Chapter 5), which provide anchors for a citizen identity. The most important of these being 'citizen' itself; that is, in addition to being an institutional nexus in the social system and a role, citizenship is a concept and a symbol – albeit, one whose substantive content is essentially contested – which functions within both the role and the institution as a means of organising them. On their own, such symbols are impotent. But if integrated into a participatory, intersubjective praxis, as an integral component of that praxis, they serve to constitute a sense of citizenship, and thus to reinforce and coordinate the citizen role and the institution of citizenship.

It is the recognition of and involvement in political interdependencies, and the place in this process occupied by discourses on citizenship and transcendent symbols, which allows citizens to take the attitude of the political community, in Mead's sense, and thus to identify as citizens and take a citizen role. There is a discourse and symbolism of citizenship and the public sphere and a participatory praxis which mobilises them and integrates them into a citizen role. Inter-subjects play the game of citizen, in a strictly Meadian sense, and they thereby become citizens, assuming the role and identity that goes with it. This game is learned as all games are (necessarily) learned, by way of communicative, intersubjective praxis. It is rooted in, preserved by and transmitted through the lifeworld.

The embeddedness of citizenship symbolism in the lifeworld is demonstrated every time a person makes reference to their rights, their citizenship or democracy. That they may do so in a conflictual fashion and may contend the meaning of their citizenship is no objection to this, providing that they still claim citizenship and thereby register its importance to their identity. Citizens don't have to agree on substantive issues, even on issues concerning the meaning of citizenship, providing that they continue to identify as citizens and continue to pursue their citizen role in the manner appropriate to the public sphere; that is, open conversation and argument. Ironically, in this sense, battles over the meaning of citizenship, such as we are witnessing at present throughout European societies, are testament to its strength and meaningfulness as a symbol. We only need worry when people stop invoking 'citizenship' in their political struggles. This would be the signal of a serious motivation or legitimation crisis.

Institution, Role and Identity

One key point that is beginning to emerge in this discussion of citizenship is the extent to which the institution, role and identity which comprise citizenship are mutually reinforcing. The institution of citizenship, as a systemic function, depends upon the embeddedness and communicative reproduction of a citizen role and identity within the lifeworld. But this role and identity depend upon political participation, which in turn depends upon the institutional facilitation of such participation. There is a strong political message in this; namely, people cannot and will not act out the role of the citizen unless that role is allowed to be genuinely meaningful. They will not feel a sense of duty and membership unless they have the opportunity of genuine participation. Societal solidarity, from this point of view, is best enhanced through the provision of good opportunities for meaningful participation in political life. We might add here, moreover, that other forms of active participation, particularly active participation in the economy by way of paid and 'recognised' work, are of equal importance. By the logic of the master/slave relation, a subject who is wholly dependent upon the state for finance and who cannot contribute financially to their community will not feel a part of that community and may feel resentment towards it because of this.

If citizenship is not realised in this way, or, rather, to the extent that it is not, individuals are disenfranchised and the system faces the possibility of a motivation crisis in the Habermasian sense. This, in itself, may not be such a problem for the social system (though it surely is for citizens). As Habermas has noted, however, motivation crises can trigger legitimation crises. And a legitimation crisis is a full-blown crisis of system integration. A state which loses its legitimation loses the very currency (power) by which it coordinates and organises social life.

Such a downward spiral need not be spread evenly through society, nor need it be as apocalyptic as I have suggested. Disenfranchisement and motivation problems can occur by degree and can vary, at least at the level of identification and role participation, between groups and individuals. Nevertheless, the possibility of legitimation crisis is not to be taken lightly and disenfranchisement should never, for ethical reasons, be ignored. Moreover, the strength of the political community of citizenship must surely depend upon its total and even integration. As both Dahrendorf (1994) and Saunders (1993) have (in different ways and for different ideological purposes) emphasised, disenfranchised groups, even if they lack the agency capacity to mount a significant challenge to the political community, nevertheless threaten that community by virtue of the reaction which their presence provokes amongst other members. Our next question, then, concerns the degree to which this system does function effectively in our society. To what extent do our societies achieve full citizenship for their members? This takes us to the next stage of our discussion, a stage inspired by the work of the neo-Hegelian intersubjectivist Francis Fukuyama.

Full Citizenship? The Fukuyama Position

In his *Citizenship and Social Class*, Marshall argued that full citizenship was achieved (for British subjects) with the institutionalisation of a set of social rights to welfare provision. This was, in his view, the last brick which needed to be put in place for the historical completion of citizenship. It eradicated the possibility that civil and political rights, which form the true core of citizenship, might be negated by social deprivation. Other writers of Marshall's era, dealing with other societies, such as Talcott Parsons (1967) in the USA, were less convinced. Parsons noted that American blacks, although they had the formal rights of citizenship, were still not yet full citizens – mainly as a consequence of the contemporary resonance of their historical oppression in the American slavery system. They were, in Parsons's view, 'second-class citizens' because although equal before the law and enjoying full political rights, they were still constituted with a less than equal status in the interactions which form the more substantive basis of social and political life. Parsons believed that this was not inevitable, however, and that it would be corrected as black cultures became accepted within the otherwise pluralistic American system. Like Marshall, then, Parsons sees an end in sight for the history of citizenship.

In recent years a far more radical version of Marshall's claim was announced with respect to Britain, the United States and the rest of the Western world (not to mention some societies in the East also). For Francis Fukuyama (1989, 1992), these societies have reached 'the end of history'. What this entails is a claim that these societies have reached a point in their evolution whereby their basic institutional and social-structural form cannot (and thus will not) be improved upon, in terms of its provision for human wants and needs. This form is liberal (capitalist) democracy. The evidence for this claim, at least in part, is the collapse of alternative models of social organisation throughout the world, particularly the collapse (in Eastern Europe) of authoritarian societies with centrally planned economies. These 'alternatives' have been selected out of the historical process, according to Fukuyama, and have been shown not to be (workable) alternatives at all.

Fukuyama's thesis does not entail the view that all social problems have been adequately resolved at this point in our history. Neither does it rule out the possibility that there are many conflicts, changes and events to come in the future of our societies. All that it entails is that basic structure of economic and political provision will not be altered. The composition of the capitalist market may well alter in years to come, particularly under the force of new technological developments, according to this position, but they will be changes within the capitalist structure, not changes towards a different form of socio-economic organisation. Likewise, the institutions and process of (representative) democracy might be altered, but not to such an extent that we would cease to constitute a representative democracy. Or rather, to invoke the slightly less self-assured thesis which also runs through *The End of History* (particularly its final chapters), there would be nothing to gain from this process. In this sense, the ending of history is not the achievement of perfection.

This thesis is extremely interesting in its own right. It is of particular interest for this chapter, however, because of the role which Fukuyama ascribes to 'intersubjectivity', 'the struggle for recognition' and 'the desire for recognition' in this process. Drawing on Kojève's account of Hegel, Fukuyama argues that, in addition to basic animal desires and reason, human beings have a fundamentally human desire for desire, a desire for recognition. Such a desire is necessary to explain a whole range of different phenomena, he argues, but most particularly it explains the human aversion to non-democratic forms of government and the consequent motivation of those in the subordinate role in such relations of government to change them. The implication of this is that human desire finds its full expression only in democratic societies and that, when it has found such a situation, the need or demand for political change will be over – though he does make a considerable qualification to this point. This is the more philosophically substantive basis for Fukuyama's proclamation of the end of history. Moreover, it establishes a very clear link between the concepts 'intersubjectivity', 'democracy', 'citizenship' and 'history'. History is viewed as an intersubjective struggle for recognition, which resolves itself in and through the achievement of mutual recognition, in the form of institutionalised democracy and citizenship.

Fukuyama's position is quite convincing at some points and certain aspects of it are quite attractive. Its attractiveness stems from the link which it forms between intersubjectivity and citizenship, and its identification of a desire and a struggle for recognition. This is attractive at one level because, in an era when the notion of human nature is being vigorously denied by many (post-structuralist and postmodern) thinkers, it posits a feasible and defensible version of the type of beings that we are and the type of needs that we have, and in doing this it seemingly posits a persuasive defence of democracy. Democracy (at all levels) is the most appropriate form of social organisation to our manner of being on this account. Moreover, citizenship is viewed as a proper and deserved status, both because we desire recognition and because we are the types of being who can only fully exist in communities with others. Such ideas, without limiting our possibilities too much, provide the basis both for a critique of some social–political relations (though Fukuyama does not particularly exploit this potential) and for a formulation of the types of social order that might be most appropriate to our needs. In doing this, moreover, it allows us to link the various analytic ideas (sociological, philosophical and psychological) that we have discussed in this book to a normative political framework. This is not to say that we need be linked to any particular political ideology of either the right or the left. It is simply to say that we have an understanding, albeit a minimal one, of the basic conditions which need to be secured if human beings are to be fully human. And it suggests that these conditions will only be secured for one person if they are secured for all, at the level of the community.

Other aspects of Fukuyama's thesis are relatively convincing. The collapse of alternatives to liberal democracy in a multitude of countries around the world is a profound fact of recent history. And the lack of realistic alternatives to liberal democracy, at the broad structural level, is undeniable. Our societies are undergoing profound changes at the moment and these directly affect economic and political organisation, but they do not tend away from liberal democracy – or, at least, the greater number do not. The majority of changes suggest, at most, that the centre of our social and political life will be shifted away from the national (party-based) level to both more global and more local levels; but there is no suggestion that this will involve a displacement of the market as the central mechanism of distribution or that basic representative democracy will give way to anything other than another form of representative democracy. Having said this, however, there is one clear historical tendency, already clearly theorised and politicised, which might have a more sustained effect: the development of technologies which remove the necessity for many types of work, and which therefore promises, at least according to its key proponents, a 'liberation' from work (Gorz 1982, 1985). There are many reasons to be sceptical regarding this thesis. The effects of new technologies upon economic and political life are always mediated by social relations and by the innovating praxes which set them up. New technologies have no necessary effects in themselves. Moreover, the growth of the service sector in the labour market, a sector which is less easily displaced by new technologies because of its dependence upon the 'human touch', indicates that the labour market may actually be shifting rather than drying up. Nevertheless it is interesting to briefly consider the possibilities of liberation, as outlined by its key theorists.

The effects of the liberation, at a political level, could be quite profound but not structural. Being liberated from work would leave citizens more time for political participation. They would be in a similar position to the citizens of ancient Greece, who had slaves and women to do their work for them (Roche 1992b). This might be further enhanced by the communicative possibilities offered by new technologies. Computer networking, as Toffler (1980) notes, opens the possibility for 'push button democracy'. Notwithstanding this, however, sheer population sizes make it unlikely that the type of democracy which this would allow would be anything other than a representative democracy – we can't all have a direct say, there are too many of us. These technologies, developed in this way, are only enhancing representative democracy. They are not shifting us away from it in any respect. The effects are potentially more profound at the economic level, however, since a liberation from work may undermine the basic structure of market capitalism (the 'liberal' aspect of liberal democracy) by eliminating the demand for labour, at least at one level and on the side of the owners of capital, without eliminating the supply for labour nor its necessity amongst the 'working' population. Workers would continue to need work, as a matter of survival, but capitalists would no longer need workers. Or rather, capitalists would need workers indirectly, since they need consumers with enough money to buy their goods, but they would not need workers to work for them (or at least not as many workers). Without this, or some equivalent intervention, our societies would face immense problems of unemployment on a scale never before witnessed. Market-based technological innovations would have effectively outgrown the market-based system of distribution and provision.

This is perhaps a rather apocalyptic scenario and, as I have already said, other contemporary changes do not appear to challenge liberal democracy in any substantive way; they are, rather, an extension and development of it. Nevertheless, it is important to flag it up for consideration. Having done this, we can shift to consider some of the more specific criticisms which can be levelled against Fukuyama's position.

My main criticism, and the one from which all the others stem, is that there is a considerable gap between the principles of liberal democracy, as enshrined in legislation and manifestos, and its actual practice. This results in a less than perfect realisation of democracy and, importantly, in the reproduction of 'second-class citizenship' for some – a situation which is harmful for the system as well as for second-class citizens. The critique which stems from this is not a critique of the idea of liberal democracy and it certainly doesn't suggest an alternative to it. It does, however, identify a need for change. It is, in some respects, a 'dysfunctionalist' critique; that is, a critique which identifies a manner in which the social system fails to deliver the goods that it promises. This is important in terms of the question of intersubjectivity because it suggests that the institutional consolidation of intersubjectivity is imperfect and requires change. Furthermore, it should point to some of the areas where change may be required.

There is not space in this chapter to cover all of the issues involved here. What I propose to do, however, is to point to three broad areas which might be considered in a critique of this kind, substantiating this with a consideration of the manner in which various forms of second-class citizenship are constituted. The areas that I consider are the institutions of citizenship (which form its key systemic component), the public sphere and the private sphere. I will concentrate particularly upon the latter two because they most directly concern intersubjective matters.

The Institutions of Citizenship

The institutions of citizenship are those which directly secure and enforce the rights and obligations of citizenship. Chief amongst these are the courts and judiciary, which secure and enforce civil duties and rights, Parliament and the political system, which secure and enforce political rights, and the welfare and taxation (insurance) systems, which secure and enforce social rights and duties. That these institutions are not beyond criticism, that they can fail to deliver the goods in a manner considered appropriate, should be apparent every time we pick up a newspaper or watch the television news. Moreover, it is quite clear that both the political/electoral system and the welfare system are candidates for considerable change in the eyes of some mainstream politicians. Second-class citizenship is a problem, at this level, insofar as ideologies such as racism are embodied in institutional processes and practices, thereby unjustly affecting their outcome (Gilroy 1992). Such institutional ideologies constitute second-class citizenship at two levels. Firstly, they limit effective access to the institutions that provide for citizenship rights and duties. Secondly, they manifest a failure of proper recognition; some groups are denied the recognition granted to the rest.

It is equally important to recognise here that the institutional base of citizenship is in transition. Indeed, as a national structure it is being undermined by social-structural changes, and in particular by a process of globalisation (Roche 1992a). National institutions of citizenship are not being eliminated by this process and there is little likelihood that they will be in the near future. Nevertheless they are finding themselves increasingly ineffective in coping with global issues and a global economy and are thus finding themselves conjoined by international institutions of citizenship. The development, in Europe, of a European Court which can overrule decisions in national courts and of a European parliament, with Euro-elections, laws and policies, is just one example of this. Clearly there are a great number of issues which will need to be addressed in relation to these changes, many of which, in turn, will spill over into the lifeworld/intersubjectivity issues raised in this chapter and in the book more generally. In particular, from our point of view, there is the problem, stated at the outset of this chapter, that the lifeworld conditions which secure the identifications and motivations of citizenship are not yet oriented to the international order. We are not yet 'fellow strangers' with our international contemporaries, just strangers (or, in some cases, historical enemies). There is a question, then, as to how we will come to identify and participate in a common political community (qua lifeworld).

It needs to be emphasised here, as I noted above, that the culture of citizenship is not one of shared beliefs, attitudes and values, and thus that the question of international citizenship is not a matter of securing cultural homogeneity or agreement of opinions – although linguistic and cultural differences clearly pose obstacles to proper discussion and agreement. Notwithstanding this, however, there is an important question concerning common recognition of the legitimacy of the international order and of the motivation to partake in it. A common language game, as well as institutions of citizenship, must be constituted, and citizens must be encouraged. Moreover, it seems inevitable that political globalisation will undermine lifeworld traditions in many national societies, even if it doesn't require homogeneity, and that the citizens of those societies, whose (citizenship) motivations are secured by those very traditions, will be expected to comply. This is a logical consequence of the idea of international policies. Following Habermas's work on the undermining of lifeworlds by system imperatives, we might predict that this will only be successful to the extent that a 'good deal' can be secured for those citizens, in that process. There is a danger even in this, however, as Habermas notes, in the sense that this tends to constitute subjects as clients rather than as citizens; that is, it is a process in which subjects are placated with (welfare) provisions, rather than taking an active citizen role.

A final point to be considered under the institutional rubric concerns the economy and the existence of a growing underclass. I do not have the space in this chapter to discuss this issue in any depth, but it is important to register the existence of this group of people and to briefly consider their effective disenfranchisement. Whatever the reason for the existence and perpetuation of this group, they are almost defined by their lack of full citizenship and participation in society. An institutional analysis of citizenship must look at this group and consider the conditions of their disenfranchisement (Roche 1992a).

The Public Sphere

I have already noted in this chapter that much of the citizen role is performed in the public sphere and that this sphere is constituted, in its entirety, by means of debate and discussion of issues of common concern. Following Habermas, I added that the vehicle of this dialogue is primarily the mass media (to which we might also add new information technology forms such as the Internet). Such media allow the simultaneous linkage of an entire population, or at least of all those who have the means and the will to turn them on. They provide the only access which the vast majority of citizens will ever have to the major events and agents in the political and economic system (though all citizens are affected by these events and actions). As such, they are the only basis from which citizens may make many of the informed choices that belong to their citizen role. It is by way of the media, primarily, that citizens recognise the commonality of their situation and can be mobilised into various forms of citizen action. Consequently, the manner in which media networks function bears directly upon the effectiveness of citizenship itself as an institution. A 'bad' media network will not allow citizenship to function effectively.

Many important issues follow from this point. And many of these stem from the fact that access to and control of media, in liberal democracies, is limited and unevenly distributed. Moreover, the specifically 'mass' media of these societies, such as the newspaper and non-public service television networks, are constituted through commercial bureaucracies, staffed hierarchically by professional bodies (each with their own professional interests), which must remain commercially viable both by competing with other media outlets and by soliciting the backing of other commercially interested bodies. News and public debate and discussion (in the media) is not the product of a spontaneous communication between commonly motivated parties, as the ideal of the public sphere might suggest. It is a socially and more particularly a financially organised system, which must achieve integration with the economic and political structures of its society, in a currency appropriate to those systems (money and power). This observation is hardly 'news' in itself, but it is important because it indicates that the discourse which composes the mass media, and thus the public sphere as we know it, is determined by other interests and forces than those of argument and conversation alone. Indeed, as the thesis of the colonisation of the lifeworld suggests, this lifeworld activity is precisely mediated by systemic imperatives via relations of money and power. Again this is not news, but insofar as citizenship is tied to this public sphere it does indicate something of a failure or dysfunctioning of citizenship.

I am not suggesting here that citizens are necessarily duped by the media, nor that the media set out to deliberately dupe them. Furthermore, I would distance myself from any suggestion that the media are necessarily biased towards a specific political persuasion. Insofar as there are biases, and clearly politicians of all persuasions believe that there are, these differ between outlets and over time. My point is simply that the interests of open and fair argument are only one set of interests informing media praxis, even, and most importantly, in those programmes or articles that are devoted to the discussion of public, political issues – clearly some articles are intended to do other things such as entertain and amuse. Moreover, it is clear that the private ownership and control of the media, not to mention editorial policies and the effects of the cultural backgrounds of those who create programmes, can lead to the exclusion of the presentation of the views of certain groups, in relation to some issues, and can therefore perpetuate or constitute certain forms of second-class citizenship. Not all views will have equal access to the public sphere.

The importance of Habermas and of his 'ideal speech situation' is evident here (cf. also Stevenson 1995). If we need an ideal speech situation anywhere, then it is surely in the public sphere, where our political debates are conducted. And yet we clearly do not have this. We have a system steered by money and power.

Having said all of this, recent innovations in information technology do open out possibilities both for a transformation of the mass media and for the development of alternative sites for the public sphere. In particular, there is a possibility that cyberspace, the space opened up by computer networking and particularly by the 'Internet', has tremendous potential with respect to the construction of an accessible public sphere. In cyberspace there is completely unregulated communication (i.e. institutionally unregulated) and the possibility of anonymity. Interlocutors need know nothing about each other, other than their views, and thus they can fight it out in the closest thing to an ideal speech situation to have emerged in Western societies to date. Moreover, there is a possibility, already taken up by some (connected) citizens, to form debating and information groups and forums of all kinds. Clearly this is not yet a proper public sphere. Many people are not connected and seem unlikely to be connected in the near future. Furthermore, it is perhaps not organised and regulated enough to function as an effective public sphere. Notwithstanding this, however, its wildly unregulated constitution (which is the cause of so much controversy at the moment) is an excellent starting point. Nothing is excluded from it at the outset and we can thus decide what we will exclude from it very carefully.

The Private Sphere

In relation to the private sphere it is worth returning to Nancy Fraser's critique of Habermas, as discussed in Chapter 5. Fraser points out that the private sphere of the lifeworld is, firstly, central to the material as well as the symbolic reproduction of society, and, secondly, that it is by no means 'innocent' in relation to social and political inequality. Families, Fraser notes, have their own internal (monetary) economies and can be key to the reproduction and even the constitution of gender inequalities.

This is important because it indicates that our citizenship qua recognition is as much affected from below as from above. Life chances and possibilities are not just fixed at the formal institutional level or the level of the public sphere, nor are they restricted only by external systemic impositions (the colonisation of the lifeworld). They are effected in and through the private sphere of the lifeworld, the world of everyday life and interaction. This sphere contains within itself the means for the reproduction and mediation of life chances, or, again, the means of restricting possibilities and participation. It is the sphere in which we are socialised with specific identities and competencies, in which our decisions are made and actions variously negotiated and blocked; where our time and space are variously filled and controlled, opened and restricted; a place where our possibilities for active participation in our world are (partly at least) determined. The lifeworld, in this respect, can foster forms of second-class citizenship which have been formally abolished and levelled at the systemic level.

This point rejoins my earlier point concerning the lifeworld constitution of citizen motivations and identifications. Just as citizenship qua role and identity is constituted in the lifeworld, so too can it be denied or insufficiently provided for – through socialisation or exclusive symbolisation – for some. Identities and competencies that are contingent and acquired can always be denied or restricted in the lifeworld. Furthermore, lifeworld relations can negate the recognition otherwise afforded within the system, thus annulling or seemingly annulling citizenship status. Sexual objectification of women, for example, may be said to undermine the subject–citizen status otherwise granted to them by precisely reconstituting them as objects. Or again, systemic discrimination and persecution of members of ethnic minorities, or the tendency amongst some groups to treat them as 'them', as a problem, negates any more substantive sense of citizenship. Without recognition in the lifeworld, citizenship is empty, formal and shallow.

Two points come out of this. Firstly, we can maintain that citizenship qua recognition has both a formal expression, in terms of the systemic inscription of rights and duties, and a more substantive dimension, which is linked to the status which certain groups enjoy within the lifeworld. True citizenship demands full recognition at both levels. Secondly, following Parsons (albeit with some modification), we must recognise that lifeworld relations can considerably 'lag' behind systemic relations and are not as easily changed or transformed. To change our laws is relatively easy compared with the often hidden and always deeply embedded structures of communication and intersubjective relations.

I do not have the space to develop these ideas here, nor to identify all of the groups who are variously implicated. Suffice it to say that these groups often identify themselves through social and expressive movements who vent their desire for recognition on the society which denies it to them. In this sense (contra Habermas) the colonisation of the lifeworld is not the only social force against which New Social Movements protest. They equally protest against conditions within the lifeworld which deny them recognition. Relatedly, citizenship is threatened not only from above (by the colonisation of the lifeworld) but from below too, by the forces of injustice at work in the lifeworld.

Many of these points would, I am sure, be conceded by Fukuyama. Certainly they do nothing to challenge the view that history has ended. They nevertheless establish that there is still much to be done before full citizenship is attained for all, and they do so, at least to some extent, by emphasising the role of the intersubjective lifeworld in the construction of the citizen.

This was the point that I began with and it is the point on which I conclude. I have, I hope, shown some of the ways in which the concepts 'intersubjectivity', 'lifeworld' and 'citizenship' are mutually illuminating and constructive. Citizenship is, I have shown, inextricably bound in the intertwining of system–lifeworld relations. Moreover, I hope that I have opened up the possibility of a more normative and political dimension to the understanding of intersubjectivity hitherto outlined in the book.

Conclusion

The Fabric of Social Becoming

In this book I have shown, by example, how different academic traditions and disciplines can converge around the issue of intersubjectivity, such that it might provide them with common ground. Furthermore, I have combined and coordinated different versions of the concept, reorganising them according to new distinctions (such as radical and egological), thereby showing them to be both compatible and mutually enriching. Finally, I have argued that a consideration of intersubjectivity can enrich our understanding of other key concepts such as 'power' and 'citizenship'. Underlying all of this, however, has been a more fundamental point, which it has been my main concern to establish; namely, that intersubjectivity is the fabric of our social becoming.

I say 'becoming' rather than 'being' to indicate both the temporal structure and the esssential incompleteness of our social world, to indicate that this world and the multiple relationships therein are always in a process of becoming something and are never static. More specifically, though, my point is that intersubjectivity is the key to understanding human life in both its personal and its societal forms. It is that in virtue of which our societies are possible and we are who we are. Moreover, it is irreducible and *sui generis*, a generative principle of our identities, our agency and of the societies in which we live. And it is something which we cannot step out of. No amount of methodological procedure, either philosophical or social scientific, can negate this or even bracket it out. We are inter-subjects. Our actions and thoughts aren't reducible to us alone. They are moves in a game which has many players, responses to a call to action which is expressed in every gesture of the other. And their significance is precisely constituted through their place in that game.

I use the word 'fabric' to denote this for a number of reasons. Firstly, to articulate with the popular expression 'social fabric'. Intersubjectivity is, I believe, precisely the fabric alluded to in this expression. It is what holds us all together in an identifiable group or unit. Secondly, 'fabric' conjures up an image of multiple overlappings and intertwinings, organised and arranged in different ways, sometimes becoming disorganised. It connotes a sense of unity and strength which is achieved by way of this overlapping. No thread is either strong or significant on its own but the intertwining gives it strength and form. It is these different forms and patterns of overlapping that are being investigated in the analysis of radical and egological intersubjectivity, language games and the various taken-for-granted assumptions of the social lifeworld. Finally, the word 'fabric' suggests a certain material basis, a corporeal intertwining, which is again evident in intersubjectivity. Human beings are embodied beings and this is quite crucial to their intersubjectivity. Moreover, their intersubjective relations take place within and include material environments.

Having said all of this we are left with the inevitable question that every conclusion must contend with: where to now? I have entertained many grandiose fantasies regarding this question during the writing of the book. In the final instance, however, the answer is both narrow and clear. There is no specific project which emerges out of a study such as this, even if there may be a few good ideas for projects tucked away in the text somewhere. Neither is there a distinct method or procedure that we might apply to the future projects we will undertake. The many studies I have discussed in the book employ a wide range of methods and analytic procedures, all of which are suited to drawing out particular aspects of intersubjectivity or issues relating to it, but none of which are either compulsory or exclusive. What I hope that the book does provide us with, however, is a way of thinking about the social–intersubjective world and about our involvement in it.

To think about intersubjectivity and to tackle the problems it poses as a concept is to confront the very question of social life itself. It is to unpick the fabric of social life and to wonder how it ever fits together in the first place, how we ever manage to coordinate ourselves through time and space, sharing thoughts and meanings, agreeing enough at least to disagree. It is to wonder what thought, meaning and action actually are, such that they can be shared or joint. It is to wonder how the human organism can ever be involved in anything which transcends its spatial boundaries. These are not just academic questions, even if they have a strong academic aspect. They are ultimately also existential questions about our very being (my being and your being particularly). To confront the question of intersubjectivity is to consider the type of beings that we are and the sort of world to which we belong. Considerations of this sort lie at the heart of all of our projects, whether academic or not.

If this book has opened up some of these issues, made them accessible and provoked some thoughts about how they might best be conceived, then it has done the job that I intended.

Bibliography

Abercrombie, N., Hill, S. and Turner, B. (1986), *Sovereign Individuals of Capitalism*, London, Allen & Unwin.

Amsterdam, B. (1971), 'Mirror Self-Image Reactions Before Age Two', *Developmental Psychobiology* 5(4), pp. 297–305.

Arthur, C. (1988), 'Hegel as Lord and Master', *Radical Philosophy* 50, pp. 19–25.

Austin, J. (1971), *How to Do Things with Words*, Oxford, Oxford University Press.

Ayer, A. (1981), 'Can There Be a Private Language?', in Morick, H. (ed.), *Wittgenstein and the Problem of Other Minds*, Brighton, Harvester, pp. 82–96.

Barrel, M. (1985), 'Self and Other: Communication and Love', *Review of Existential Psychology and Psychiatry*, xviii (1–3), pp. 155–80.

Beauvoir, S. de (1988), *The Second Sex*, London, Picador.

Benjamin, J. (1991), *The Bonds of Love*, London, Virago.

Blair, T. (1995), 'The Conservative Party Seems Neither to Understand Nor to Act Upon the Concept of Duty' (*The Spectator*/Allied Dunbar Lecture), *The Spectator*, 25 March, p. 18.

Bourdieu, P. (1977), *Outline of a Theory of Practice*, Cambridge, Cambridge University Press.

Bourdieu, P. (1979), 'The Economics of Linguistic Exchanges', *Social Science Information* 16(6), pp. 645–68.

Bourdieu, P. (1984), *Distinction: A Social Critique of the Judgement of Taste*, London, Routledge & Kegan Paul.

Bourdieu, P. (1992), *Language and Symbolic Power*, Cambridge, Polity.

Bourdieu, P. (1993), *Sociology in Question*, London, Sage.

Bourdieu, P. and Passeron, J.-C. (1993), *Reproduction*, London, Sage.

Bruner, J. (1991), 'Nature and Uses of Immaturity', in Woodhead, M., Carr, R. and Light, P. (eds), *Becoming a Person*, London: Routledge, pp. 247–75.

Buber, M. (1958), *I and Thou*, Edinburgh, T. & T. Clark.

Budd, M. (1989), *Wittgenstein's Philosophy of Psychology*, London, Routledge.

Burns, T. (1992), *Erving Goffman*, London, Routledge.

Butler, J. (1990), *Gender Trouble*, London, Routledge.

Case, R. (1991), 'Stages in the Young Child's First Sense of Self', *Developmental Review* 11, pp. 210–30.

Cashmore, E. and Troyna, B. (1983), *Introduction to Race Relations*, London, Routledge & Kegan Paul.

Castoriadis, C. (1987), *The Imaginary Institution of Society*, Cambridge, Polity.

Castoriadis, C. (1990), 'An Interview', *Radical Philosophy* 56, pp. 35–43.

Castoriadis, C. (1991), 'An Interview', *Free Associations* 2(4), pp. 483–506.

Clarke, R. (1978), 'The Transition From Action to Gesture', in Lock, A. (ed.), *Action, Gesture and Symbol*, London, Academic Press, pp. 231–57.

Clegg, S. (1989), *Frameworks of Power*, London, Sage.

Cohen, D. and Mackeith, A. (1991), *The Development of Imagination*, London, Routledge.

Coulter, J. (1971), 'Decontextualised Meanings: Current Approaches to *Verstehende* Investigations', *The Sociological Review* 19(3), pp. 301–23.

Coulter, J. (1973), 'The Ethnomethodological Program in Contemporary Sociology', *The Human Context* 5, pp. 103–22.

Coulter, J. (1975), 'Perceptual Accounts and Interpretive Asymmetries', *Sociology* 9(3), pp. 385–96.

Coulter, J. (1979), *The Social Construction of Mind*, London, Macmillan.

Coulter, J. (1982), 'Remarks on the Conceptualisation of Social Structure', *Philosophy of the Social Sciences* 12, pp. 33–46.

Coulter, J. (1989), *Mind in Action*, Cambridge, Polity.

Coyle, M. (1987), 'An Experiential Perspective on the Mother–Infant Relationship: The First Eight Months', *The Focusing Folio* VI, pp. 1–28.

Crossley, N. (1993), 'The Politics of the Gaze: Between Foucault and Merleau-Ponty', *Human Studies* 16(4), pp. 399–419.

Crossley, N. (1994), *The Politics of Subjectivity: Between Foucault and Merleau-Ponty*, Aldershot, Avebury.

Crossley, N. (1995a), 'Body Techniques, Agency and Intercorporeality: On Goffman's *Relations in Public*', *Sociology* 29(1), pp. 133–49.

Crossley, N. (1995b), 'Merleau-Ponty, the Elusive Body and Carnal Sociology', *Body and Society* 1(1), pp. 43–63.

Crossley, N. (1995c), 'Embodiment and Communicative Action', paper presented at the *Theory, Culture & Society* 'TCS Berlin 95' conference.

Crossley, N. (1996), 'Body-Subject/Body-Power', *Body & Society* 2(1).

Dahrendorf, R. (1994), 'The Changing Quality of Citizenship', in van Steenbergen, B. (ed.), *The Condition of Citizenship*, London, Sage, pp. 10–19.

Davies, M. (1993), 'Healing Sylvia: Accounting for the Textual Discovery of Unconscious Knowledge', *Sociology* 27(1), pp. 110–21.

Davies, M. (1995), *Healing Sylvia: Child Sexual Abuse and the Construction of Identity*, London, Taylor & Francis.

Dean, M. (1991), *The Constitution of Poverty*, London, Routledge.

Descartes, R. (1969), *Discourse on Method* and *The Meditations*, Harmondsworth, Penguin.

Dews, P. (1987), *The Logics of Disintegration*, London, Verso.

Dillon, M. (1978), 'Merleau-Ponty and the Psychogenesis of Self', *Journal of Phenomenological Psychology* 9, pp. 84–98.

Donzelot, J. (1980), *The Policing of Families*, London, Hutchinson.

Easton, S. (1987), 'Hegel and Feminism', in Lamb, D. (ed.), *Hegel and Modern Philosophy*, London, Croom Helm, pp. 30–55.

Edie, J. (1987), *Merleau-Ponty's Philosophy of Language*, Washington, University Press of America.

Elias, N. (1978a) *The Civilising Process, Vol. 1*, Oxford, Blackwell.

Elias, N. (1978b), *What is Sociology?*, London, Hutchinson.

Elson, D. (1988), 'Socialisation of the Market', *New Left Review* 172, pp. 3–45.

Evans, F. (1993), *Psychology and Nihilism*, New York, State University of New York Press.

Fanon, F. (1986), *Black Skin, White Masks*, London, Pluto.

Fein, G. (1991), 'The Self-Building Potential of Pretend Play, or "I Got a Fish, All By My Self"', in Woodhead, M., Carr, R. and Light, P. (eds), *Becoming a Person*, London, Routledge, pp. 328–46.

Fernando, S. (1988), *Race and Culture in Psychiatry*, London, Croom Helm.

Fernando, S. (1991), *Mental Health, Race and Culture*, London, Macmillan.

Fogel, A. (1977), 'Temporal Organisation in Mother–Infant Face-to-Face Interaction', in Schaffer, H. (ed.) *Studies in Mother–Infant Interaction*, London, Academic Press, pp. 119–52.

Foucault, M. (1965), *Madness and Civilisation*, London, Tavistock.

Foucault, M. (1979), *Discipline and Punish*, Harmondsworth, Penguin.

Foucault, M. (1980), *Power/Knowledge*, Brighton, Harvester.

Foucault, M. (1981) *The History of Sexuality Vol. 1*, Harmondsworth, Penguin.

Foucault, M. (1982), 'The Subject and Power', in Dreyfus, H. and Rabinow, P. (eds), *Michel Foucault: Beyond Structuralism and Hermeneutics*, Brighton, Harvester, pp. 208–26.

Foucault, M. (1987), *Mental Illness and Psychology*, Berkeley, University of California Press.

Fraser, N. (1989), *Unruly Practices*, Cambridge, Polity.

Freeman, M. (1993), *Rewriting the Self*, London, Routledge.

Freud. S. (1984), 'Formulations on the Two Principles of Mental Functioning', *Pelican Freud Library 11: On Metapsychology*, Harmondsworth, Penguin, pp. 29–45.

Fukuyama, F. (1989), 'The End of History', *The National Interest*, Summer, pp. 3–18.

Fukuyama, F. (1992), *The End of History and the Last Man*, Harmondsworth, Penguin.

Gadamer, H.-G. (1989), *Truth and Method*, London, Sheed & Ward.

Garfinkel, H. (1967), *Studies in Ethnomethodology*, Englewood Cliffs, NJ, Prentice Hall.

Giddens, A. (1979), *Central Problems in Social Theory*, London, Macmillan.

Giddens, A. (1981), *A Contemporary Critique of Historical Materialism, Vol. 1: Power, Property and the State*, London, Macmillan.

Giddens, A. (1982), 'Labour and Interaction', in Thompson, J. and Held, D. (eds), *Habermas: Critical Debates*, London, Macmillan, pp. 149–61.

Giddens, A. (1984), *The Constitution of Society*, Cambridge, Polity.

Giddens, A. (1993), *New Rules of Sociological Method*, Cambridge, Polity.

Gilroy, P. (1992), *There Ain't No Black in the Union Jack*, London, Routledge.

Goffman, E. (1959), *The Presentation of Self in Everyday Life*, Harmondsworth, Penguin.

Goffman, E. (1961), *Asylums*, Harmondsworth, Penguin.

Goffman, E. (1963), *Behavior in Public Places*, Glencoe, IL, Free Press.

Goffman, E. (1968), *Stigma*, Harmondsworth, Penguin.

Goffman, E. (1972a), *Relations in Public*, Harmondsworth, Penguin.

Goffman, E. (1972b), *Interaction Ritual*, Harmondsworth, Penguin.

Goffman, E. (1981), *Forms of Talk*, Oxford, Blackwell.

Goldberg, D. (1993), *Racist Culture*, Oxford, Blackwell.

Gorz, A. (1982), *Farewell to the Working Class*, London, Pluto.

Gorz, A. (1985), *Pathways to Paradise*, London, Pluto.

Gramsci, A. (1982), *Selections from the Prison Notebooks*, London, Lawrence & Wishart.

Habermas, J. (1974), 'Labour and Interaction: Remarks on Hegel's Jena *Philosophy of Mind*', *Theory and Practice*, London, Heinemann, pp. 142–69.

Habermas, J. (1987a), *The Theory of Communicative Action, Vol. Two: System and Lifeworld*, Cambridge, Polity.

Habermas, J. (1987b), *Towards a Rational Society*, Cambridge, Polity.

Habermas, J. (1988a), *Legitimation Crisis*, Cambridge, Polity.

Habermas, J. (1988b), *On the Logic of the Social Sciences*, Cambridge, Polity.

Habermas, J. (1990), *The Philosophical Discourse of Modernity*, Cambridge, Polity.

Habermas, J. (1991a), *The Theory of Communicative Action, Vol. One: Reason and the Rationalisation of Society*, Cambridge, Polity.

Habermas, J. (1991b), *Communication and the Evolution of Society*, Cambridge, Polity.

Haley, J. (1969), *The Power Tactics of Jesus Christ*, New York, Avon.

Hall, S. (1984), 'The Rise of the Representative/Interventionist State', in McLennan, G., Held, D. and Hall, S. (eds), *State and Society in Contemporary Britain*, Cambridge, Polity, pp. 7–49.

Hall, S. (1987), 'Gramsci and Us', *Marxism Today*, June, pp. 16–21.

Hammond, M., Howarth, J. and Keat, R. (1991), *Understanding Phenomenology*, Oxford, Blackwell.

Hanfling, O. (1989), *Wittgenstein's Later Philosophy*, London, Macmillan.

Harland, R. (1987), *Superstructuralism*, London, Methuen.

Harman, C. (1989), 'The Myth of Market Socialism', *International Socialism* 42, pp. 3–63.

Harré, R. and Gillet, G. (1994), *The Discursive Mind*, London, Sage.

Hebdidge, D. (1988), *Subculture*, London, Routledge.

Hegel, G. (1971), *The Philosophy of Mind*, Oxford, Clarendon.

Hegel, G. (1979), *The Phenomenology of Spirit*, Oxford, Clarendon.

Heinzig, D. (1987), 'Maurice Merleau-Ponty and Ludwig Wittgenstein: A Synthesis', *Auslegung* 14, pp. 19–36.

Heritage, J. (1984), *Garfinkel and Ethnomethodology*, Cambridge, Polity.

Hindess, B. (1982), 'Power, Interests and the Outcome of Struggles', *Sociology* 16(4), pp. 498–511.

Hindess, B. (1988), *Choice, Rationality and Social Theory*, London, Unwin Hyman.

Hirst, P. and Wooley, P. (1982), *Social Relations and Human Attributes*, London, Tavistock.

Hochschild, A. (1979), 'Emotion Work, Feeling Rules and Social Structure', *American Journal of Sociology* 85, pp. 551–75.

Hochschild, A. (1983), *The Managed Heart*, Berkeley, University of California Press.

Honneth, A. (1995), *The Struggle for Recognition*, Cambridge, Polity.

Hunter, J. (1971), 'Forms of Life in Wittgenstein's *Philosophical Investigations*', in Klemke, C. (ed.), *Essays on Wittgenstein*, Chicago, University of Illinois Press, pp. 273–97.

Husserl, E. (1970), *The Crisis of the European Sciences and Transcendental Phenomenology*, Evanston, IL, Northwestern University Press.

Husserl, E. (1991), *Cartesian Meditations*, Netherlands, Kluwer Academic Publishers.

Irigaray, L. (1991), *The Irigaray Reader* (ed. Whitford, M.), Oxford, Blackwell.

Irigaray, L. (1993), *An Ethics of Sexual Difference*, London, Athlone.

Joas, H. (1985), *G.H. Mead*, Cambridge, Polity.

Joas, H. (1988), 'The Unhappy Marriage of Functionalism and Hermeneutics', *Praxis International* 8(1), pp. 34–51.

Kaye, K. (1991), 'The Parental Frame', in Woodhead, M., Carr, R. and Light, P. (eds), *Becoming a Person*, London, Routledge, pp. 129–43.

Kearney, R. (1991), *The Poetics of Imagining*, London, Harper Collins.

Kelly, G.A. (1965), 'Notes on Hegel's Lordship and Bondage', *Review of Metaphysics* 19, pp. 780–802.

Kojève, A. (1969), *Introduction to the Reading of Hegel*, New York, Basic Books.

Kripke, S. (1982), *Wittgenstein on Rules and Private Language*, Oxford, Blackwell.

Lacan, J. (1989), *Écrits: A Selection*, London, Tavistock.

Lamb, D. (1987), 'Sense and Meaning in Hegel and Wittgenstein', *Hegel and Modern Philosophy*, London, Croom Helm, pp. 70–102.

Lash, S. and Urry, J. (1988), *The End of Organised Capitalism*, Cambridge, Polity.

Lee, J. (1987), 'Prologue: Talking Organisation', in Button, G. and Lee, J. (eds), *Talk and Social Organisation*, Philadelphia, Multilingual Matters, pp. 19–54.

Lefort, C. (1990), 'Flesh and Otherness', in Johnson, G. and Smith, M. (eds), *Ontology and Alterity in Merleau-Ponty*, Evanston, IL, Northwestern University Press, pp. 3–13.

Levin, D. (1991), 'Visions of Narcissism: Intersubjectivity and the Reversals of Reflection', in Dillon, M. (ed.), *Merleau-Ponty Vivant*, New York, State University of New York Press, pp. 47–90.

Levinas, E. (1969), *Totality and Infinity*, Pittsburgh, Duquesne University Press.

Levinas, E. (1985), *Ethics and Infinity*, Pittsburgh, Duquesne University Press.

Levinas, E. (1987a), 'Intersubjectivity: Notes On Merleau-Ponty', in Johnson, G. and Smith, M. (eds), *Ontology and Alterity in Merleau-Ponty*, Evanston, IL, Northwestern University Press, 1990, pp. 55–60.

Levinas, E. (1987b), 'Sensibility', in Johnson, G. and Smith, M. (eds), *Ontology and Alterity in Merleau-Ponty*, Evanston, IL, Northwestern University Press, 1990, pp. 60–6.

Levinas, E. (1987c), *Time and the Other*, Pittsburgh, Duquesne University Press.

Levinas, E. (1989), 'Martin Buber and the Theory of Knowledge', in Hand, S. (ed.), *The Levinas Reader*, Oxford, Blackwell, pp. 59–74.

Lloyd, G. (1985), 'Masters, Slaves and Others', in Edgely, R. and Osborne, R. (eds), *Radical Philosophy Reader*, London, Verso, pp. 291–309.

Lyon, D. (1988), *The Information Society*, Cambridge, Polity.

Lyotard, J.-F. (1984), *The Postmodern Condition*, Manchester, Manchester University Press.

McCarthy, T. (1991), *On Reconstruction and Deconstruction in Contemporary Critical Theory*, Cambridge, MA, MIT Press.

Malcom, N. (1981), 'Wittgenstein's Philosophical Investigations', in Morick, H. (ed.), *Wittgenstein and the Problem of Other Minds*, Brighton, Harvester, pp. 45–81.

Mandel, E. (1970), *An Introduction to Marxist Economic Theory*, New York, Pathfinder.

Mandel, E. (1980), *The Second Slump*, London, Verso.

Marshall, T.H. (1992), *Citizenship and Social Class*, Cambridge, Polity.

Mauss, M. (1979), 'A Category of the Human Mind', *Sociology and Psychology*, London, Routledge, pp. 57–94.

Mead, G.H. (1967), *Mind, Self and Society*, Chicago, University of Chicago Press.

Meltzoff, A. and Moore, M. (1977), 'Imitation of Facial and Manual Gestures by Human Neonates', *Science* 198, pp. 75–8.

Meltzoff, A. and Moore, M. (1983), 'Newborn Infants Imitate Adult Facial Gestures', *Child Development* 54, pp. 702–9.

Meltzoff, A. and Moore, M. (1991), 'Cognitive Foundations and Social Functions of Imitation, and Intermodal Representation in Infancy', in Woodhead, M., Carr, R. and Light, P. (eds), *Becoming a Person*, London: Routledge, pp. 111–28.

Merleau-Ponty, M. (1962), *The Phenomenology of Perception*, London, Routledge.

Merleau-Ponty, M. (1964a), *Sense and Non-Sense*, Evanston, IL, Northwestern University Press.

Merleau-Ponty, M. (1964b), *Signs*, Evanston, IL, Northwestern University Press.

Merleau-Ponty, M. (1965), *The Structure of Behaviour*, London, Methuen.

Merleau-Ponty, M. (1968a), *The Visible and the Invisible*, Evanston, IL, Northwestern University Press.

Merleau-Ponty, M. (1968b), *The Primacy of Perception and Other Essays*, Evanston, IL, Northwestern University Press.

Merleau-Ponty, M. (1969), *Humanism and Terror*, Boston, Beacon.

Merleau-Ponty, M. (1973), *Adventures of the Dialectic*, Evanston, IL, Northwestern University Press.

Merleau-Ponty, M. (1974), *The Prose of the World*, London, Heinemann.

Merleau-Ponty, M. (1979), *Consciousness and the Acquisition of Language*, Evanston, IL, Northwestern University Press.

Merleau-Ponty, M. (1985), 'The Experience of Others, and Phenomenology and Psychoanalysis', *Review of Existential Psychology and Psychiatry*, xviii (1–3), pp. 33–72.

Merleau-Ponty, M. (1988), *In Praise of Philosophy* and *Themes from the Lectures at the Collège de France*, Evanston, IL, Northwestern University Press.

Merleau-Ponty, M. (1992), *Texts and Dialogues*, Princeton, NJ, Humanities Press.

Merquior, J. (1985), *Foucault*, London, Fontana.

Meyer, J. (1991), 'Power and Love: Conflicting Conceptual Schemata', in Davis, K., Leijenaar, M. and Oldersma, J. (eds), *The Gender of Power*, London, Sage, pp. 21–41.

Mitchell, J. (1975), *Psychoanalysis and Feminism*, Harmondsworth, Penguin.

Natanson, M. (1973), *Edmund Husserl: Philosopher of Infinite Tasks*, Evanston, IL, Northwestern University Press.

Nettleton, S. (1992), *Power, Pain and Dentistry*, Milton Keynes, Open University Press.

Newson, J. (1977), 'An Intersubjective Approach to the Systematic Description of Mother–Infant Interaction', in Schaffer, H. (ed.), *Studies in Mother–Infant Interaction*, London, Academic Press, pp. 47–62.

Newson, J. (1979), 'The Growth of Shared Understandings Between Infant and Caregiver', in Bullowa, M. (ed.), *Before Speech*, Cambridge University Press, pp. 207–22.

O'Neill, J. (1986), 'The Specular Body: Merleau-Ponty and Lacan on Infant, Self and Other', *Synthèse* 66, pp. 201–17.

Offe, C. (1984), *Contradictions of the Welfare State*, (ed. Keane, J.), London, Hutchinson.

Offe, C. (1985), *Disorganised Capitalism*, Oxford, Polity.

Parsons, T. (1960), *Structure and Process in Modern Societies*, Glencoe, IL, Free Press.

Parsons, T. (1967), *Sociological Theory and Modern Society*, New York, Free Press.

Passerin d' Entrèves, M. (1992), 'Hannah Arendt and the Idea of Citizenship', in Mouffe, C. (ed.), *Dimensions of Radical Democracy*, London, Verso, pp. 145–68.

Perkins, M. (1981), 'Two Arguments Against a Private Language', in Morick, H. (ed.), *Wittgenstein and the Problem of Other Minds*, Brighton, Harvester, pp. 97–118.

Pfuetze, P. (1961), *Self, Society, Existence: Human Nature and Dialogue in the Thought of George Herbert Mead and Martin Buber*, Westport, CT, Greenwood.

Piaget, J. (1961), *The Language and Thought of the Child*, London, Routledge & Kegan Paul.

Pollner, M. (1974), 'Mundane Reasoning', *Philosophy of Social Science* 4, pp. 35–54.

Pollner, M. (1975), 'The Very Coinage of Your Brain: The Anatomy of Reality Disjunctures', *Philosophy of Social Science* 5, pp. 411–30.

Poster, M. (1990), *The Mode of Information*, Cambridge, Polity.

Rawls, A. (1987), 'The Interaction Order *Sui Generis*: Goffman's Contribution to Social Theory', *Sociological Theory* 5, pp. 136–49.

Ricoeur, P. (1967a), *Husserl: An Analysis of His Philosophy*, Evanston, IL, Northwestern University Press.

Ricoeur, P. (1967b), 'New Developments in Phenomenology in France: The Phenomenology of Language', *Social Research* 34, pp. 1–30.

Ricouer, P. (1991), *From Text to Action*, London, Athlone Press.

Roche, M. (1973), *Phenomenology, Language and the Social Sciences*, London, Routledge & Kegan Paul.

Roche, M. (1987), 'Citizenship, Social Theory and Social Change', *Theory and Society* 16, pp. 363–99.

Roche, M. (1990), 'Motherland or Motherhood', *New Socialist*, Oct./Nov., pp. 10–12.

Roche, M. (1992a), *Rethinking Citizenship*, Cambridge, Polity.

Roche, M. (1992b), 'Rethinking Social Citizenship', paper presented at the XIIth World Congress of Sociology (New Classes and Social Movements Section), Madrid, July 1990.

Romanyshyn, R. (1982), *Psychological Life*, Milton Keynes, Open University Press.

Rose, N. (1985), *The Psychological Complex*, London, Routledge.

Rose, N. (1989), *Governing the Soul*, London, Routledge.

Rosenthal, S. and Bourgeois, P. (1991), *Mead and Merleau-Ponty: Toward a Common Vision*, New York, State University of New York Press.

Ryle, G. (1949), *The Concept of Mind*, London, Penguin.

Sacks, H. (1989), '1964–65 Lectures', *Human Studies* 12(3–4).

Said, E. (1978), *Orientalism*, Harmondsworth, Penguin.

Sandywell, B., Silverman, D., Roche, M., Filmer, P. and Phillipson, M. (1975), *Problems of Reflexivity and Dialectics in Sociological Enquiry*, London, Routledge & Kegan Paul.

Saretzki, T. (1988), 'Collective Action vs Functionalism: Some Remarks on Joas' Critique', *Praxis International* 8(1), pp. 52–72.

Sartre, J.-P. (1948), *Anti-Semite and Jew*, New York, Schocken.

Sartre, J.-P. (1969), *Being and Nothingness*, London, Routledge.

Sartre, J.-P. (1972), *The Psychology of Imagination*, London, Methuen.

Saunders, P. (1993), 'Citizenship in a Liberal Society', in Turner, B. (ed.) *Citizenship and Social Theory*, London, Sage, pp. 57–90.

Schaffer, R. (1991), 'Early Social Development', in Woodhead, M., Carr, R. and Light, P. (eds), *Becoming a Person*, London, Routledge, pp. 5–29.

Schutz, A. (1964), *Collected Papers 2: Studies in Social Theory*, The Hague, Martinus Nijhoff.

Schutz, A. (1970), *Collected Papers 3: Studies in Phenomenological Philosophy*, The Hague, Martinus Nijhoff.

Schutz, A. (1972), *The Phenomenology of the Social World*, London, Heinemann.

Schutz, A. (1973), *Collected Papers 1: The Problem of Social Reality*, The Hague, Martinus Nijhoff.

Schutz, A. and Luckmann, T. (1973), *The Structures of the Life-World*, Evanston, IL, Northwestern University Press.

Singer, P. (1983), *Hegel*, Oxford, Oxford University Press.

Spurling, L. (1977), *Phenomenology and the Social World: The Philosophy of Merleau-Ponty and Its Relation to the Social Sciences*, London, Routledge & Kegan Paul.

Stern, D. (1977), *The First Relationship: Infant and Mother*, London, Open Books.

Stern, D., Beebe, B., Jaffe, J. and Bennet, S. (1977), 'The Infant's Stimulus World During Social Interaction: A Study of Caregiver Behaviours with Particular Reference to Repetition and Timing', in Schaffer, H. (ed.), *Studies in Mother–Infant Interaction*, London, Academic Press, pp. 177–202.

Stevenson, N. (1995), *Media Culture: Social Theory and Mass Communication*, London Sage.

Stewart, A. (1995), 'Two Conceptions of Citizenship', *British Journal of Sociology*, 46(1), pp. 63–79.

Suchman, L. (1987), *Plans and Situated Actions*, Cambridge, Cambridge University Press.

Taylor, L. and Cohen, S. (1993), *Escape Attempts*, London, Routledge.

Taylor, L. and Walton, P. (1971), 'Industrial Sabotage: Motives and Meanings', in Cohen, S. (ed.), *Images of Deviance*, Harmondsworth, Penguin, pp. 219–45.

Theunissen, M. (1984), *The Other*, Cambridge, MA, MIT Press.

Thompson, E. (1967), 'Time, Work-Discipline and Industrial Capitalism', *Past and Present* 38, pp. 56–61, 70–3, 90–6.

Thompson, J. (1983), 'Rationality and Social Rationalisation: An Assessment of Habermas's Theory of Communicative Action', *Sociology* 17(2), pp. 278–94.

Toffler, A. (1980), *The Third Wave*, London, Pan.

Trevarthen, C. (1977), 'Descriptive Analyses of Infant Communicative Behaviour', in Schaffer, H. (ed.), *Studies in Mother–Infant Interaction*, London, Academic Press, pp. 227–70.

Trevarthen, C. (1979), 'Communication and Cooperation in Early Infancy: A Description of Primary Intersubjectivity', in Bullowa, M. (ed.), *Before Speech*, Cambridge, Cambridge University Press, pp. 321–47.

Trevarthen, C. and Hubley, P. (1978), 'Secondary Intersubjectivity: Confidence, Confiding and Acts of Meaning in the First Year', in Lock, A. (ed.), *Action, Gesture and Symbol*, London, Academic Press, pp. 183–231.

Turner, B. (1990), 'Outline of a Theory of Citizenship', *Sociology* 24(2), pp. 189–217.

Volosinov, V. (1986), *Marxism and the Philosophy of Language*, Cambridge, MA, Harvard University Press.

Vygotsky, L. (1986), *Thought and Language*, Cambridge, MA, MIT Press.

Walzer, M. (1986), 'The Politics of Michel Foucault', in Hoy, D. (ed.), *Foucault: A Critical Reader*, Oxford, Blackwell, pp. 51–68.

Weights, A. (1981), 'Max Weber's Sociology and the Conceptualisation of Social Agents', Unpublished PhD thesis, University of Liverpool.

White, S. (1988), *The Recent Work of Jürgen Habermas*, Cambridge, Cambridge University Press.

Wilson, E. (1985), *Adorned in Dreams*, London, Virago.

Winch, P. (1958), *The Idea of a Social Science*, London, Routledge & Kegan Paul.

Wittgenstein, L. (1953), *Philosophical Investigations*, Oxford, Blackwell.

Wittgenstein, L. (1958), *The Blue and Brown Books*, Oxford, Blackwell.

Wittgenstein, L. (1961), *Tractatus Logico-Philosophicus*, London, Routledge & Kegan Paul.

Wittgenstein, L. (1969), *On Certainty*, Oxford, Blackwell.

Young, I. (1980), 'Throwing Like a Girl', *Human Studies* 3, pp. 137–56.

Index